VICTORIA STRICKLAND

CW00796664

LETHE'S LAW
JUSTICE, LAW AND ETHICS
IN RECONCILIATION

LETHE'S LAW
Justice, Law and Ethics in Reconciliation

Edited by

EMILIOS CHRISTODOULIDIS
AND
SCOTT VEITCH

·HART·
PUBLISHING

OXFORD · PORTLAND OREGON
2001

Hart Publishing
Oxford and Portland, Oregon

Published in North America (US and Canada) by
Hart Publishing
c/o International Specialized Book Services
5804 NE Hassalo Street
Portland, Oregon
97213-3644
USA

Distributed in Netherlands, Belgium and Luxembourg by
Intersentia, Churchillaan 108
B2900 Schoten
Antwerpen
Belgium

© The Contributors jointly and severally 2001

The Contributors jointly and severally have asserted their rights under the
Copyright, Designs and Patents Act 1988, to be identified as
the authors of this work.

Hart Publishing is a specialist legal publisher based in Oxford, England.
To order further copies of this book or to request a list of other publications
please write to:

Hart Publishing,
Salters Boatyard, Folly Bridge, Abingdon Rd,
Oxford, OX1 4LB
Telephone: +44 (0)1865 245533 Fax: +44 (0) 1865 794882
email: mail@hartpub.co.uk
WEBSITE: http//:www.hartpub.co.uk

British Library Cataloguing in Publication Data
Data Available

ISBN 1 84113-109-1 (hardback)

Typeset by John Saunders Design & Production, Reading
Printed and bound in Great Britain by
Biddles Ltd, www.biddles.co.uk

Contents

Part III Memory and the Ethics of Reconciliation

List of Contributors

Jennifer Balint is in the Research School of Social Sciences, Australian National University, Canberra, and has recently been a Fellow at the Collegium Budapest. She is currently working on comparative analyses of genocide.

Leora Bilsky is a senior lecturer in the Faculty of Law at Tel Aviv University. Her main areas of interest are feminist legal theory, child law, Holocaust and the law and political trials. As a Fulbright Scholar, she attended Yale University Law School, completing her J.S.D. in 1995. In her work on political trials she has looked at the history of Israeli law and the legacy of the Holocaust and the work of Hannah Arendt. She is currently writing a book tentatively titled Political Trials: The Struggle over Israel's Collective Identity.

Emilios Christodoulidis is Reader in Law at the University of Edinburgh. He has published in the area of philosophy of law and political theory. His book *Law and Reflexive Politics* (1998) won the European Award for Legal Theory and the SPTL prize for 'outstanding legal scholarship.'

Adam Czarnota is Senior Lecturer in the Faculty of Law, University of New South Wales, Sydney. He has published widely on Eastern European trans-formations and is co-editor of two recent collections on political and sociological interpretations of transitions in former communist states. He is currently engaged in a project on law, time and collective memories.

Francois du Bois is Senior Lecturer in the Faculty of Law at the University of Cape Town since 1996. Prior to that, he taught at the School of Oriental and African Studies, University of London after studying law at the Universities of Stellenbosch and Oxford. His main research interests lie in the fields of legal theory and comparative law. He has published in the areas of jurisprudence and environmental law and is currently working on legal dimensions of the Truth and Reconciliation Commission.

David Dyzenhaus is Professor of Law and Philosophy at the University of Toronto. Recent monographs include *Legality and Legitimacy: Hans Kelsen, Carl Schmitt and Herman Heller in Weimar* (OUP, 1997) and

Judging the Judges, Judging Ourselves: Truth, Reconciliation and the Apartheid Legal Order (Hart, 1998). He is editor most recently of *Recrafting the Rule of Law: The Limits of Legal Order* (Hart, 1999).

Klaus Günther holds the Chair of Criminal Law at the University of Frankfurt where he teaches criminal law, legal philosophy and criminology. He has published extensively, amongst other things arguing for the need for, and possibly of, an "enlightened" reform of the criminal law from both philosophical and legal perspectives. Amongst his publications are The *Sense of Appropriateness: Application Discourses in Morality and Law* (SUNY, 1993) and *Die Sprache der Verstummten: Gewalt und performative Entmachtung.*

Valerie Kerruish taught law at various universities, most recently at the University of Western Australia and then Macquarie University, Sydney. She has written many articles in critical legal theory and the philosophy of law and is the author of *Jurisprudence as Ideology* (Routledge, 1991). She moved to Germany in December, 1999 and is working on a monograph titled The Wrong of Law.

Alexander McCall Smith is Professor of Law at the University of Edinburgh. He is a recognised expert in the areas of medical law, criminal law and the law of delict. Amongst his many publications are (with J K Mason) *Law and Medical Ethics* (5th ed., Butterworths, 1999), and (with D Sheldon) *Scots Criminal Law* (2nd ed., Butterworths, 1997). He is also a well-known author of novels, short stories and children's books.

Burkhard Schäfer is Lecturer in Law at the University of Edinburgh. His main interest is the methodology of comparative law and the use of computer technology for transborder legal issues. He has published widely on topics both in the field of AI and law and comparative politics and law.

Bert van Roermund is Professor of Legal Philosophy at Tilburg University, the Netherlands. Apart from his permanent interest in law and language (See *Law, Narrative and Reality. An Essay in Interceptive Politics* (1997)) he is presently involved in questions of legal authority, especially in transnational contexts.

Scott Veitch is Reader in Law at the University of Glasgow. He has published in the area of philosophy of law and is the author of *Moral Conflict and Legal Reasoning* (Hart, 1999), for which he won the European Award for Legal Theory.

Introduction

EMILIOS CHRISTODOULIDIS

AND

SCOTT VEITCH

We have called this book Lethe's Law because it is a book about law, memory (or the loss of it) and truth. Lethe, in the modern Greek usage of the term too, stands for oblivion and forgetting. The early mythic appearances of Lethe are recounted by Hesiod in the *Theogony*. Lethe, daughter of Eris (dissension), is imagined as a river; drinking its water does not quench thirst, mortals thirst as they drink and by drinking they forget their lives and lineages. Socrates recalls Lethe in Plato's *Republic*. "The soul in this situation, as Plato writes of it, lives in a futile effort to replenish itself with immediacies that flow away as they come to presence. Its life is like an unremitting effort to be here now, continuously unsatisfied, thirsting for what Lethe gives in withdrawal."[1]

But there is more to the significance of Lethe and it comes with the connection to truth in the notion of "un-concealment". We will go back to Heidegger for this: truth is Dasein's disclosedness, "aletheia"—the Greek word for truth—its unconcealment. Notice Heidegger's coinage, his wonderful par-etymology here, his word-welding: a-lethe-ia, where "a" is the pre-fix "un", that which negates in this case: Lethe, the recovery of an original memory or in any case the pushing back of the borders of oblivion. If Lethe connotes the moment when meaning and imagery fall away and are lost to awareness, "a-letheia" as reversal of forgetting, signals the recovery of an original knowledge. Truth becomes unconcealment and, in Heidegger, reveals its true nature as an *Erschlossenheit*—a sudden openness to what was removed from view—a moment when obscurity falls away.

The aim of this book, and of the project from which this book originated, is to explore the logic of law's disclosures and concealments, its tapping of memory and, when this is the case, its facilitating oblivion. We found that the focus on transitional justice fruitfully brought to the fore crucial questions in this respect, in the sense that limit situations force law to manifest what under normal conditions might have remained latent. It is this, to return to Heidegger for a last time, that in this context makes transitional justice "worthy of question", ethically and politically.

---

[1] C. Scott, *The Time of Memory* (Albany, SUNY Press, 1999), p. 33.

The contributions to this volume address this set of pressing contemporary problems. From a philosophical, primarily, perspective, and in the context of a variety of jurisdictions each with its full compliment of particularities and concerns, the authors seek to delineate and often to challenge traditional understandings of the relation between law and justice. In this sense the nature of legal judgment is itself brought under scrutiny at a number of levels. At one level there will be a focus on how responsibility is attributed in accounting for past crimes, and, more specifically, the role of punishment or its lifting through amnesty. At a second level, these questions of responsibility are raised more generally both as a matter of how to do justice to the past in the service of peaceable futures, and particularly, the sense in which legal institutions can facilitate or inhibit this task. Finally, at a third level, we focus on how the politics of memory articulate with the ethics of reconciliation. This demands thinking through a series of questions which interrogate the very premises of the other two levels.

In the first group of chapters the exploration of guilt and its relationship to forgiveness leads in the direction of an ethico-juridical reflection on the relationship of *penalty to responsibility*. It is worth noting that what is amongst other things crucial here is a shift in the consciousness of fault (if fault is the right term to capture the guilty conscience of a collective) from a situation in which responsibility is understood as collective to an ethico-juridical schema of guilt where fault is attributed on an individualistic basis. Then, to paraphrase Ricoeur, the "we" subsides and makes evident the loneliness of the guilty conscience.

One key argument here is that because of the increasing demand that the past be dealt with for the sake of a shared future, and due to the inability of conventional notions of justice to succeed in this context, law is being forced to incorporate a structural and symbolic element of forgiveness. This results in a new demand being placed on law, on an unprecedentedly grand scale, to be merciful rather than just in the conventional sense. This change involves law in a huge, explicitly symbolic effort of a type it ordinarily shuns. The demand on law has as much to do with forgetting as it has with remembering: paradoxically, if the past is too alive it will never be past, yet, the truth has to be remembered first in order that it can be forgotten. (It is not simply coincidental that the granting of amnesty—from "amnesia", forgetfulness, oblivion—has been so prevalent a feature of transitional justice.) Thus as law becomes seduced into temporal paradoxes, and as its sense of justice must struggle with the unlikely task of reconciling tragedy at a national level, so the logic of amnesty appears increasingly to negotiate the problem of memory and forgetting.

Amongst other legal aspects that are considered the discussion focuses on how, in coming to terms with the past, conventional criminal notions of punishment based in retribution have been disrupted and seen variously to be inefficacious, impossible or undesirable. As such, different sets of demands are placed on legal systems as the stakes are tied not to individual retribution or the restoration of value, but instead to demands for truth, for reconciliation, and for national unity in the face of a divided past.

Klaus Günther and Burkhard Schäfer explore from different perspectives the connections between the criminal law's attribution of guilt and the rationale for amnesty, with their focus on recent German cases. Günther concentrates on the question of amnesties for offences in the former GDR, and argues that while the demand for punishment asks too much, the request for amnesty asks too little. Only be reference, it is argued, to a conception of democratic citizenship can we gain proper purchase on the attribution of guilt and the role it can play in the politics of memory.

Burkhard Schäfer's chapter engages directly with Günther's. He provides an analysis which asks us to re-think the conceptual relations between law, amnesty and mercy. It questions the extent to which amnesty and mercy are concerned, as several authors have suggested, with responding to issues of particularity, or instead embody a series of discretionary possibilities which can be used as political tools. With reference to Germany since the fall of the Berlin Wall, and specifically to the treatment of the Red Army Faction (RAF), Schäfer provides a reading of the use of amnesties for political ends which sees "kind" treatment—through the lifting of punishment—being used strategically as a means of weakening political opposition.

The next chapter by Scott Veitch situates the legal regulation of amnesty within the broader context of legal theory and, specifically, of legal reasoning. The intimate dependency of the meaning and application of amnesties on prevailing political conditions are considered with reference to South Africa and some recent developments in Northern Ireland. He argues that a certain paradox underlies the logic of amnesty which has to do with the specific use of time in renegotiating *mens rea*; it relies on an *a posteriori* rationalisation of motive that involves the retrospective imputation of political objective, as deemed appropriate to current requirements of reconciliation. Whilst current democratic aspirations necessarily have a bearing on the justification for redressing past wrongs, and legal mechanisms are stretched in order to bear this responsibility, the application of legal categorisations nonetheless exposes an institutional limit to law's capacity to carry this through.

The concluding chapter of this part sees Alexander McCall Smith pose the following question: What is the effect of the passage of time on guilt? Through a consideration of when and why crimes become "stale", the argument opens out into a discussion of the ability, and in certain cases the duty, of criminal law to exercise forgiveness. For McCall Smith, there are limitations to what the criminal law can undertake to do within its own boundaries, yet the sensitivity towards a need for forgiveness necessitates a delicate re-assessment of the underpinning rationales of the application of the criminal law. In these senses, the chapter brings together several of the concerns already canvassed and links the issue of accounting for past crimes to themes developed in later sections of the book.

These problems, unique in their detail, are perhaps best seen in the context of the recent phenomenon of nations coming to terms with their past within a new, international, culture of human rights. This still aspirational culture itself grew out of the immense problems of coming to terms post-1945 with the traumatic events of the Holocaust. Since then the need to deal with the past has been reproduced in the aftermaths of revolutions, genocides, civil wars, and even peacefully negotiated settlements. A variety of approaches has been tried in places as diverse as Central and South America, Eastern Europe, and Africa. In all this, law has been centrally implicated, as legal mechanisms ranging from civil law restitution to criminal prosecution and blanket amnesties have been utilised, and their reception greeted with diverse appreciations of relative success or failure.

Take, for example, the work of the Truth and Reconciliation Commission (TRC) in South Africa that has brought to the fore important questions of how a nation deals with its past. In the case of South Africa this is, clearly, a difficult past to come to terms with and to account for in the present. Yet a failure to do so might appear not only to be unjust, but could seriously jeopardise hopes for future reconciliation. "Doing justice" to a divided and violent past could be seen to be not only the mark of an ethically, perhaps legally, responsible community, but the very condition of the South African nation coming to terms with itself in a reconciled future.

David Dyzenhaus and Francois du Bois look separately at the South African experience, making particular reference to the conceptions of justice and legality which underpinned the work of the TRC. Dyzenhaus's chapter provides a critical account of the TRC's legal hearing: the three-day official inquiry into the legal order during the apartheid era and into those who sustained (and, occasionally, challenged) it. It begins with a much needed discussion of context: the nature of its mandate, the legal hearing and its purpose, the justice of the reasons for calling judges and lawyers into account. Does an investigation of judges unduly risk politicising the judiciary in a way which comprises their role in the future? In this context the author recounts the fascinating story of the South African lawyer Bram Fischer, whose commitment to legality led him, paradoxically perhaps, down the revolutionary path of armed struggle. The author's philosophical concern is with the concept of legality. Law, claims Dyzenhaus, is primarily an exercise in reciprocity between law-giver and citizen and in effect one that elevates the principles that establish that reciprocity—the features of the rule of law—as nothing less than constitutive of legal practice itself. The commitment to this internal link sustains and organises his argument. It informs a second central idea: that the judges had a duty to resist handing down what were in appearance only "legal" decisions, since a more fundamental commitment to legality would require them to observe the principles of reciprocity and act according to principles of equality, equity and respect for the dignity of the oppressed. Dyzenhaus ends the chapter with reference to the Israeli Supreme Court's understanding of the legality of the regulations which permitted certain interrogation practices of the General Security Service, an understanding which is, he suggests, illustrative of the notion of the rule of law he defends.

Du Bois's chapter provides a stimulating re-assessment of the project attempted by the Truth and Reconciliation Commission in South Africa. It is not, he points out, a reflection upon the actual workings of the Commission, but rather an investigation into the principles which underlie it. In processes of transition to democracy the South African model is often held up as the most advanced of its kind, a means of negotiating a way between punishment and impunity in coming to terms with the past, and one which concentrates on the role of multiple truths in stimulating a process of constructive justice and social reconstruction. The questions raised here are not so much did it work, but could it work; is there a viable "third way" between victors' justice and victors' mercy? Du Bois's provocative argument is that there is not. In setting out why, his analysis explores the relationship between truth and justice, and as such engages the very core of the problematics encountered in the process of truth and reconciliation.

The context of political transitions is significant, as we said, because it throws into relief paradoxes and incongruities in practices and understandings that tend to go unscrutinised under ordinary political conditions. In all this, dealing with the past tests the limits of a conventionally conceived jurisprudence of formally equally rights and duties, and exposes notions of universal legal rationality to radical conflicts based, amongst other things, on contested truths, histories, and identities. Both Adam Czarnota's and Jennifer Balint's chapters explore these themes.

Czarnota notes that the use of quasi-judicial institutions is a prevalent feature of transitional justice. While such institutions vary in their composition and goals, they draw on legal means for legitimacy, yet at the same time differ enormously from the formalities of conventional legal proceedings. But his emphasis is equally on the social conceptions of time (an overlooked variable, he suggests, in the conceptualisation of law) and the notion of collective memory as developed by Maurice Halbwachs. In all this Czarnota sees a very specific role for law in its regulation of collective memories, with conventional justifications for law's legitimacy being challenged as law seeks to re-conceptualise the past in order better to control the present and the future. And it is this set of problems that Balint thematises in the context, specifically, of responses to state crimes, genocide and gross violations of human rights. This is carried out with reference to research on a number of historical instances, but with particular emphasis on responses to genocides which have weighed less in the public conscience, such as Rwanda, Armenia and Australia. The main impact of her argument is that legal mechanisms, while capable of opening spaces for institutional and societal reconstruction, do have clear limits when thinking through deeper questions of reconciliation.

The final part of the book considers how political and ethical issues coalesce in the medium of judgment. Leora Bilsky's re-telling of the Kastner trial is a fascinating account of how a trial was politicised to undermine a fragile reconciliation in Israel. She shows how a simple libel trial, and one which was prior to those more publicly familiar "Holocaust" trials, became a forum for the opening of historical questions of complicity and community, and a re-awakening of Zionist nationalism. This was achieved through a strategic use of legal discourse in the courtroom and one which used a reversal of familiar legal techniques in the service of a politicisation of judgment. There is, as she notes, an implicit linking of legal discourse and silence, one that goes well beyond sociological analyses of disempowerment in the courtroom, and bears on the very possibilities of what stories could be told, what could be collectively voiced and what would come to be the subject of a collective amnesia. In her words, the Kastner trial "postponed the frank and free discussion of a traumatic past for many decades, it perpetuated myths and closed an entire chapter of history to serious deliberation".

What is reconciliation and what are the conditions of undertaking it? Bert van Roermund takes his cue from an ambivalent etymology to argue that reconciliation bears a double relationship to truth. It is bound to cover and to uncover the facts of an oppressive past on behalf of the former victims. But what presuppositions would underpin the victims' attitude of forgiveness? Why would they engage in a process that is clearly at odds with some principles that, according to well-established legal theory, derive from the rule of law? He argues that the paradoxical answer is that by doing so they establish the very basis of a legal order, in an account of human relationships that is radically different from the economics of social contract theories. This conceptual deep-structure (or "grammar" in Wittgenstein's sense) of reconciliation is neatly revealed by various phenomena that occurred in the process of "truth and reconciliation" presently taking place in South Africa.

Valerie Kerruish asks the question of reconciliation in the Australian context of Aboriginal dispossession, and its legal embodiment *terra nullius*. Drawing on a notion of reconciliation from Hegel, she develops an intricate analysis that connects the meaning of colonisation to the form of law's authority and the stake of reconciliation to the concept of property rights. Reconciliation, she argues, "is not its own end. Its conceptual link is to freedom, in this context, decolonisation". Reconciliation must therefore be re-thought in a way which challenges unitary thinking, that engages with a proper recognition of (Aboriginal) laws, and thus which exposes the ethics of reconciliation to underlying aspects of political economy and justice.

"The *owners of history* have given time *a meaning*: a direction which is also a significance . . . those for whom irreversible time has existed discover within it the *memorable* as well as the *menace of forgetting*", wrote Guy Debord.[2] Emilios Christodoulidis's chapter on "Law's Immemorial" engages with the question of time and memory, and asks whether memory might be recalled in a way that disrupts and challenges established histories, "their direction and meaning", and might thus redress "the menace of forgetting". More specifically it seeks to explain the concept of the "immemorial" which Lyotard defines as "that which is remembered as forgotten". Does this make the forgetting irreversible and futile any attempt to recount the past as a resource for emancipation and praxis? The chapter is an analysis of the connection between time and memory in legal discourse and explores the legal mechanisms that reconcile the past to the present and future and repress memory's disruptive potential.

In clarifying and drawing out the conceptual roles of truth, justice and reconciliation which are at play, and by analysing the legal methods in use, it may be seen not only that key problems and paradoxes emerge, particularly around the notions of memory and forgetting, but that law itself is being challenged to provide a new form of justice. In this, what remains most crucially at stake is a certain reflexiveness about, and responsiveness to, the past, that allows it to remain open, accommodating of re-interpretations, never conclusively determined. But performative attitudes towards the past do, of course, run the risk of dangerous revisionism, and this too ought not to be downplayed; there was a saying in the Soviet Union under Stalin, apparently, that is was impossible to predict the past.

The sensitivity with which we conceive and theorise ethico-juridical responses to the past therefore appears as an obligation not only to memory but to the conditions of the political horizons that will define the future. The essays in *Lethe's Law* engage with this obligation, and do so through an exploration of the varied roles which law can play, and an assessment of its limits and its possibilities.

The book grew out of two workshops that we organised in Edinburgh and Sydney. They were occasions of fruitful intellectual exchange and we would like to thank all those who participated for making them so rewarding. We would also like to thank those who gave financial support to the project, the University of Edinburgh through the Lindsay Bequest Fund, and the Law Foundation of New South Wales and Macquarie University, Sydney. Finally, our sincere thanks go to those who contributed to this volume and to our publisher, Richard Hart.

---

[2] Guy Debord, *Society of the Spectacle*, (Detroit, Black and Red, 1983), 132–3.

Part I

Criminal Law, Amnesty and Time

1

The Criminal Law of "Guilt" as Subject of a Politics of Remembrance in Democracies*

KLAUS GÜNTHER

INTRODUCTION

There is one important caveat for my ideas on the topic of "amnesty". As far as I discuss amnesty at all, and in particular, amnesty for possible criminal offences in the former GDR, I presuppose that these acts are the subject of criminal liability in the first place. I know this is contested, and that therefore some authors refuse to speak about amnesty at all in this context, since they deny that the actions under consideration were unlawful. I am not going to discuss this here. My arguments for and against an amnesty therefore simply assume that the acts under consideration were illegal in the sense of the criminal law.

With that, we have already introduced an important feature of the concept of amnesty. Amnesty presupposes that there is a legal system, which is based on punishment as legal consequence for criminal acts. Johann Georg Schätzler has thus defined amnesty as a "legal norm which, for an indefinite number of cases, either revokes (or reduces) the lawful punishment of convicted offenders, terminates continuing proceedings or prevents cases coming to court at all".[1] An amnesty is therefore not concerned with a particular case, but requires a general law enacted by the legislative power. Furthermore, an amnesty does not necessarily require a court verdict, but also addresses cases where the proceedings are not yet terminated or even started. These two features distinguish amnesty from mercy: mercy is a decision of the executive power to revoke the criminal sanction of a court verdict in a particular case.

In what follows, I will focus on the differences between the two possible consequences of an amnesty, the difference between waived punishment

---

* The text was translated from the German by Burkhard Schäfer.
[1] J G Schätzler, *Handbuch des Gandenrechts*, (München, C H Beck, 1992), pp. 17, 208.

and waived legal proceedings. Waiver of punishment presupposes a legally valid conviction. And this means that it has been publicly determined who violated the criminal law, which offences were committed, and how these offences were attributed to the offender. In short: a person's guilt has been determined. This differs from waiver of criminal proceedings. Here, we omit everything that could result in the attribution of (criminal law) guilt in the first place. Admittedly, an amnesty is neither an acquittal, nor the pronouncement that a (possible) perpetrator is innocent. An amnesty does not revoke the court verdict as such, nor does it revoke the guilt of the offender.[2] But the decision not to prosecute has the consequence that a possible criminal liability is not determined publicly.

Hence, in the first case, waiver after a court verdict, an amnesty addresses (only) the question of punishment. In the second case, waiver of legal prosecution, an amnesty has to deal with the issue of guilt. Even if the consequences of an amnesty (as defined in German law) are always both, waiver of attribution of guilt and waiver of punishment, I will argue that there are better reasons for a revocation of punishment than for relinquishment of the determination of guilt. I admit that this argument is to some extent fictitious and unrealistic. There are, however, two reasons to carry through such an argument. First, because I think that in the public debate on amnesty, the problems of punishment overshadow the debate about guilt. Since it is much easier to argue against punishment, the possible reasons for a public determination of guilt are left aside. The reason for this might be that it is assumed that the determination of guilt must result in a punishment. In the same way in which punishment presupposes guilt, it is assumed that conversely, guilt must result in punishment. But if this relation does not hold, then, and this is my second reason, we can analyse if there are better ways of determining guilt than by legal proceedings, which end in an acquittal or a conviction.

THE PROBLEMS OF PUNISHMENT

The reasons against punishment are obvious.[3] We have to distinguish however between reasons against punishment in general, and reasons against the punishment of offences which are prosecuted after dramatic societal changes, as in the case of the former GDR. Already the reasons for punishment in general are dubious. The most important are retribution and prevention. We can immediately discount retribution as vengeance, since it will do nothing but create new injustice. Punishment for revenge relies on mystical constructions of a re-balancing, from the concrete "an

---

[2] *Ibid.*, p. 208.

[3] See e.g. Lüderssen, *Abschaffen des Strafens?* (Frankfurt, SuhrKamp, 1995), Stratenwerth, *Was leistet die Lehre von den Strafzwecken?* (Berlin, de Gruyter, 1995).

eye for an eye", to the abstract "negation of negation" of injustice. But why should we adopt such archaic modes of thought? To avenge harm with another harm doesn't make sense at all. Harm does not "re-balance" anything, nor does it replace a loss, or re-establish violated law. This would be possible only if we attribute in suspicious, if not to say magical ways, a hidden "message" to the harm inflicted. But these messages can be conveyed without inflicting harm on anybody.

Punishment as prevention creates the same doubts. They are especially prominent concerning the correction of the perpetrator. Nobody today seriously believes that punishment could further this goal. One prison visit should easily convince you of that. Effective therapy is possible only outside prison walls, and requires voluntary collaboration by the offender. And in the case of criminal acts committed by a government, there will often be no need for re-socialisation.

As a final rationale for punishment, we end up with general prevention. There are two different versions of this concept. According to the first, third parties are deterred from committing crimes. The fear of suffering the same fate as a convicted offender should influence their decision whether to commit an offence. According to the second, punishment has a beneficial result on the general public. The punishment of the offender re-asserts the trust of the public in the validity of the legal norms. None of these results is confirmed empirically. They work only in those fields where they are least important: when a rational deliberation between risks and profits takes place, and the outcome directly motivates the acceptance or violation of the norms. Already in the Middle Ages, the public execution of petty thieves did not deter others from stealing the occasional purse. Even more contested is the empirical reality of reinforcing public trust through punishment. And in the case of criminality by governments, there is no need for either.

To conclude, it is not necessary that offences must result in punishment, and no justification of punishment withstands closer examination. If there are therefore good reasons to revoke punishment, are there equally compelling arguments to renounce criminal proceedings, understood as the public determination and attribution of guilt? To answer this question, we have first to determine what this would mean.

RENOUNCING CRIMINAL PROCEEDINGS

Criminal proceedings normally conclude with a verdict, which either acquits the defendant, or determines legal consequences (punishment). Before this is possible, the court must do two things: it must determine the facts of the case and evaluate them legally. But we must not take this description literally. Facts are not established with reference to absolute truth, but are constructed and attributed according to specific rules. Furthermore, not all facts are established, but are rather selected and described with a legal evaluation in mind. The process of (selective) determination and construction of the facts is governed by the concept of "attribution". An event is attributed to a person. This happens in three stages. First, the results of an action of the person in question must be attributed to her, objectively and subjectively.[4] She must stand in a certain internal and external nexus to the events. Secondly, it must be determined whether these attributed actions were in line with the law or not. Finally, the individual responsibility must be established. If this is the case as well, a person is responsible in the sense of the criminal law.

What are the reasons for this schema? If one starts the business of attribution, one has made a fundamental decision. Attribution is possible in two ways: an action-event can be attributed to a *person,* or to a *situation.* This binary coding permeates the entire process. In the first case, the person is the active centre, from which the actions do not only emanate, but from which they are also directed. In the second case, the person is passive, the true reasons for her actions are to be found in the situation, the circumstances or the actions of third parties. In the first case, a person acts, in the second case, a person experiences a situation.[5] Legal attribution only starts when one has decided to attribute an action to a person. Legal attribution is of course only one form of attribution. Attribution takes place permanently in society; it structures our social perceptions. And despite the crudeness of the binary scheme, this very crudeness allows us to react quickly when directly confronted with other people in day to day interaction. The appropriateness of an attribution will often be contested. Well-known and extensively researched is the difference between actor and observer. Actions with detrimental or illegal consequences are typically attributed to the actor by the observer, while the actor himself tends to attribute it to the situation.[6]

Amnesty means only a forfeiture of *legal* attribution, not of attribution in general. An amnesty for crimes in the GDR would not end the process of public attribution of guilt, and the debate about its adequacy. From the informer to the politburo, the two possible forms of attribution will always collide. Are there now reasons to prefer legal attribution to informal attribution in society? Legal attribution always focuses on the individual person and abstracts from the circumstances of the situation, especially if these are seen as rather remote from the concrete illegal act in question. The geo-political situation for instance will not be considered by a court to

[4] This is the German equivalent to *actus reus* and *mens rea.*
[5] Luhmann, "Erleben und Handeln", in *Soziologische Aufklärung 3* (Wiesbaden, Westdt. Vlg., 1981), pp. 67–80, Heidenescher, "Zurechnung als soziologische Kategorie", (1991) 21 *Zeitschrift für Soziologie* 440–55.
[6] Jones and Nisbett, "The Actor and the Observer", in E Jones *et al.* (eds), *Attribution: Perceiving the Causes of Behaviour* (Morriston, 1972).

determine whether the concrete killing of a fugitive by a soldier can be attributed to him, or must be attributed to the situation. On the other hand, legal attribution is rule bound, facts must be established, and hence, a certain rationality is created. Now, two things are possible. The decision not to attribute guilt in a legally organised way can reduce the desire to attribute guilt at all, that is increase the collective desire for forgiveness. Then, an amnesty would indeed pacify a society. Or it can result in a situation where informal attribution is intensified, and most notably, irrational attribution (e.g. by mooting conspiracy theories or by attributing "collective guilt"). Then, an amnesty could increase tensions in a society, and might even prepare the ground for new violence. Irrational attribution of collective historical guilt for instance was at the very heart of the conflict in Yugoslavia. Legal attribution, because of its increased rationality, can then often interrupt the spiral of guilt and retribution. Waiver of legal attribution on the other hand seems to be the more pacifying solution when both parties have gone through the circle of escalation, revenge and counter-revenge, have totally exhausted themselves and the enemy, and when "gain" and "loss" are more or less evenly balanced. Different from this is the situation when there is a clear distinction between perpetrator and victim, winner and loser. In this situation, an official amnesty can be the catalyst for self-help and uncontrolled vengeance by the victims.

Admittedly, there are other non-legal but rational forms of attribution, especially through historiography, where academics establish attribution of actions to persons and situations in a methodological, rule-governed way and in adherence to scientific standards of objectivity.[7] Historical attribution can be found in all cultures that define themselves through a shared tradition and shared memory. An amnesty will not stop this process of historical analysis; the attribution of actions to people, and on the basis of this, normative judgements made by the wider public. We should note however that the historical discussion of the Holocaust in Germany, for instance, was initiated to a large extent by the starting of legal procedures.[8] There are nonetheless crucial differences between legal and historical attribution. Historical attribution avoids normative judgements. It stops with the attribution of causal responsibility. Legal attribution is directed towards the individual actor, and more specifically, towards his core personality. It ends with a normative judgement, that the perpetrator was responsible for his actions. Other forms of societal attribution, including historical attribution, single out specific groups or individuals. Legal attribution establishes

---

[7] On this debate between lawyers and historians see Chandler *et al* (eds), *Questions of Evidence: Proof, Practice and Persuasion across the Disciplines* (Chicago, Chicago University Press), 1994.

[8] Frei, "Der Frankfurter Auschwitz Prozess und die deutsche Zeitgeschichtsforschung", in Fritz Bauer Institute (ed), *Auschwitz—Geschichte, Rezeption, und Wirkung* (Frankfurt, Campus Verlag, 1996).

for every individual actor the degree of her involvement, and asks about her ability to have acted otherwise.

GUILT

The meaning of "guilt" is at least as contested as the rationale for punishment. It might even be that the fixation of the public discourse on the question of punishment tries to avoid this difficult issue. Hassemer, in his *Introduction to the Foundations of Criminal Law*, for instance, writes that the notion of guilt is the most difficult and cryptic instrument in our criminal law system.[9] Nor does our everyday experience help a lot. Guilt is often confused with shame, especially in public speeches commemorating the atrocities of Nazism.[10] The whole concept of guilt is often rejected and understood in the context of a masochistic Protestant "conscience", or the internalisation of a frightening, overpowering and repressive authority.[11]

None of these fits the self-understanding of the modern enlightened citizen and a secular democracy under the rule of law. Attribution through the criminal law now differs from other forms of societal attribution in determining guilt only negatively. Criminal law does not say what guilt might be, but only states negative conditions under which the attribution of guilt is ruled out. Three elements are decisive here: a person must be in a psychological state to understand the unlawfulness of her actions; secondly, she must know that her actions violate law;[12] and finally, adherence to the law must not present unendurable hardship. If none of these conditions is violated, then a person will be declared "guilty of her actions" at the end of the proceedings.[13]

Despite the reluctance of the criminal law to define guilt, the guilty verdict has positive connotations and a more direct definition of the notion of guilt in the criminal law is unavoidable. German criminal law doctrine has developed in the main two contrasting positions. One of them starts with our everyday understanding of the notion of guilt, and focuses on the ability of a person to act otherwise in the moment of the offence. A perpetrator should *only* be punished if she decides of her own free will to commit the offence. It is however not entirely clear what this freedom could mean, and it is clearly not understood as an empirical claim about

[9] Hassemer, *Einführung in die Grundlagen des Strafrechts* (München, C.H.Beck, 1990), p. 217.

[10] See for the connection and differences Taylor, *Pride, Shame and Guilt—Emotions of Self-Assessment* (Oxford, Clarendon, 1985).

[11] Crawford and Quinn, *The Christian Foundations of Criminal Responsibility. A Philosophical Study of Legal Reasoning* (New York, Edwin Mellen Press, 1991); Sigmund Freud, "Totem und Tabu", in *Studienausgabe* (Frankfurt, 1982), pp. 228–444.

[12] Under German law, *ignorantia iuris nocet*, at least in principle.

[13] Code of Criminal Procedures, art 260 at 4.

the state of mind of an individual offender. Rather, it is a fiction, which is oriented at the self-understanding of the other members of a society. Guilt comes close to moral self-determination and autonomy. According to this fiction, the guilty party acts against her own good reasons, and is therefore tied up in a self-contradiction. An offender can be found "guilty" if she doesn't use her capacity for moral self-determination. This blurs the boundaries between law and mores: the separation of law, ethics and morality, constitutive of liberal democracy under the rule of law, is threatened. The offender is not any longer only a legal person, but a moral person as well. The second position avoids these difficulties and ignores the subjective situation of the offender entirely. Guilt is seen as nothing but a rational reconstruction of the need to punish, punishment again justified through its preventive and deterrent effect. Guilt is nothing but a fiction, a mere label. And it fails to the extent that the arguments for punishment, discussed above, fail.

GUILTY PERSONS OR GUILTY CITIZENS?

Guilt as autonomy imports too much morality into the criminal law, guilt as function faces a gap in legitimisation, because punishment can not be justified. This dilemma can be avoided if the concept of guilt is linked to the notion of the person as citizen and the idea of democratic legitimisation.[14] Democratic procedure grounds the legitimacy of law in public discourse and decision-making procedures, in which all citizens can participate as of right. Citizens in a democracy are not only subjected to norms, but are also authors of legal norms. This dual function of norm addressee and norm author is based on a conception of the person. Part of this conception is her ability to question critically and evaluate actions and utterances. This ability for rational critique applies both to one's own actions and to those of other people. This is what we mean by "freedom" of a person. I call an opinion "critical" if it is based on reasons. A person who has the ability to evaluate actions from such a distanced, critical attitude I call a "deliberative" person.[15] She can form a reasoned opinion, and she is able to act according to this opinion. Both elements are connected via the notion of "reason". Reasons are (amongst other things)

[14] The following discussion brings together ideas from Habermas, *Faktizität und Geltung* (Frankfurt, Suhrkamp, 1992), ch 3; Rawls, *Political Liberalism* (New York, Columbia University Press, 1993), pp. 35–40 and 47–88; Gerstenberg, *Deliberative Demokratie* (Frankfurt, Suhrkamp, 1997). See also Günther, "Individuelle Zurechnung im demokratischen Verfassungsstaat", (1994) 2 *Jahrbuch für Recht und Ethik* 143–57.

[15] For a justification of this definition see Habermas, *Theorie des kommunikativen Handelns* (Frankfurt, Suhrkamp, 1981), vol 2, pp. 115–17; Günther, "Communicative Freedom, Communicative Power and Jurisgenesis", (1996) 129 *Cardozo Law Review*, 1035–58.

defined as something which can change our attitude towards the world and which can motivate our actions. But apart from that, it is left deliberately open which sorts of reasons we consider admissible.

To summarise, a deliberative person is able to form a critical opinion of her own and other's actions, she is able to justify this opinion with reasons, which she can check in the role of a fictitious participant in a discourse, she can act according to those reasons she accepts, and can therefore become the author and source of her actions. This again allows these actions to be truly attributed to her. Democratic proceedings now link the creation of universally valid norms to procedures which presuppose everyone's capacity to form a critical opinion of assertions (e.g. proposals for new laws) of others. This ability becomes the constitutive and operative element of the procedures. Democratic procedures allow the argumentative investigation of reasons and counter reasons, they create a market-place of reasons and competition to create better ideas. To the extent to which persons can participate in this market-place, they become authors of the norms created by these procedures.

Since, however, democratic procedures do not correspond totally with ideal discourses (they enable for instance decision-making in limited time), the deliberative person requires other necessary elements. Legal norms are valid even for those persons who did not, or not exhaustively, participate in the democratic process. Legal norms demand respect if the correct procedures have been followed, even if the factual agreement of all concerned is missing. The specific features of the democratic process, which distinguish it from discourse, and the specific nature of legal norms (as opposed to other reasons for actions), distinguish the deliberative person as *citizen* and *legal person*, as author and addressee of legal norms, from other forms of the deliberative person (e.g. the ethical or moral person).

The deliberative concept of personhood that informs the notion of citizen finds its mirror image in the concept of the legal person as addressee of norms. Again, it is not necessary that the deliberative person make the norms as reasons for actions into *her* reasons. Norms need not be interpreted as an act of self-binding one's own free will. She need not follow norms as a moral person. The duty to obey legal norms requires only that the addressee is able in principle to evaluate critically her own actions and statements. She can choose whether to follow the norms at all, and for which reasons. But the law obliges her not to violate through her actions the norm which she rejects. Hence it requires nothing more than the ability to assess critically *one's own* actions. And therefore, the law can threaten sanctions in the case of a violation of the norms. Sanctions preserve the freedom of a person to reject a norm, and become relevant only if her actions violate that norm. The robber who aborts her attempt to rob a bank because she sees the policeman standing nearby obeys therefore as a rational actor also the relevant legal norm, which prohibits bank robbery.

The democratic process is distinguished from all other forms of legitimisation of norms in unifying the notion of citizen and the notion of legal person in the concept of the deliberative person. It is the *external* violation of norms by deliberative persons which constitutes the guilt of that person as legal person. There is of course a long way to go from this very abstract and general conception of a deliberative person to the notion of guilt in the sense of the criminal law. But from now on, it is the citizen himself who is responsible for this journey. But the introduction of conditions which rule out guilt shows that obedience to legal norms depends on the critical evaluation of norms.[16] And they determine *how* the ability to evaluate norms critically is attributed to the actor: she must be informed about the relevant laws, she must be in a position to change her plans because of the critical assessment of these norms, and her obedience to the norms must not constitute an unbearable hardship. In other words: a violation of a norm can be attributed to a person only if she has the cognitive capacity to understand the norms, and she must be able to change her plans because of this cognitive act. Finally, she must not be in a situation where obedience to the norms would violate other, disproportionally more important values. These conditions which might negate the duty to obey the laws, therefore determine how to attribute guilt. The criminal law notion of guilt is therefore born out of a circle, such that citizens recognise each other as free and equal, and at the same time decide how they recognise each other as free and equal. With the concept of guilt, citizens take over the responsibility to determine how to attribute to each other responsibility. The criminal law notion of guilt is always concerned with the understanding of citizens of their own capacity to assess critically their own and others' actions. It concerns the extent to which they confer on each other this freedom. In short, the notion of guilt concerns the self-understanding of citizens as free and equal legal persons.

NEUTRALISATION

The notion of "neutralisation", borrowed from social psychology, is particularly suitable to illustrate the functioning of this circle in the public discourse.[17] It is equally a trivial and deeply disturbing fact that human rights have seen in this century violations of the utmost severity. This fact

---

[16] I follow here the spirit, if not the words, of Hart, "Legal Responsibility and Excuses", in *Punishment and responsibility* (Oxford, Clarendon, 1988).

[17] Sykes and Matza, "Techniken der Neutralisierung: Eine Theorie der Delinquenz", in Sack and König (eds), *Kriminalsoziologie* (Frankfurt, 1974), pp. 360–71; Döbert and Nunner-Winkler, "Performanzbestimmende Aspekte des moralischen Bewusstseins", in Portele (ed.), *Sozialisation und Moral* (Weinheim, 1978), pp. 101–21. On the relevance of neutralisation for justification and excuse of macro-crime see esp. Jäger, "Bedingungen und Mechanismen der Neutralisierung", in *Makrokriminalität* (Frankfurt, 1989), pp. 187–213.

is well known. More astonishing is the multitude of more or less demanding attempts to transfer accountability in these cases from the human actors to the circumstances of the situation. One of the most frequently used legal figures is that of the *historical philosophy of emergency*. Here, it is attempted to excuse human rights violations by saying that they are necessary and inevitable in the present, to guarantee a better future. Depending on the nature of the emergency, we can distinguish excuses from justifications. In the argument that it is necessary to violate certain human rights to enable "true" or "higher" human rights in the future, we are dealing with a justification. In the argument that a specific emergency "regrettably" prevents us from respecting human rights for the time being, we are dealing with an excuse. Especially in the case of excuses, the question of the critical attitude of persons towards their own actions, and hence their freedom, becomes important. The reference to the "Cold War" is not intended to justify the violation of the human right of free movement, but describes the desperate situation, in which (allegedly) people found themselves when they obeyed orders to shoot at people fleeing the country, a situation which did not give them a choice.[18] In the public discourse on guilt, citizens determine the validity of such neutralisations. State emergencies can of course be a valid excuse. But how far this carries, to what extent citizens mutually attribute to each other freedom, even under difficult circumstances, depends on a public debate of the borderline between freedom and coercion. If the debate on the appropriateness of a given excuse is withdrawn from the public domain, unjustified excuses might become prevalent as a neutralisation in a society. This can be avoided only if in each separate case, personal responsibility is determined, if in each separate case, the ability to act in a concrete situation is investigated, and the reasons for a possible exclusion of guilt are scrutinised. This does not at all mean to reject excuses in all cases. On the contrary, naïve attribution of guilt is simply another form of neutralisation. Here, the individual person is seen as the sole party which incurred guilt, and the responsibility of third parties or society is blended out. Society neutralises its own guilt by judging the individual offender.

With the communicative concept of guilt in mind, it becomes evident why forfeiture of criminal proceedings by way of an amnesty are so dangerous. But my analysis would be incomplete if I did not discuss also the dangers of a naïve insistence on the notion of guilt. Of these dangers I want to discuss two: guilt as stigmatising element of social memory, and the interrelation of guilt and power.

[18] But this argument was accepted in mitigation in the case against the GDR, Generals Baumgarten *et al*. See FAZ 13 September 1996.

GUILT AND MEMORY

Guilt is a form of memory. Nietzsche understood guilt, especially the feeling of guilt, as a mnemotechnique: "only that which does not stop hurting remains in our memory".[19] Guilt shows the irreversibility of time in human affairs: the violation of the norm cannot be undone. Guilt makes us remember not only the action that violated the norm, but also the offender. Attribution of guilt takes place in the present, but refers to events past. For the person in the present, that means that she is identified with her former self. "Guilty", she is chained to the past and to her offence. I think that the importance of guilt in this context is to enable a society to organise their past along the lines of the binary schema of attribution to persons and situations. To quote Maurice Halbwachs: "the collective memory forms the internal perspective of a group, whereas the historian adopts an external perspective. It is a continuing mode of thought—whose continuity is not at all artificial since it preserves in living memory only those elements of the past which are still alive and able to survive in the memory of the group which sustains it".[20] I think that legal attribution of guilt is one element of this collective memory. It is an expression of the interest that the group itself has in its past. This living memory is important for the group as a whole—not only for the victims. It makes a difference for a society if it attributes past atrocities to the conflict between societal systems during the Cold War, or individual persons. It is even more important for the victims, whose only alternative to the attribution of guilt to a third person is the fatalistic recognition of injustice suffered as an inevitable fate, or even where she feels herself responsible for what happened to her.

This function of guilt for the collective memory also points to one of its dangers. Guilt chains a person to her past, and this reduces her freedom to start anew, to "turn a new page".[21] To be able to begin something new is one of the meanings of "freedom". The originally open identity of a person remains static, labelled forever by her guilt. Now similar consequences can occur for a society which remains in a state of conflict and shuns reconciliation. Given this danger, we must ask whether or not Herman Lübbe's "communicative silencing" of the past is better than moralistic attribution of guilt to specific individuals.[22] But the

---

[19] Nietzsche, "Genealogie der Moral", in Karl Schechta (ed.), *Gesammelte Werke* (München, 1969), vol. 2, p. 208.

[20] Halbwachs, *Das kollektive Gedächtnis* (Stuttgart, 1967), p. 68.

[21] As Hannah Arendt has shown. See her *Vita Activa* (München, Piper, 1981), para. 33.

[22] Lübbe, "Der Nationalsozialismus im deutschen Nachkriegsbewusstsein", (1983) 236 *Historische Zeitschrift* 579–99. Critically Blanke, "Der Rechtshistorikerstreit um Amnestie", (1985) 28 *Kritische Justiz* 131–50.

preference, which he and other authors similarly attribute to harmony and integration, is unjustified and gets its prima facie plausibility only against the picture of civil war, which these authors describe. This danger will only occur if legal attribution is understood as a moralistic fight against "the evil".[23] But this form of attribution is itself irrational and non-legal. The source of discontent is precisely not the attribution of guilt but the attribution of guilt outside the fair procedural arrangements of the legal process. Democracy does not survive by harmony at all costs, but by prudent ways of dealing with conflict.[24] The notion of guilt is such a conflictual concept, which enables a debate about the self-understanding of the citizens in a democracy. It forces them to make reasoned decisions between attribution of actions to persons or to situations. The danger of civil unrest as a result of enforced reconciliation or collective "omerta" is as great as the danger of civil war as a response to irrational public attribution of guilt.

Without public conflict over the attribution of individual guilt, we also lose a perspective which might open a possible way to become liberated from the past. Recognition of guilt, so Hannah Arendt argued, is also a precondition for forgiveness.[25] Attribution of guilt then is not the end of a process, but the beginning of a new communicative exchange, which can end with the negation of guilt through forgiveness by those directly concerned. But this perspective also has a certain danger for the communicative process in a democracy under the rule of law. The law cannot require acceptance of (one's) guilt and forgiveness; here, law reaches its final limits. The offender cannot be forced to recognise his guilt, the victim cannot be forced to forgive. But this process can nonetheless *be started* by a rational legal procedure.

CONCLUSION

In insisting on the gap between legal attribution of guilt and the recognition of guilt by the offender, I come finally to my last point, the entanglement of power and guilt. One of the bitter experiences that we had during the twentieth century was not only the denial of guilt and the neutralisation of human rights violations, but also conversely, the domination of guilt by power. Power had seen its greatest triumph when the loser was forced to confess his "guilt". This was the case for instance in the public confessions of guilt in the "legal" proceedings under Stalin. For those not prepared to succumb, however, power has another means: they are declared

[23] Against this tendency see my "Kampf gegen das Böse? Zehn Thesen wider die ethische Aufrüstung der Kriminalpolitik", (1994) 27 *Kritische Justiz* 135–57.

[24] Dubiel, "Gehegte Konflikte", (1995) 49 *Merkur* 1095–1106.

[25] Arendt, above n. 21, paras 33, 34.

to be insane. This is, from Nietzsche to Foucault, the great problem for the modern notion of guilt, which focuses on the inner judgement of conscience and the unconditional confession of guilt. This allows power to infiltrate the innermost centre of a person.

This entanglement of power and guilt brings me back to the communicative concept of guilt and its basis, the deliberative notion of personhood. On the one hand, a person needs besides their inner voice also an external voice, to participate in the proceedings which determine the norms. On the other, she must herself participate in the precise definition of the concept of the legal person, and the frontier between freedom and coercion. Society must reclaim the notion of guilt from power. We have to determine the limits of guilt *against* all powers which require from us a confession before them.

If this would be possible, I would say that the demand for punishment of an offender asks too much, the request for an amnesty asks too little.

2

"Sometimes You Must be Kind to be Cruel"
Amnesty between *publicae laetitiae* and *damnatio memoriae*

BURKHARD SCHÄFER

INTRODUCTION

This chapter started as a response to ideas expressed at the Workshop on Mercy and Law held at Edinburgh University, some of which are published in this volume. As a contribution to an on-going discussion, the argument was triggered most notably by Klaus Günther's impressive analysis of a "politics of remembrance". It seemed to me then, as it does now, that most of the contributions shared a number of highly plausible implicit assumptions about the nature of amnesty and mercy in law, which nonetheless might be in need of further scrutiny. Essentially, my questions concern the alleged "special status" of amnesty and mercy in the law, the dichotomy between law, mercy and amnesty, and a discussion which accepts too easily widespread public perceptions of a deep conceptual dichotomy between amnesty and mercy on the one hand, and law on the other. Indeed, the very identification of mercy and amnesty with legal benevolence is, I think, more complicated than it seems, and most of what follows is best understood as a series of observations and questions to test the idea of the exceptionality of amnesty as a legal concept. German law distinguishes between "*Amnestie*" and "*Gnade*", amnesty and mercy.[1] One of the claims I am making is the importance of this analytical distinction for a theory of amnesties. The other is that both, each in a different way, can be used to punish (certain forms of) criminal law actors, not to reward them.

---

[1] Mercy follows a judgment in a particular case, amnesty is a general law covering an abstractly defined group of people possibly before a conviction: Schaetzler, *Handbuch des Gnadenrechts* (Munchen, CH Beck, 1992), pp. 17, 208.

BACKGROUND TO THE DISCUSSION

A quick Internet survey reveals that over the past ten years, literature on law, amnesty and mercy has mushroomed to an extraordinary extent.[2] The Truth and Reconciliation Commission (TRC) in South Africa, the legal problems created by Germany's reunification and the demise of several military dictatorships in Latin America necessitated a more thorough analysis of concepts which had previously been at the margins of legal-theoretical thought, of interest more to the legal historian, and a reminder of the time when absolute sovereigns celebrated their coronation and similar *"occasionae publicae laetitiae"*.[3] These times of amnesty as a form of public celebration however are over, and this same decade has seen quite often embittered public debate on the merits and demerits of concrete proposals for amnesties. In South Africa, for example, initial enthusiasm has been replaced by an increasing sense of disillusion, and a feeling that the TRC has left the country as divided as before. In Chile, an amnesty of a very different kind, the self-amnesty of its former dictator Pinochet, was initially seen as a necessary condition for a peaceful transition to democracy. But when the British House of Lords had to decide its very lawfulness under international law, the grief of his victims regained its voice and showed the world a Chile whose transition to democracy remains precarious—because of, not despite, the amnesty. Finally, in Germany the debate over the legal response to the crimes of the former GDR opened old wounds when the—inevitable but misguided—comparison to the abject failure of the criminal justice systems to deal with the atrocities of the Nazi dictatorship entered into the public debate.[4]

The discussion in Germany soon widened its scope, from the question of the appropriate legal response to past crimes of the communist East to a general discussion of crimes committed as a result of the Cold War, in East and West. This included a proposal from the Social Democratic Party to

---

[2] See e.g. the extensive bibliographies in Smith and Amargalit (eds), *Die Politik der Erinnerung* (Frankfurt, Suhrkamp, 1997), O'Donell and Schmitter (eds), *Transition from Authoritarian Rule: Tentative Conclusions about Uncertain Democracies* (John Hopkins Univ. Press, 1986); Boraine, Levy and Schaffler (eds), *Dealing with the Past. Truth and Reconciliation in South Africa* (1994).

[3] Schaetzler, above n. 1, p. 253. This is not entirely a thing of the past, though. France in particular celebrated since 1959 the elections of de Gaulle, D'Estaing and Mitterand with amnesties for petty crime. See Spies, "Amnestiemassnahmen und deren Verfassungsmaessigkeit in Frankreich und Deutschland", (PhD thesis, Freiburg 1991). Austria still enacts amnesties for public festivities, the last in 1985 to celebrate 40 years of independence.

[4] So Blanke, "Der Rechtshistorikerstreit um Amnestie", (1995) 28 *Kritische Justiz* 140; Wassermann in [1993] *Neue Juristische Wochenzeitung* 897. Critical Limbach, "Fatalismus ist nicht gestattet", in [1991] *Recht und Politik* 142.

incorporate convictions of past demonstrators against NATO under an amnesty which would try to "draw the final curtain" over the history of Germany's partition.[5] More surprisingly, the then conservative Head of State, President von Weizsäcker, proposed to include a reconciliatory approach towards the surviving left-extremist terror groups in Germany, most notably the Red Army Faction (RAF).[6] While both proposals foundered after an overwhelmingly hostile, public reaction, the Weizsäcker proposal was later resurrected. Interestingly enough, it was the Secret Service who spotted its potential for ending thirty years of RAF terrorism, initiating a "drop-out programme" which resulted ultimately in the winding up of the RAF by its remaining members.

This chapter will focus on these two attempts for an amnesty law to argue for a conceptual rethink in the debate on amnesty and mercy in law. I will argue that some of the most commonly held assumptions about amnesties and mercy in law, in public discourse and in the academic dispute mirroring it, are failing to explain the inner working of amnesties in these cases.

THE AMNESTY DEBATE IN GERMANY

It is probably fair to assume that the debate over the need for an amnesty in Germany was at least partly due to the feeling that the response of the state in both cases had at least compromised the ideal of the *"Rechtsstaat"*, and that both courts and police had been playing fast and loose with constitutional and human rights guarantees out of political expediency. The following is an attempt to describe this *perception,* which was shared by parts of the liberal, centre-left and left of the political spectrum. For the purpose of the argument it is not necessary to see this perception as accurate, fair, or justified, so long as it is acknowledged that as a perception, it played a significant role in German politics and society. Dissatisfaction with the overreaction of the state against the emerging protest movement played, for instance, an important role in the formation of the hugely successful Green movement in Germany.[7] This was particularly clear in the case of the "Pershing" protestors.[8] In this instance, the

---

[5] So Hirsch and Daeubler-Gmelin, BT prot. ("Parliamentary protocol") 11/222, pp.17499, 17542. For an earlier attempt by the Green party, see Schaetzler, above n.1, p. 252.

[6] Even if he remained sceptical regarding a general amnesty for crimes committed in the GDR. See R *v*. Weizsaecker, Interview in (1995) 4 *Der Spiegel* 22.

[7] Acknowledged to a certain extent by the Verfassungsschutz (literally, Constitution protection agency, the German equivalent to MI5) analysing the recruitment of left-wing extremists (admittedly the newer groups) at schools and universities, see "Militante Linksextremisten rekrutieren Nachwuchs Schauplatz Schule und Jugendtreff" at http://www.verfassungsschutz.de.

[8] After all, their solicitor was to become the first Green foreign minister in Germany.

courts had bent over backwards to secure a conviction for unlawful duress, stretching on the one hand the meaning of the notion of "violence" to its utter limits, whilst on the other ignoring the explicit requirement of one of the offence elements, that the force used and the aim attempted should be grossly disproportional. In the case of the Pershing protestors, the problem was a "*Lex Mutlangen*", a highly questionable decision by the courts to deal with a very specific group of people in a very specific historical and political context.[9] But the decision does not seem to have created a precedent above and beyond the protest against nuclear armament—no attempt was being made for instance to prosecute farmers for blocking roads as part of their protest against the government's agricultural policy.

The situation regarding the RAF is more complex, the damage to the rule of law more indirect. In comparison with the Mutlangen decision, the situation is almost the inverse. Here, the problem is less the investigation, classification and adjudication of the crimes committed by the RAF, but rather the impact which legislation, brought into force as a response to their terror campaign, has or could have for totally unrelated and largely peaceful social movements and political protest.[10] To force the state into an authoritarian response, in the hope of "exposing" the structures of the state as inherently fascist, and to trigger a public uprising in response, was a conscious aim of the extreme left and the RAF in particular. As far as the first part of this proposition is concerned, they were surely successful. Tighter legislation, the creation of new criminal offences and the dramatic increase of powers for the police followed the assassination of Herrhausen, Braunmuehl and Rohwedder. In particular, the notorious article 129a of the Criminal Code re-introduced criminal liability for the expression of

---

[9] In this case, the question was whether "human road blocks" by protestors, which forced the drivers of the Pershing rocket launchers to use a different road, amounted to "unlawful duress". Court of first instance and Federal Court of Appeal (BGH) both decided that the threat of psychological harm a driver of a 30 ton military vehicle would suffer when driving through a human wall, forcing him to take a detour, constituted violence. They apparently also decided (without discussing it in much detail) that this harm was disproportionate to the goal the protestors wanted to achieve (i.e. saving mankind from a nuclear holocaust). The Constitutional Court quashed the conviction and referred the case back to the BGH, deciding that mere psychological harm did not constitute violence in the sense of art. 240 of the Criminal Code (StGB). The BGH however, far from now acquitting the accused, affirmed its earlier verdict, arguing now that while the first driver in a column was only subjected to psychological duress, his halting his van would cause a physical, not only psychological, barrier to all drivers behind him. These then were not only psychologically, but physically forced to abandon their route. This decision, apart from its dubious interpretation of the law, violates some of the most elemental rules of statutory interpretation (e.g. the rule to interpret the same notion uniformly throughout the Code) and blatantly undermined the authority of the Constitutional Court.

[10] With a very strong left-wing bias, but nonetheless a good overview, see the discussion at http:"www.argonsoft.de/~cogito/heft3_4/10.html. See also the paper of the Bundesarbeitsgemeinschaft Kritischer Polizistinnen und Polizisten (Association of Critical Police Officers), *Das politische Strafrecht*.

political opinions, if these could be understood as supporting a terrorist organisation.[11] However, the RAF radically misinterpreted the public reaction to these legislative measures. Far from resulting in a public revolt, these measures were by and large enthusiastically welcomed by the broader public. If there was a hostile reaction at all, this was limited to the "liberal left", especially in the student population and among certain members of the "educational upper class", academics, journalists and artists. While it undoubtedly helped the RAF to recruit new members at the fringes of the student movement, most of these critics were absorbed by mainstream political parties, most notably by the Green movement.

It is against this background that we must understand the proposals for amnesties for RAF terrorists and members of the peace movement alike. Public opinion, aided and abetted by the tabloid press, voiced its outrage over proposals which were seen as a "reward for criminals", a "special treatment for politicals" while "ordinary people" would continue to feel the harsh hand of the law with all its force.[12] The *Rechtsstaat* was perceived to be in a dilemma: either the legal case against the accused was dubious, in which case an amnesty would be seen as a public acknowledgement of the failure of legal guarantees and as implicit criticism of prosecution, police and judiciary (none of the big political parties wanted to risk adopting this perspective in the ensuing discussion);[13] or, the potential beneficiaries had committed the crimes they stood accused of, and in this situation "the law is the law" and any exceptions to its general rules amounted to undermining the very fabric of legality.[14]

Academic discourse, in Germany and elsewhere, mirrors this perceived dilemma, even in those cases where the general attitude towards amnesties is positive. We can equate the public feeling that amnesties allow exceptions from the rule of law for specific, individual offenders, with a theoretical analysis which emphasises the particularist nature of amnesties; a way

---

[11] One has to be careful though in claiming a causal relation between the RAF campaign and these laws. In Britain, the recently proposed anti-terrorism legislation by Jack Straw closely mirrors the German precedent, especially in criminalising "ideological" support for organisations engaged in criminal activities. Here as in Germany, the main danger of these laws are the potential for criminalising, say, discussions of the destruction of GM crops by Greenpeace. However, the British laws were enacted at a time when terrorism was at an all time low, with the peace process in Northern Ireland still looking healthy. Home Secretaries do not need much of a reason to curtail civil liberties, it comes naturally to them.

[12] The contrast of having to pay for traffic violations while "politicals" can get away with murder became a particularly popular topic in readers' letters.

[13] The social democratic SPD which had first proposed an amnesty for anti-nuclear weapons protestors, wanted explicitly to "draw the final curtain", that is, avoid a debate about rights and wrongs. Once it became obvious that the proposal had started that debate, the proposal was dropped. Only the left-extreme PDS and the Greens continued to argue for amnesties beyond those for GDR spies, discussed by Günther in Chapter 1 above.

[14] On the rejection by the general public see Schaeuble, *Der Vertrag* (Stuttgart, Deutsche V.-A, 1991), p. 268.

of doing "justice to particulars" in the positive reading, "the tombstone on the grave of the rule of law" in the negative reading.[15] The public apprehension of political interference with the legal process results in the widely accepted dichotomy of mercy and law, amnesties being conceptualised as outside the legal process, and law conversely as free of an understanding of the political context in which it operates.[16] Implicit in academic and public discourse, is the assumption that "mercy" and "amnesty" can be equated, that the party receiving an amnesty is in one way or the other "rewarded", "let off the hook" or at least subject to a more favourable treatment. Once these dichotomies are accepted, once we think of amnesties as benefits for individual offenders outside the legal process, the consequences drawn by Günther become inevitable: in situations where law becomes precarious, where punishment, for whatever reasons, is sensed to be inappropriate, an amnesty is always going to offer too little, and punishment is going to be too much.[17] But if we have reasons to reject this dichotomy, if we can find examples of amnesties which are best understood *as part* of the legal process, general in nature and not wholly beneficial to the receiving party, we can overcome this problem. In particular, it is the assumption that amnesties benefit in one way or another the receiving party which seems to be the most natural and commonsensical. However, as I will argue, these assumptions are not sufficient nor indeed necessary to conceptualise the legal notion of amnesty.

This means that I have to show:

(a) that there are other forms of non-punishment in the legal system, which also constitute favourable treatment of individual offenders, but which are nonetheless not normally discussed together with amnesties. Traditional theoretical analyses of amnesties are not able to distinguish them sufficiently from other forms of discretionary waiver of punishment in the law. A convincing theory of amnesties must therefore either discuss amnesties as part of a broader analysis of legal discretion, or enrich its conceptual vocabulary to allow the necessary distinctions to be made:

(b) that there are amnesties which do not display any of the three characteristics used to define amnesties: particularity, extra-legality and "beneficiality" for the accused. In particular this means showing that we can think of amnesties which are intended to harm, not to benefit, the receiving party.

---

[15] Wilhelm Kahl, quoted in Quaritsch, "Ueber Buergerkriegs—und Feindamnestien", [1998] *Der Staat* 198.

[16] For many others, Hillenkamp, "Offene oder Verdeckte Amnestie. Humbold Forum Recht" at http//www.humboldt-forum-recht.de/6-1997/Drucktext.html.

[17] See Günther in Chapter 1 above.

CONCEPTUAL PROBLEMS WITH TRADITIONAL
DISCUSSIONS OF AMNESTIES

In the following, I will have a closer look at the three elements identified above, which in traditional discourse build the conceptual foundations for the notion of amnesty. In each case, I will argue primarily that there are legal vehicles other than amnesties which display the relevant feature. The second aspect to my argument, that there are amnesties which display neither, will largely be postponed until the RAF amnesty is discussed as a case study.

(a) Amnesties are not outside the system of legal rules, and do not make exceptions for individuals. Of all the three, the notion that amnesties bring a specific particularity to the legal system—that they are an alternative to general, abstract rules—is the most easily dealt with. Not only do we find examples of particularistic decision making in other forms of legal adjudication, but amnesties are in fact a rather poor example of "taking the individual into account" and are actually more rule-based and general than probably most decisions reached in courts. Under German or French law, to give just two examples, amnesties themselves would indeed have the form of a general law, and amnesties for named individuals are considered illegal.[18] As a consequence, an amnesty would apply to a group of people defined by the same general, abstract characteristics typically found in offence elements in the criminal law. Moreover, by defining this group, Parliament can ignore conceptual distinctions which typically permeate criminal law, being less, rather than more, discerning than normal criminal procedure. In the case of the Mutlangen protestors mentioned earlier, the relevant criminal law, properly applied, would have at least made a distinction between those protestors who acted because of their sincere concern for human survival, and those who were simply eager to pick a fight with the police. Furthermore, if the statutory provision—the "disproportionality" between the threat applied and the goals intended—had been interpreted as a subjective offence element, it would have enabled the judge to investigate and thematise the motivation and beliefs of individual suspects, and the meaning each of them attributed to their actions. Hypothetically, however, even those involved in the process with a valid defence—for instance duress—would be treated under an amnesty law in exactly the same way as the "true" offenders.

Apart from this individualistic element of the German law on criminal duress, in deciding on the concrete punishment, judges in general have wide discretion to take a multitude of individual factors into account: from the degree to which the individual was involved in the act (sitting at the

---

[18] Marxen, *Rechtliche Grenzen der Amnestie* (Heidelberg, Forum Rechtswissenschaft Bd 13, 1984), pp. 29–42.

centre or the side of the road), to an assessment of individual responsibility (intellectual ability to understand that a law was violated, intoxication, and the notorious "troublesome childhood"), and the effect the punishment would have on the individual offender (age, chance of re-socialisation, claustrophobia which makes prison harder to bear etc.). An amnesty law again would gloss over these differences between individual offenders; it is in its form more general, more law-like than established forms of decision-making *within* the court process.

It is this ability of amnesties to treat unlike cases alike that contributes to the potential of amnesty laws to be used as a weapon, a punishment rather than a reward. Regarding the Mutlangen protest, some of the accused might well prefer a conviction which, through a more lenient sentence, acknowledges the difference between those with politically acceptable motives and those without—a sentence which would have been an indirect but noticeable public recognition of the political, if not legal, validity of their argument. An amnesty, especially an amnesty which precedes a verdict, would have made this impossible. To use an analogy, nothing is more unnerving for a child to be told by his parents that what he did was wrong, but that he is forgiven, while he still trying to argue that it was in reality his sibling who caused the damage.

We can think of more radical examples which take the idea, mooted by Germany's Social Democrats of a "final curtain", one step further: one amnesty, for instance, for left-wing and right-wing terrorism alike would not be appreciated by either, establishing an essential similarity between the two and undercutting their conceptual framework of "good" and "bad" terrorism. We might in passing compare the situation in Northern Ireland, where the early release scheme under the Good Friday agreement targets loyalist and republican terrorists simultaneously. If my analysis is correct, then both sides by accepting the *joint* release abandoned, or at least weakened, a self-understanding which saw the one side as a legitimate defender, the other as an illegal aggressor. The politicians of both sides, by voluntarily accepting this definition, removed an important element of justification from their own paramilitary wings and distanced political from terrorist activities much more radically than they themselves were probably aware. They established an equality between terrorist acts of both sides, which as ("illegitimate") "third parties", the British and Irish justice systems, merely by punishing them alike, could not possibly communicate to the two communities.

(b) Amnesties are not (necessarily) outside the court system and its fact-finding process. A different version of the dichotomy discussed under (a) asserts the exceptional status of amnesty legislation by contrasting not so much the form of the substantive laws, but the way of their implementation and adjudication. On this reading, amnesties are located outside, or even opposed to, the normal court process. This in particular is at the heart of

Klaus Günther's argument, which, rightly I think, points out that the legal process of fact-finding is a very powerful and effective vehicle for establishing a nexus between people and their actions, and can have an important contribution to the public interpretation of the past.[19] If, however, this analysis is correct, *and* amnesties are also with necessity outside the normal court procedure, then any proposal for an amnesty must be aware that it gives away a powerful tool for a highly effective and desirable public accounting of individual actions. The South African Truth and Reconciliation Commission (TRC) can be seen as a partial response to this problem, employing the traditional techniques of the legal process, but with an amnesty as pre-established component, and institutionally separated from the South African court system. Günther's own solution follows the line of the TRC, and differentiates between amnesties which only cover the actual punishment, and those which prevent the attribution of guilt. But he also points out that this solution will not always be available. Countries with a well-established legal tradition will most certainly face constitutional obstacles for such special tribunals. German constitutional law would, for instance, clearly prevent such an approach to deal with the crimes committed in the former GDR and indeed, we saw similar challenges in South Africa as well. Nor do we want to force the accused into insincere acts of public contrition. The alternatives again, so it seems, are problematic: either an amnesty before a verdict is granted by an ordinary court, and hence there is no public recording of guilt; or, there is an amnesty after an ordinary court reaches its verdict. But which self-respecting judge could carry out a trial in the knowledge that whatever verdict she reaches, the political decision over an amnesty is already taken? And even were it possible, how could we avoid the parallel to the public remorse requested from those convicted in the political trials under communism?

But again we must ask if this problem is characteristic for amnesties. Most jurisdictions leave the decision whether to prosecute in the individual case to a special office, for instance the Staatsanwaltschaft in Germany or the Crown Prosecution Service in England. Here again, the relevant officials have wide discretion in taking individual factors of the case into account in reaching a decision as to whether the prosecution would be in the public interest. Sometimes, as in Germany, they will also be subject to orders by a government department, institutionalising a representation of political considerations in the court process. If these officials take the political decision not to prosecute an abstractly defined group of alleged offenders, we do indeed speak sometimes of a "hidden amnesty".[20] More

---

[19] K Günther, "Der strafrechtliche Schuldbegriff als Gegenstand einer Politik der Erinnerung in der Demokratie", in Gary Smith and Avishai Margalit (eds), *Amnestie oder die Politik der Erinnerung in der Demokratie* (Frankfurt am Main, Suhrkamp, 1997), pp. 48–89, at p. 83.

[20] See, for "hidden amnesties", Hillenkamp, above n. 16.

typical will be the situation where highly individual features of the particular case make a prosecution seem undesirable; the fear, for instance, that
even a successful prosecution of a person with great public appeal could
bring bad publicity for the legal system. Or even more prosaic considerations which are alien both to the alleged offence and the person of the
alleged offender, for instance budgetary considerations, or a flu epidemic
which forces prosecutors to concentrate on the more urgent cases. As
already discussed, these forms of non-prosecution will be even less law-like
and general than amnesties. They are, moreover, only to a small degree
subject to judicial review. Amnesties, on the other hand, being formal laws,
could, under German law, be subject to scrutiny by the constitutional
court. A general theory of amnesties, so it seems to me, must deny that
these forms of non-prosecution are essentially the same as amnesties. But
then, our suspicion of amnesties must be caused by other not yet discussed
conceptual characteristics. Alternatively, we would have to develop a
general theory of non-prosecution, with formal amnesties as a special case.
But in this case, every conclusion drawn regarding the problematic status
of amnesties would equally apply to the most common features to be
found in modern criminal justice systems, and if amnesties are perceived to
be illegitimate, this illegitimacy would spread far beyond current discussions of legal systems in transition.

Coming back however to Günther's dilemma between punishment and
amnesty, we now have to consider the second case: amnesties (or similar
non-prosecutions) which are integrated into the legal process, and make
use of its fact-finding ability. We can find at least two models in German
law which fit this description. One, Crown witness regulations, it shares
with many other jurisdictions.[21] As it was also at the heart of the RAF
drop out programme, I will discuss this later. The other is even more
intriguing. German law provides the possibility for people who have
committed criminal offences under the tax law regime to avoid punishment
if they institute legal proceedings against themselves and make a full
confession.[22] This is not a form of discretional mitigation by a judge for
co-operative behaviour, since there is a guarantee of non-punishment. Nor
is it simply a criminal law defence; only the punishment is affected, not the
legal evaluation of guilt.

Both of Günther's conditions are therefore met: the waiver of punishment where punishment is inappropriate, full establishment of guilt, and
the use of the fact-finding and publicity mechanisms of the ordinary justice
system. But it does not require a public display of remorse, which might
anyway look rather odd in cases of tax evasion. What makes this legal

---

[21] The expression "Crown witness" is the literal translation of "*Kronzeuge*". It is widely
used, including by the government and its agencies, this notwithstanding the fact that
Germany does not have a crown.

[22] Hillenkamp, above n. 16, p. 14.

instrument unique is that the offender has a legal guarantee of a pardon. Thus, finally, we have a legal regulation which in abstract and general terms sets out the conditions for an amnesty, and which is not subject to the discretionary exertion of mercy by a political power.

AMNESTY AND DAMNATIO MEMORIAE

When the then German President Richard von Weizsaecker first mooted the idea of a possible reconciliation with terrorists of the RAF, the public outcry was deafening, and the idea was immediately dropped in mainstream political discourse. Despite the high personal reputation of the President, the wider public did not feel a need to "reconcile" with the historic losers of the Cold War. In not prosecuting politically motivated criminals, nothing could be gained, and the integrity of the legal order could be lost—or so it was felt. The German Verfassungsschutz however saw things differently. Despite the considerably increased investigative powers of the police, successes in the fight against terrorism had been rather limited. Police actions against left-wing terrorism had been only of limited success, but the break-down of communism and the Warsaw pact, Germany's reunification and the continuing discovery of human rights violations in the GDR had severely shaken left-wing ideology, making extremist groups more vulnerable than any investigative successes could have done. Furthermore, it became apparent that not only had the GDR protected members of the RAF, but they had also integrated them into a life-style which was as *"petit bourgeoise"*, as dull and unglamorous as one could imagine. School teachers living in council house estates in a garden gnome idyll, in the state which under Margaret Honecker[23] had oppressed Rock n' Roll music for excessive hedonism, were not figures likely to inspire a new generation of left-wing terrorists. The Verfassungsschutz correctly sensed that if they wanted to capitalise on this ideological insecurity, overly aggressive actions by the police and the criminal justice system could only offer a new rallying point, an ersatz-ideology, and had therefore to be avoided.[24] As a consequence then, it revived the Weizsaecker initiative, no longer in the terminology of "reconciliation", but under the heading of a more efficient fight against terrorism. In offering leniency or even waiver of prosecution to members of the RAF and its wider environment in exchange for co-operation, either as part of on-going criminal procedures (the Crown witness programme) or outside (the *Aussteigerprogramm*, or "drop

---

[23] Wife of the then Head of Government of the GDR, Erich Honecker, and stalwart of sexual probity during her reign in his Cabinet.

[24] For the problems of left-extremist groups to deal with the de-escalation, while understanding it as an attempt to undermine its claim for legitimacy, see "Interview mit der Antifa". At http://www.xs4all.nl/~radical.

out" programme) it succeeded in dragging the internal ideological debate and insecurity into public.[25] While the Crown witness programme was originally intended to result in measurable success regarding new prosecutions, a careful interpretation by the courts allowed this avenue even if only "general information about the operative structures" of the RAF were offered.[26] This made it easier for individuals to participate, and more difficult for the remaining commando structure to denounce this co-operation. And indeed any criticism of members who chose to participate in these programmes was remarkably muted and restrained.

Not only does the accused have to earn the more lenient sentence by contribution to the fact-finding process—one of Günther's conditions—but this seems to be all that is required. The conditions for participation are described objectively, without reference to a subjective notion of "remorse". In offering leniency to *individual* members, it succeeded where previous court cases had failed, by defining as private a conflict which for the RAF had always been a political conflict. While in previous cases, the state had tried to make the political legal, it succeeded this time in making the legal and political private, thus inverting a central plank in the self-understanding of the left. What the left traditionally understood as the predominance of the political in shaping private life now became the public story of a misguided political life as a result of personal accidents. The terrorist self-understanding of heroic struggle against the system, sounded now in the public statements of former RAF members like a wasted political life, shaped by highly personal problems: terrorism as an excessive response to teenage angst.[27]

The success of the programme was immense. In 1992, the RAF denounced violence against persons. In the following year, the programme got the support of prominent RAF prisoners, most notably Brigit Hogefeld and Helmuth Pohl, who asked publicly for the dissolution of the RAF.[28] But only when Christopher Seidler used the programme to give himself up, claiming that he was never a member of the RAF in the first place (a claim supported by another RAF prisoner, Eva Haule, who was equally criticised for this statement by the RAF), did the official RAF react. In a statement sent to Agence France Press, and a letter to the Berlin Newspaper *Neue Welt*, the RAF aggressively criticised the programmes, but also admitted

---

[25] Crown witness offers for terrorists required legislative initiative, and was offered to accused standing trial. The drop out programme was more of an administrative decision by the Verfassungschutz to help people in hiding to return from illegality.

[26] E.g. http://www.spiegel.de/spiegel/0,1518,23324,00.html The author states that no convictions, but a number of rather embarrassing acquittals, resulted from the programme—factually correct, but if the analysis presented here is convincing, a wrong conclusion.

[27] See e.g. Brigitte Hogefeld during her trial, at
http://pages.ohz.north.de/kombo.k_30hoge.htm

[28] Hogefeld, however, refused the offered Crown witness status; she was sentenced to life imprisonment.

that "the very concept of the RAF is outdated", and "there can be no return to old strategies".

Specialists from the Security branches and the police uniformly interpreted these letters as the *de facto* dissolution of the RAF, and the Bavarian Verfassungschutz officially declared the RAF dead. The Verfassungsschutz[29] and RAF agree on the effectiveness of the two programmes: according to the RAF:[30]

"The Aussteigerprogramm and Crown Witness Regulation are two sides of a coin. It intends to transform members in hiding and prisoners to tools of the secret service, betraying not only their comrades, but also their own history".

It added:

"There is a lack of distance to such 'programmes', and this is not only a problem for the disintegration of our political context, but a problem for the entire political left. For many, this is the end of an era, and they do not find themselves personally any longer represented in the radical struggle against the system and/or illegal structures of the left".

And finally:

"Probably, you will criticise us because we wrote against the 'prattling' in the media. Of course, we do not mind if comrades bring their personal experience into films, conferences etc., and how they experience the past, and how they see this today, and what lessons we should learn from this. On the contrary. But it is a problem for us if for a great number of our comrades, the RAF is already history".

These quotes clearly show that the programmes hit a nerve. A group which defined itself primarily as negation of the state, and its struggle as against state pressure, loses its foothold once this pressure is removed.[31] The RAF understood this in identifying the Crown witness programme— superficially an investigative measure—with the partial amnesty of the drop out programme. Hogefeld came to a similar conclusion when she wrote that the state needed groups like the RAF, not the least to justify its own violence.[32] We saw earlier, of course, that the converse is equally true:

[29] For the Verfassungsschutz, see http://www.verfassungschutz.nrw.de/vs_raf.htm The impact on the RAF becomes particularly clear in numerous Internet articles published by the wider support groups of the RAF, especially the "Angehoerigen Info" at http://www.nadir.org?nadir?periodika/angehoerigen_info/ai-130.html p. 2.

[30] In a letter to the Berlin newspaper *Junge welt*. To be found e.g. at
  http://www.verfassungschutz.nrw.de/news/raf_jw.htm

[31] One of the imprisoned RAF terrorists clearly saw this in her statement made during her trial (http://pages.ohz.north.de/kombo/k_30hoge.htm p. 6), when she speaks about the "exclusive orientation of our [i.e. the RAF's] policy as negation", which essentially relies on a black and white scheme of things.

[32] Hogefeld at http://pages.ohz.north.de/kombo/k_30hoge.htm p. 8: the state need groups like the RAF.

that it was a main plank in the RAF's insurrectionary agenda to provoke the state into oppressive measures. As a consequence, the state needs (if at all) the RAF as much as the RAF needed the oppressive state: without public and symbolic prosecution by the state, the RAF could not survive.

For a conceptual theory of amnesty, we should note the following points: the original description by Weizsaecker of a "reconciliation" was not dropped by accident. Reconciliation and mercy have a different logical structure. Reconciliation is a symmetrical relation. I can be reconciled with you only if you are reconciled with me. Therefore, it requires as a minimum condition, if not an equivalence in power, then at least the survival of both sides in the process of reconciliation. Mercy, on the other hand, is not a symmetrical relation. I can show mercy to you, without any corresponding relation from you to me. While reconciliation does not require that the parties in the process are of equal power, mercy is typically shown by the stronger to the weaker, by the victor to the defeated. In Northern Ireland, the "early release scheme" did not take the form of an amnesty—and with good reasons. A Royal Pardon would not have impressed the republican movement, it was not for the Queen to show mercy to a defeated enemy. Instead, we got a scheme which looks more like an exchange of prisoners, and which did not undermine the self-understanding of the IRA as an army unbeaten in battle. Amnesties have the same structure as mercy, it is granted by the stronger side to the weaker. This does not preclude the possibility that an amnesty might eventually result in reconciliation; only that it is not an act of reconciliation in itself. Typically, it will require that the receiving side can repay the amnesty in kind, show mercy itself and thus can transform the unilateral act into a symmetrical relation.

Phenomenologically, we have to distinguish between amnesties which negate a legal classification and the attribution of guilt, and those which do not. Both can take place, as argued, inside and outside the legal process. In particular, amnesties which do not negate the attribution of guilt reinforce asymmetrical power relations The party that offers the amnesty is strong enough to enforce *its* definition of the events, and then shows mercy for the acts as *defined by the party that grants amnesty*. In the case of the RAF amnesty, it therefore doubly undermines the mechanism which sustained the RAF: first, by defining *in co-operation* with the accused his/her acts as criminal and not political acts; denying that is, in the criminal law process, the political its voice; secondly, by cutting through the nexus between the criminal law classification and the punishment. But even amnesties which do not follow an official attribution of guilt can be, as we have seen, a double-edged sword. In Günther's criticism, it seems to be always the party granted an amnesty which avoids the attribution of guilt. But given the unequal power structure of amnesties, this need not be the case. An amnesty in the Mutlangen case for instance would prevent the demonstrators in an appeal challenging the attribution, or raising issues of police wrongdoing. An amnesty for former GDR spies would settle, by implication at least, the question of their guilt, even if it is doubtful that a conviction could have been secured. Amnesties therefore can be a means for the granting party to imply guilt where it has not been established yet—the opposite result, in other words, from those cases Günther discusses. As Horst Sendler put it rather pointedly: "It is particularly necessary to grant an amnesty for things which were not illegal in the first place".[33]

Günther is right in emphasising the important contribution the legal process can make in establishing and attributing guilt. And he is right in comparing the legal process to the methodologically guided discourse of the historian. But the consequences of this similarity are more far-reaching then he imagines. Historians, like lawyers, are primarily concerned with the past. It is only the allocation of punishment which introduces a forward-looking element into the legal process, e.g. in determining chances of re-socialisation. If it is clear during this process that punishment will not be of primary concern, then the acts in question are indeed primarily of historical interest. In engaging with the legal process of fact-finding, the accused members of the RAF also subscribed to an understanding which sees the RAF itself as "mere" history, and thus a thing of the past—an understanding correctly identified by the RAF in the above quotation.[34] And again, we see an application of the power differential, especially regarding the power to impose understanding and definitions inherent in amnesties which can be turned to the disadvantage of the receiving party.

Amnesties, when granted to collective actors, can result in the destruction of this actor if its identity is defined by a conflict-relation with the granting power. In the most astonishing comment on the RAF, the authors deny that such a thing as the RAF as a well-defined group had ever existed.[35] Apart from the dubious conspiracy theories associated with this claim, it means the most radical destruction of the idea of the RAF possible, denying not only their future existence, but also threatening its past; a view which after the self-termination of the RAF got increasing support even by rather conservative authors, and was made the subject of a parliamentary debate. This should not surprise us. Since time immemorial,

---

[33] Quoted from Hillenkamp, above n. 16, p. 7. For the discussion on amnesties in cases where a criminal law conviction seems dubious see Blanke, above n. 4, p. 132; Luederssen, "Zu den Folgen des Beitritts fuer die Strafjustiz der Bundesrepublik Deutschland", [1991] *Strafverteidiger*, 483; Wassermann, *NJW*, 1994, 2669. These authors argue that amnesties are illegitimate for actions which were not illegal. For the opposite view, see Hillenkamp, above n. 16. More nuanced Günther, in a case comment on the "Mauerschuetzen decision" BGH 3 November 1992, [1993] *Strafverteidiger* 18.

[34] Particularly so in Hogefeld's declaration, which is criticised by the RAF precisely for its emphasis on the "historical aspects" of the RAF terror campaign.

[35] Wisniewski, Landgraeber and Sieker, *Phantom RAF* (Berlin, Knaur, 1993). For further references to the public reception of this idea, see the author's web page at http://ourworld.compuserve.com/Homepages/Gerhard_Wisnewski_3/raf.htm.

the "politics of forgetting" was an instrument of the victor to eradicate the defeated more thoroughly than mere victory on the battlefield could have.[36] In ancient Rome, the "*damnatio*" or "*abolitio memoriae*" meant the destruction of statues and pictures of the enemy of the state, his name erased from official documents, plaques and inscriptions. If he was in life the Caesar, his signature under his laws and ordinances would be deleted and the laws themselves abolished.[37] Amnesty, from "*amnesia*", describes the same process of publicly sanctioned forgetting, even if we got used to seeing it as a benevolent act when used for centuries to celebrate the birthdays of royalty. But as the example of the RAF shows, the Janus face of amnesties is still very much with us.

[36] See Simon, "Verordnetes Vergessen" quoted in Smith, above n.2, p.21.
[37] Vittinghoff, *Der Staatsfeind in der roemischen Kaiserzeit* (Berlin, 1936).

3

The Legal Politics of Amnesty

SCOTT VEITCH

It was written that "there shall be on the one side and the other a perpetual Oblivion, Amnesty, or Pardon of all that has been committed since the beginning of these Troubles", and that "all that has pass'd on the one side, and the other, as well before as during the War, in Words, Writings, and Outrageous Actions, in Violences, Hostilitys, Damages and Expences, without any respect to Persons or Things, shall be entirely abolish'd in such a manner that all that might be demanded of, or pretended to, by each other on that behalf, shall be bury'd in eternal Oblivion". "Moreover, all Prisoners on the one side and the other, without any distinction of the Gown or the Sword, shall be releas'd after the manner it has been covenanted, or shall be agreed between the Generals of the Armys, with his Imperial Majesty's Approbation."

It was also written that, excepting certain crimes—amongst which were "murder or piracy unconnected with the late wars, buggery, rape, forced marriage, bigamy, and witchcraft"—subjects or their offences were to "be pardoned, released, indemnified, discharged and put in utter oblivion", by an Act of free and general pardon, indemnity and oblivion.

Finally, it was "enacted by the Queen's most Excellent Majesty, by and with the advice and consent of the Lords Spiritual and Temporal, and Commons, in this present Parliament assembled, and by the authority of the same," an Act "to make provision about the release on licence of certain persons serving sentences of imprisonment", if their offences were committed as part of the political conflicts of the past.

Three wars, three amnesties. The terms of the first were included in the nation-state-enhancing Treaty of Westphalia in 1648. The second, some twelve years later, were introduced by the English Parliament after the restoration of King Charles II in the wake of the Interregnum. The terms of the last are included in the Northern Ireland (Sentences) Act 1998.

Amnesties, like wars, are not new. If violent conflict provides an irregular heartbeat to human co-existence, amnesties come to lighten the burden. And if we have lost the use of oblivion from our political vocabulary, we have not lost the need for something like its function. Amnesties, lest we forget, are here to stay.

There is a sense of executive decree about the older amnesties, a grand, instrumental use of law's authority, the traces of which can still be found in the royal holiday lists which empty out prisons, the presidential self-pardons, and in general (and often Generals') blanket amnesties. Certain modern amnesties appear, however, to be more subtle. They are often conditional amnesties, or are amnesties which are themselves conditioned by the claims of a superior, usually international or human rights, law. They are, moreover, sometimes conditioned by judicial proceedings, subject to the scrutiny of those more used to applying than suspending the conventional law. In such cases the issue appears to be not merely the content of the amnesty, but the process: how to sharpen the legal tools for the desired social purpose—how, in other words, to condition the oblivion legally.

Such amnesties appear at the meeting point of law and politics. They express a set of political desires which legal categories may be stretched to comprehend. They do so, moreover, in a way which exposes the ambivalent and normally submerged temporal perspectives of law and judicial decision-making. For they appear to demand simultaneously of law a backward- and forward- looking temporal sensitivity, both of which are overlain by a political teleology which would see the law somehow deliver a future redemption from the wrongs committed in the past.

What is engaged in these processes? What understandings about law do we need to bring to processes which appear to challenge conventional understandings of law's morality and temporality? Conversely, how does amnesty disrupt these very understandings? It is these types of questions which are explored here. In order to do so, I will focus initially on a partic-ular recent instantiation of amnesty, one which draws in directly the above concerns.

In the main, this chapter will attempt to conceptualise some aspects of the recent South African amnesty process—established by the Promotion of National Unity and Reconciliation Act 1995—from a legal philosoph-ical perspective. As an element of the negotiated settlement from minority rule in South Africa, the amnesty process was a result of a political compromise formulated in the transitional period. As one of three commit-tees of the Truth and Reconciliation Commission (the TRC), the task of the Amnesty Committee was to grant amnesty to applicants if their actions were found to meet the criteria set out in the founding Act.[1] Of all the procedures set up within the brief of the TRC, this Committee was the

---

[1] These criteria will be elaborated on in the course of the chapter. The other two commit-tees of the TRC were the Human Rights Violations Committee and the Reparation and Rehabilitation Committee. The most comprehensive overview of the institution itself, its mandate and findings, remains the five volume *Truth and Reconciliation Commission Report* published in 1998. The work of the Amnesty Committee remained (and remains) unfinished, and the final report from it is still awaited.

most "legal" in its operations and outcomes: it was subject to judicial review (and approval) by the Constitutional Court, it was staffed by professional lawyers and judges, it involved the application of statutory sections to applications that came before it, and its decisions had immediate legal effect.

That said, this chapter will seek to establish the meanings of the operations, goals, and outcomes of the process from the perspective of more conventional understandings of the role and application of law. For the process is, I will suggest, an anomaly, riddled with paradox, and thus fascinating in what it can tell us about the capacity of law and legal mechanisms when a society is faced with coming to terms with a past of extensive human rights abuses. And with this in mind, I hope to draw out an analysis of amnesty which might help uncover more generally some of the founding dynamics of law in transitional phases.

THERE BUT FOR THE GRACE OF LAW

Amnesty law works as a touch that liberates rather than dominates. In its application amnesty lifts not only the application of the "normal" law—be it criminal or civil—but also the *possibility* of the application of that law.

In the South African model there are two scenarios. First, there are those applicants currently serving jail sentences for "crimes" committed prior to the cut-off date prescribed in the Act (as amended). (These applicants make up at least three-quarters of all applications for amnesty.) For those who are successful, amnesty frees; it lifts a penal sanction that has already been imposed. It acts as a legal "cure" for an original legal wrong, where that wrong is itself now declared wrong by way of being transformed from a "crime" to "an act committed in association with a political objective in the conflicts of the past", and the applicant is set free.

Secondly, there are those who "confess". These are those who committed wrongs under the old regime but who were never caught or sentenced or subject to the legal process by way of any sanction; who are, legally, already free. These are a much smaller category than the first, typically from the old state security or police forces. Amnesty for them is not the lifting of a legal sanction, but is instead the lifting of the possibility of a legal sanction being imposed. Although technically free, they are further liberated from the *potential* of legal action (either by the state or by private civil litigants) in the future.

Is such an operation unique to amnesty? By way of comparison to the law of tort, we might note that it is possible for individuals or corporations or states to disclaim their liability for wrongs that occur for which they could otherwise be held liable according to the normal legal rules of negligence. But there are two major differences from amnesty. One is that in tort these kinds of actions are typically the result of executive rather than judicial application: it is not usually a court whose legal act will suspend liability. The court may—or may not—*recognise* and enforce the disclaimer of liability, but that is different from establishing or creating—being the source of—the disclaimer, of that which suspends liability.

The other difference is more significant. Normally, disclaimers of liability are future-oriented, that is, they act to disclaim liability *in advance* of the tort occurring. The sense of this is obvious: as a matter of knowl-edge—of rights and liabilities, of being able to plan rational action (personal, economic, whatever), and for making contingency plans in the event of the tort's occurrence—all matters of *prior* knowledge on which the possibility of rational action according to law depends.

The granting of amnesty differs in both these respects and suggests *prima facie* that the *application* of law to *suspend* law remains an original feature of the amnesty process. Amnesty remains the legally authorised (by statute) decision not to apply valid law.

But let us return for the moment to the temporal point. The main reason why law is conventionally future-oriented, why retrospectivity is shunned, is that law's normativity is bound up with the possibility of obeying or disobeying its demands. Normativity is in its essence the "ought" quality of legal (as opposed to physical) laws; that is, it demands that something "ought to be done". Retrospective "laws"—laws which could not have been obeyed at the time because it was not possible to know that that was the law and thus no-one could have realised that they "ought to have been followed"—fail to be normative in this sense.

In what sense then, is amnesty law law? It is quite clear that at the time of the offence or wrong no-one could have followed that law, and *yet*, the consequence of the successful amnesty application is to re-write that event and its legal significance. But that this can be re-written *now* is one of the paradoxes of amnesty. The operation is something like this: *that is what happened then and that is what happened then now.*

This mode is distinguishable from pardoning, although it may seem more similar to it than to other legal mechanisms. For with amnesty there is no explicit statement of a "miscarriage" of justice, no sense of a valid law wrongly applied *at the time*, of an error made then and now in need of rectification. Amnesty law starts in the present and looks back the way.

If this is true, then it is also clear that amnesty law as law is really a paradigm case of normative direction to an official (now). It is not a law directed at the citizens—although it does demand that they understand and re-tell their actions in a specified way (now) in order that their case be cognised in the right manner, a point we will come to presently. It is not a law that demands of them that they "ought to have done something or other". The Act therefore specifies that such and such ought to be the case for the law to apply (the act must have been associated with a political objective etc.) and the judge must determine whether this is true of the present case, and if so, then certain consequences ought to follow.

The symbolism of this is therefore quite different from conventional legal proceedings. The applicant is not in court to show that he or she has a right and the other party a duty to do or forbear from doing something, nor is he or she there to be proven guilty—or innocent—of some offence. (The amnesty process seems quite barren ground for arguments about rights and duties.) The applicant is there, in that other literal meaning of the term, to plead, to plead with the judicial committee to exercise its grace and to lift the sanction (or the possibility of sanction) from its attaching to the applicant.

This is an "image in negative" of conventional legal mechanisms: operations which now bring back to life the dead souls of society's "criminals", whose point of legal application is precisely a non-violent touch, and thus an invisible, un-touching, anti-violent touch: a momentary instance of the uncoupling of law and violence.

In a sense it could not be otherwise. For amnesty law *not* to be retrospective, its logic must be non-coercive except in relation to the official's acts. But it does not follow from this that its mode of cognition cannot be retrospective, that the application of amnesty law does not involve, literally, a recognising of the events of the past. To explore this further we must examine more closely some elements of the decisions of the Amnesty Committee.

AMNESTY AND LEGAL REASONING

One of the most prominent features of decisions of the Amnesty Committee is the paucity of legal reasoning. These, generally short, decisions place heavy emphasis on the reading of "facts", of placing events gleaned through evidence in such a form as to make them coherent as a narrative.[2] Here it is not only the credibility or lack of credibility of witnesses' testimony that is considered, but whether they have made "full disclosure of the relevant facts" (a prerequisite for the grant of amnesty). Decisions consist mainly of the judge's reading of what has happened, followed frequently by jumps between fact and decision. There is scant evidence of close reasoning from the applicable law, there appears to be little sense of normative consistency in relation to the application of the relevant sections across judgments, and a common lawyer would look largely in vain for reasoning from precedent. There is, finally, a strong sense in which outside—or at least hidden, unknown, and thus unargued—factors influence the outcome.

---

[2] Narrative coherence has been deemed to be a vital element in common law reasoning generally. See indicatively B Jackson, *Law, Fact and Narrative Coherence* (Merseyside, Deborah Charles Publications, 1988).

We seem to be dealing, in other words, with a decision-making procedure that falls a long way short of formal rationality, to use Weber's typology. Perhaps the overwhelming reason for this is not the inability of judges to find the law—the law from the statute is reasonably clear in its expression—but rather the way in which the *content* of the rules to be applied affects the nature of the reasoning, legal or otherwise, available to the judges. The application of the relevant legal rules requires an assessment of "what took place" as reconstructed *in the light of* these rules.

There are two disjunctures here, one explicitly recognised, the other not. Consider first, the following statement by the judicial panel in a decision of the Amnesty Committee on an application for amnesty by a former apartheid state policeman:

> "Almost all policemen giving evidence before the Amnesty Committee referred to their background and at the end of their testimony expressed regret for what they had done. This may be very relevant in an ordinary criminal hearing when extenuating factors are considered but these factors or any other factors relating to morality that may lend colour to an offence do not in terms of Act 34 of 1995 render one offence more justified than another. They are not requirements or relevant factors to be considered in the granting of amnesty or refusal thereof. They may however be factors that could contribute to reconciliation and a better understanding of the conflicts of the past and for this reason the Committee allowed the evidence to be led".[3]

The goal of the amnesty process is to aid the promotion of national reconciliation, yet the *mechanism* is concretised to allow only individuals to be applicants and grantees. Thus when thirty-seven ANC members, including some of the current leadership, applied for amnesty for human rights violations without giving details of what these were—without, that is, any attempt at "full disclosure"—such a "blanket" amnesty was denied. But whilst an individualisation must occur, the acts for which a successful amnesty is to be granted must not be understood to engage the moral culpability of the applicants. In other words, it is not for the panel, in "de-sentencing", to consider the moral worth or motive of the applicant; to consider those moral aspects which, rather ominously put one might think, "lend colour to an offence". Of course, as the panel acknowledge, such information may help the process of reconciliation in its broader context, but, in what might be conceived as a positivist move to hold distinct the moral from the legal, the panel refuses to judge the moral appropriateness of the violation in the context of the past. Instead, it must determine whether the offence was "associated with a political objective". Only this can negate criminal culpability as the re-alignment of *mens rea* is effected by the legal conditions of the amnesty.

The sense of this (more traditional) distinction between law and morality seems to be an even-handedness of approach to the conflicts of

[3] Amnesty Decision: Cronje, JH (2773/96).

the past, maintained, interestingly, by a quite specific separation between *politics* and morality. Judges are then seen not to make an explicit value-judgement vis-à-vis the particular applicant, yet will nonetheless allow for that applicant to be treated *as* an individual. But here is an apparent irony. The applicant can neither be treated as a member of a class (because of the need for full disclosure which is dependent on the uniqueness of the case), nor not be treated as a member of a class (for the purposes of the political criteria of the offence). That is, judges must make an overt judgment about the "political objective" of the offence, and in so doing they necessarily engage a collective meaning for both the offence and the applicant's role in its commission; yet, this must somehow be understood to fit the "full disclosure" unique to the applicant. This makes the coalescence of universal and particular appear both paradoxical and necessary if law is to be kept pure, untainted from any possibility of its *own* moral culpability.

This we might term the legal politics of amnesty. The constraints apparent in reasoning exist because the assessment of "acts associated with a political objective" cannot be determined except by a close reading of "facts" which are themselves already predisposed by an evaluation of what is to count as "political". This is so even though the assessment of the latter is shot through with evaluative, if often unarticulated, criteria.

This can best be explained by the second disjuncture I foreshadowed: that is, between truth and memory. The granting of amnesty is premised on "full disclosure" in line with the TRC's modus operandi that the revelation of "truth" is a prerequisite for getting on the "road to reconciliation". Full disclosure appears to involve an act of memory, of remembering or bringing back to mind and then to the attention of the panel, the detailed truth of the events which took place in the past. But as Charles Scott has noted, "Memory's 'truth' appears to be its manifestation, not its object or an aspect of its object. Memory seems to occur as the manifestation of things in their significance and meaning—to infuse their meaning and significance—in both their generality and their particularity."[4] If we go with this reading, truth is *not* the object to be uncovered in the contemporary hearings on amnesty, but rather what is to be articulated is the truth of the manifestation of memory. Moreover, *this* memory is not itself simply an object, since it is inseparable from the performative process that recalls it as event and therefore which constitutes the very object of legal scrutiny: "memory", as Scott added, is also "a mediator of passed events rather than an immediate enactment of truth."[5]

The locus of the process of memory is vital, and in determining the "truth" of memory's manifestation that locus is in this instance no less than the decision-making process of the amnesty panel. And this involves the construction of a "legal memory" now, *and for the first possible time,*

---

[4] C Scott, *The Time of Memory* (Albany, SUNY Press, 1999), p. 7.
[5] *Ibid.*, p. 284.

40   *Scott Veitch*

which is itself inseparable from the legal politics on which amnesty depends. Failure to recognise this leads to apparent inconsistency and mystification.

Compare the following two decisions. The "Biko" decision noted that "There can be no doubt that the death of Biko resulted from head injuries sustained on the 6th of September 1977 when his head collided with an object in room 619, Sanlam Centre, Port Elizabeth . . . In any event, we are not satisfied that the Applicants have made a full disclosure . . . Applicants' version as to the cause of the scuffle and the manner in which Biko sustained the fatal head injury is so improbable and contradictory that it has to be rejected as false . . . they have clearly conspired to conceal the truth of what led to the tragic death of Biko." The panel decided, moreover, that the restraining acts of the applicants, even though unknown to the panel in their detail, did not amount to pursuit of a political objective and were "not political in nature but formed part of normal police duties".[6]

However, the "Benzien" decision noted this: "Benzien's evidence did not convey a clear picture of the events or the sequence in which they occurred. There are inconsistencies and even contradictions on some aspects . . . part of the explanation for this may be, that Benzien was giving an account of a fast moving scene ten years after the event". The actions (of killing Kriel) were "negligent" "and in torturing and assaulting his victims Benzien believed that he was doing his duty as a policeman . . . There can be no doubt that his action related to a political objective".[7]

These two descriptions may seem merely inconsistent. Yet they display something more revealing about the amnesty process. The question they refuse to engage with is this: What is the standard by which "full disclosure" is deemed to have occurred? Given that in both cases, there is no yardstick of truth by which to measure "full disclosure", how does the panel know that full disclosure is not being made? Both acknowledge that it is a lack of knowledge that in important respects lies at the core of their decision, and yet the cases are decided differently (Biko's murderers do not get amnesty while Benzien does). Benzien's decision suggests that the details do not have to be perfect, Biko's murderers' that they do.

Yet what is exposed here is the very essence of the problem: the referent of memory is not the event but the truth of memory; that which, in law, is to be accounted for demands not the truth of the event but of its accounting. "Full disclosure" is the unconcealment of *this*, and not of the event—the latter remains, from the point of view of adjudication, unknown and unknowable.

---

[6] Amnesty Decision: Snyman, H (3918/96); Siebert, DP (3915/96); Beneke, JJO (6367/97); Marx, R (3521/96).

[7] Amnesty Decision: Benzien, JT (5314/97).

In this sense it is "legal memory", conditioned by the process of legal politics, rather than the "facts" on which amnesty depends. This is precisely the disjuncture between memory and truth. It is not the "object" of memory, the event itself, which allows for amnesty to be granted: the process is somehow already bound up with its own possible outcomes that require not truth but the fulfilment of an expectation of a legal memory that could not have had an original correspondent legal truth. This is because of the *political* condition of the recall, which is dependent on the political reconciliation at one level having *already taken place* in order to decide whether the plea constitutes an act associated with a political objective. And there is no correspondent "truth" which could have pre-existed that reconciliation.

The need to re-cognise the events of the past—this re-alignment of the *mens rea* within a different set of legal co-ordinates—in this way not only signals the impossibility of understanding testimony before the panel in the context of a linear, progressive notion of time, but also, we might note in passing, shows how the amnesty process formally questions a more simple conceptual connection between "truth" and reconciliation.

This is why applicants coming before the judicial panel need to "frame" their acts accordingly. How the politics of the acts are understood by the panel is itself a matter of political judgement. In one case, for example, the panel decides that shooting a suspected informer "was not justified" since "appropriate disciplinary action could have been taken against him".[8] In another, they decide that stoning a white American woman to death when the applicants "lost control of themselves and got caught up in a frenzy of violence" in the context of a political disturbance, "was related to a political objective" namely, "sending a serious political message to the government".[9]

The point here is not to question the wisdom of these decisions, nor to make a trite point about the lack of consistency. But this itself formally questions the notion that the judges have somehow kept their process "purely" legal, distanced from assessing qualitatively the applications that come before them.

And again, this is not surprising. For the amnesty process is geared—despite its conventionally conditioned (if, again, an "image in negative") technique of individualisation—to an explicitly formulated goal of "*national* unity and reconciliation". A goal—albeit spawned from its specific statutory creation—in other words, that must engage with the creation of a *collective* memory. But the "legal memory" that the process must deliver is already, we should note, necessarily engaged in having formulated and applied the collective: it must answer the question "What happened then?" by reference to an understanding of *contemporary*

---

[8] Amnesty Decision: Ndithini Thyido (755/96) and Zwelitsha Mkuhlwa (665/96).

[9] Amnesty Decision: Ntamo, VS (4734/97); Peni, NA (5188/97); Nofemela, EM (5282/97); Manqina, MC (0669/96).

politics. Unlike the TRC's other sub-committees, the Amnesty Committee must already have had a sense of the meaning of the conflicts of the past in order, simply, to decide cases. And that that is political no-one should doubt.[10]

The difficulty with this process is not with the aim, but with the manner in which legal mechanisms are explicitly used to challenge conventional legal operations and reasoning. The explicit insertion of a conditional re-reading of the events of the past requires a determinedly political assessment of the legal response. The legal truth, always at one remove from a "factual" truth, is here further displaced in the production of a legal memory that sees process indistinguishable from outcome. The amnesic result for the successful amnesty applicant—that "any entry or record of the conviction shall be deemed to be expunged from all official documents or records and the conviction shall for all purposes . . . be deemed not to have taken place"[11]—is then the corollary of the legally regulated memory which is now read into, and sealed into, the collective record of South Africans' process of truth and reconciliation. For those who, on the other hand, fail in their application, they are left to the normal operations of the civil and criminal law, as potential defendants or criminals or, simply, as criminals.

The *telos* of a collective reconciliation is a substantive goal that impacts on the mode of decision-making available to the amnesty process. Unless we are to say that this makes the amnesty process illegitimate, we must be willing to conclude that in the process of transition and coming to terms with the past, law and legal institutions afford an elasticity that challenges a reading of law—and arguably the rule of law—to a novel demand of justice corresponding to the perceived needs of the transitional period. The politics of legal memory negotiate the transitional phase, but in so doing necessitate law's role as a mediating process which cannot but depart, even in its ideal form, from a formally rational notion of law application, as it both re-reads and re-writes the past for the sake of the future. Nonetheless, we must also see how in coming to (legal) terms with the past, the legal operations involved do come up against a normal, though usually under-exposed, limit: the intimate dependency of any successful legal operation on a settled politics.

Few amnesty processes have been so open, so judicial, as that in South Africa. The British Government's release of political prisoners under the Northern Ireland (Sentences) Act 1998 was far less public and far more low key. There is a host of reasons why this may be so, but it can be observed that whereas in South Africa the TRC came at the end of the conflict, the

---

[10] Witness the BWB's (Boer radicals) response to the refusal to grant amnesty to two former Conservative Party members for the killing of Chris Hani, the then leader of the Communist Party, to see them as now being "Boer prisoners of war".

[11] Promotion of National Unity and Reconciliation Act 1995, s.20 (10).

aftermath of the Good Friday Agreement is politically and institutionally still unsettled. The meaning of the amnesty process in Northern Ireland, as well as the legal conditions which are used in it, are, it is now clear from a comparison with South Africa, different, since the trajectory of the peace process is as yet incomplete. Significantly, for example, prisoners are released "on licence"—which is not the case in South Africa's amnesty process—and this is itself indicative of the institutional-political risk which still pervades the contemporary politics of Northern Ireland.[12]

In Northern Ireland, a re-cognition of the truth of the conflicts of the past cannot, as far as legal mechanisms are concerned, be carried out in any new or truly transitional sense because the politics of the present have not been sufficiently stabilised in their meaning. Instead, the amnesty is a non-judicial administration of the release of prisoners based on existing United Kingdom law, one which involves *no* re-reading of past events in which the actors were involved—no attempt, in other words, to find out the "truth" of what happened or to invite "confessions" from non-prisoners—but relies for its point of reference solely on the *already existing legally*-determined *status* that they have; that is, as inmates with criminal convictions. This is why the release of prisoners there, as Schäfer points out in Chapter 2 above, is an amnesty which is more like an exchange of prisoners, a strategic political move in a political conflict that is not yet over. The fact that the prisoners who are released are limited to those whose status of "criminality" was politically based, and not to "ordinary" criminals, may give the lie to years of official British policy which treated "terrorists" not as political actors at all, but simply as criminals,[13] but it does not in itself signal an amnesty process which is involved either with establishing memory or, indeed, which is post-conflict.

Unlike in South Africa, the conditions then are all tentative, all individualisation—licensing—really in fact forward-looking, an act of mercy and hope rather than one of detailed legal scrutiny of what might have happened. Temporally speaking, the ship of the old nation-state is still going forward, there is insufficient transitional stability to look too closely at what has passed, and there is no doubt about who is still claiming authority at the helm. Given all this, it can, of course, make no sense to talk of the legal writing of a collective memory; for that is still impossible to begin far less achieve.

[12] For example, s. 3(5) of the 1998 Act states one of four conditions for the licence, namely: "if the prisoner were released immediately, he would not be likely (a) to become a supporter of a specified organisation, or (b) to become concerned in the commission, preparation or instigation of acts of terrorism connected with the affairs of Northern Ireland".

[13] Margaret Thatcher's famous "A crime is a crime is a crime" was supported by, amongst many others, the Criminal Law Revision Committee, which stated in 1980 that violence is often "alleged to have been committed either directly or indirectly for political purposes . . . [but] in our opinion putting these criminals into a special category would tend to encourage their claim that they have special status, a claim we would reject": Cmnd 7844, p. 58.

Yet for three related elements of analysis in our enquiry—law, morality, politics—certain issues do appear the same. Steve Biko's family and others questioned the morality and constitutionality of the amnesty provisions in South Africa.[14] Likewise in Northern Ireland, certain voices in the process saw the disruption to law's conventional institution and the putative disjuncture between politics and morality as too abhorrent to endure. In the debate on the Northern Ireland (Sentences) Bill, for example, it was argued by one Member of Parliament that "there is no moral justification for the early release of prisoners. When we pursue policies in a moral vacuum, we run the risk of courting trouble. I do not accept that crimes of violence are less serious, or that their perpetrators can be treated more leniently, if they have been committed for political motives. The Bill . . . is incompatible with the rule of law; it marks the triumph of terror". On the issue of reconciliation he added, quoting, "'It will be a society which bends morality and justice for political expediency' . . . This is not the way to build a just and stable society".[15]

The argument here is clearly about the future; the past, and in particular of all things the legal past on which the rule of law depends, ought not to be tampered with and unsettled. To build the stable society, so the argument goes, the law—its history, culture and specifically the meaning of its decisions—must be set in stone.

It is interesting to note then that one counter made to this argument was by Tony McWalter MP in his observation to the House of Commons that, "Nelson Mandela was once deemed to be a terrorist and is now honoured as the President of South Africa. People may have one status at one time and a different status at another".[16]

In South Africa the process is clearly, in this sense, that much further on. Whilst the TRC was also strongly committed to the future it was also prepared to engage in a dialectic of memory and forgetting which depended on getting its hands dirty in a political re-assessment of the past. It was willing to engage, in other words, with the possibility that in retrospect things were different all along; even although, from a specifically legal point of view, only now; never then.

This is why the "deemed" legal status—terrorist—may change (now), and the oblivion result. But we see law's limit situation here; for from another point of view, so common, so universal—one of self-definition— the status may have never truly changed: never a terrorist, always a freedom fighter.

The judicial role may only be stretched so far. In the legal politics of amnesty in South Africa, unlike, as yet, in Northern Ireland, the future could not be faced without memory. But ultimately, legally, in one last

---

[14] *AZAPO* v. *President of RSA* 1996 (8) BCLR 1015 (CC).

[15] Mr Andrew Hunter, MP for Basingstoke, *Hansard* 1791 (10 June 1998), col. 1116.

[16] *Ibid.*, col. 1130.

temporal paradox, that memory must be, and have been, of the right sort (now).

The jurisprudential significance of the TRC's amnesty process lies precisely in exposing the need for a sense of justice which is alive to the demand for memory; something the older-style amnesties, in their invocation of "perpetual oblivion", overlooked. Doing this solely through legal mechanisms will indeed encounter limits, yet it is perhaps the desire today for a democratic legitimacy, in which law is clearly implicated, which, more than anything else, will ask for a justice which has a performative attitude towards the past.

"Law," wrote Robert Cover, "may be viewed as a system of tension or a bridge linking a concept of reality to an imagined alternative", adding that "our visions hold our reality up to us as unredeemed".[17] But, we might add to this insight, there are always two ways across a bridge, and it is not only our present and future which appears to us as unredeemed. It may indeed be that the future for democratic aspirations, of even or even especially, "stable" societies, is to be caught up in pasts whose visions and realities—so variously enslaving, imperial, liberationist—can no longer be suppressed. In that sense, there are many pasts still waiting to happen.

---

[17] Robert Cover, "Foreword: *Nomos* and Narrative" in (1983) 97 *Harvard Law Review* 4–68 at 9.

4

Time, Guilt and Forgiveness

ALEXANDER McCALL SMITH

It is clear that we have a strong interest in redressing the wrongs of the past. This interest may be expressed at the level of societies and of states—as is demonstrated by the movement for historical reparation in North America and Australia—or it may focus on the investigation of old, personal wrongs, as in the case of the prosecution, many years after the event, of a war criminal or a sex offender.[1] The features of redress and its objectives will be very different at the social and the personal level, but there is a common feature present in both. In each case what we see is an attempt to define our relationship with events which may have taken place a considerable time ago but which continue to resonate in the present. These processes, which include both applications of punishment and the provision of compensation, are attempts at settling unresolved relationships with other persons or groups of persons. In so far as these gestures take place within a legal framework, the law is invoked to normalise a situation in which some previously unanswered demand for justice has made itself known. This, the law declares, is the end of the matter. So it was that a French court in the final year of the twentieth century sentenced Maurice Papon, an eighty-six-year-old former civil servant, to a term of imprisonment in respect of his participation in deportations in Vichy France over fifty years previously;[2] so it was too that the Belgian Senate in 1994 acknowledged the fact of the Armenian genocide of 1914.[3] In the one case, punishment is brought to an individual who bore a measure of guilt for one of the great crimes of the twentieth century; in the other, a government, for the benefit of the historical memory of an oppressed people, acknowledges the fact of a crime which took place before the birth of the vast majority of those making the demand. In each case, the passage of

---

[1] The issue of redressing wrongs by the state is discussed in G Sher, "Ancient Wrongs and Modern Rights", (1981) 10 Philosophy and Public Affairs pp. 3–17. For a particularly useful discussion of the Maori claims in New Zealand, see A Sharp, *Justice and the Maori*, (Auckland, Oxford University Press, 1997).

[2] For an account of the Papon affair, see M Slitinsky, *Le Proces Papon, le devoir de justice,* (Paris, Editions de l'Aube, 1997).

[3] Belgian Senate Resolution, 1-736/3 (1997–98).

time seems to play little role: the requirement that justice be done is not defeated by the historical distance separating event from its final resolution. Indeed, in some cases, historical distance seems to sharpen the sense of anger which the victims, or their descendants, feel.

What is the effect of the passage of time on guilt? Rather surprisingly, this question has not received a great deal of attention, and yet it is a question which almost inevitably emerges in any period in which political change leads us to examine the way in which power has been exercised in the past. The process of scrutiny can focus on the major contours of our historical experience, or it can be concerned with the intimate and the local. In the final decades of the twentieth century, both these forms of scrutiny took place. Not only was there a coming to terms with the implications of European colonialism and its off-shoots, but there was also, at the level of individuals and their dealings with one another, an examination of wrongs done to those who had been subjected to exploitation and abuse, principally sexual, by more powerful others. It is not inappropriate to link these two forms of wrong, and response to them, even if they are very different in terms of scale and historical significance. The factor which leads to a calling to account in each case is a growth in our understanding of how people become victims of others. In each case there is a belief that a wrong has been committed and that by bringing the wrong into the open and doing something about it the victim will somehow be helped and we, ourselves, will be collectively improved. To an extent, this is the logical conclusion of a belief in the therapeutic implications of confronting memory, both personal and collective; there are direct links, it might be argued, between each manifestation of this process.

My concern here is principally with wrongs against individuals, the sort of wrongs which are the subject of criminal prosecution. The issue is addressed at a largely theoretical level—asking the question as to why time may affect the guilt of the wrongdoer and why there should be reluctance to prosecute in such cases. This is followed by a discussion as to the role of forgiveness in criminal justice, as the exercise of forgiveness militates against the further pursuit of old wrongs. But first, to put the matter in the context of actual systems of criminal justice, we shall look at some examples of how the question of time and guilt becomes a practical concern of the criminal law.

STALE CRIMES: DIFFERING APPROACHES

A number of systems of criminal justice do not set out limits as to the time during which a crime must be prosecuted by the state. This is the case, with the exception of homicide (the prosecution of which is *never* subject to time limits), in the United Kingdom, Canada and Australia, and indeed in a number of other countries influenced by the common law tradition. By contrast, in the USA and in countries in the civil law mould, codes of criminal law or criminal procedure usually state clear limits to the period that can elapse between the commission of a crime and the offender's being brought to court to face criminal charges.[4] Again there is normally an exception made for homicide, which may be prosecuted no matter how long ago it was committed.

The implications of this difference can be striking. In Canada, for example, a sexual assault may result in prosecution even if the offence is brought to light twenty years later. Immediately over the border, a similar crime committed in the USA would not normally be prosecuted once a period of perhaps eight years had elapsed (the precise period depends on the terms of the statute of limitations in the state concerned). What is interesting here is that in two societies which, in spite of important political and cultural differences, nonetheless have many shared values, there should be such a different view of prosecuting crimes in these circumstances. One possible explanation of this is that this is the result of legal-historical factors rather than a difference of contemporary moral outlook. It could be argued that the USA adopted a statute of limitations because the philosophy behind such an approach suited a revolutionary state with a strong sense of the future and an ideological distaste for historical baggage.[5] English criminal law in the early nineteenth century was relatively static; it was bypassed by the enthusiasm for codification that occurred in the late eighteenth and early nineteenth centuries and there was little impetus to reform until the late nineteenth century efforts of James Stephen. The fact that English law happened to have no statute of limitations, and nor did most of its common law off-shoots (with the exception of American law), may furnish the explanation for current differences in approach rather than any substantial difference of current moral outlook. Yet even if this is so, it is hardly possible to ignore the very different results which the two models produce. The fact that the Canadian perpetrator of the assault is imprisoned for his offence means that a moral stance has been taken in relation to his crime and a decision has been made that he should suffer punishment; does the fact that his American counterpart escapes punishment mean that a different view is taken of the offence?

---

[4] In the USA, the rules on prescription vary from state to state. The Texas provisions are fairly typical: serious felonies cannot be prosecuted after ten years have elapsed since the commission of the crime; a three-year period applies for misdemeanours: Texas, Code of Criminal Procedure, 12.01 [1998]. For an example of the approach adopted in the civil law world, see the Italian *Codice Penale*, art.157: the periods vary from 20 years (for crimes punishable by periods of imprisonment over 24 years) to two years (for crimes punishable by a fine).

[5] For historical discussion, see Note, "The Statute of Limitations in Criminal Law: a Penetrable Barrier to Prosecutions", (1954) 102 *University of Pennsylvania Law Review* 630.

Has it ceased to matter, or is the time limitation merely an arbitrary procedural rule which carries no moral significance? Do the different results which the two legal systems achieve have a different impact on the victims? These questions take us to the heart of a number of intriguing issues of guilt and forgiveness in the criminal law. They also point to a number of profound policy choices for criminal justice and for society in general, raising the issue of our relationship with the past and our use of the past for the purposes of the present or future.

CRIMINAL LAW, THE PAST AND GUILT

Human affairs are conducted in a spatial and temporal framework. For the criminal law, this framework provides a sense of the law's boundaries—a sense of what it can reasonably undertake to do. In this respect, the law is no different from those theories of morality which recognise limits to the claims upon the moral actor. As these theories would suggest, the moral claims which others may make upon us are subject to the interest which we have in pursuing our own projects. Morality, then, is limited to what is psychologically and practically feasible: we simply cannot live meaningful, satisfying lives if we cannot distinguish between those situations in which we are in a relationship of moral proximity with others, and those in which we are relative moral strangers. The criminal law has traditionally made a similar calculation: crimes committed in other countries are no concern of the courts, although states may make arrangements amongst themselves allowing for the extradition of offenders. This has been the general rule; in many countries this principle has recently been weakened by the development of substantial extra-territorial jurisdiction over certain offences committed abroad (torture, war crimes, drug offences and sexual offences against children are examples of crimes which have prompted legislatures to extend national jurisdiction—or to create international jurisdictions—to encompass crimes committed abroad). Subject to this qualification about expanding extra-territorial jurisdiction, the restriction of criminal jurisdiction in spatial terms is not only an acknowledgment of limited power but also an acknowledgment of limited moral *locus standi*. We may disapprove of wrongs committed in other places, but we recognise that we simply cannot assume responsibility for righting them. This is not to say that it is not open to us to try: attempts at eradicating the evil of, say, child labour or debt bondage abroad reflect creditably on those who make them, but such efforts will often be seen as supererogatory. The observation might be made, though, that these efforts represent a welcome widening of the area of moral concern to embrace humanity in general, rather than that narrow section of humanity which makes up our own moral backyard (our immediate neighbours, our co-religionists, our fellow nationals or citizens). Yet the practical limit remains: our prime responsibility is for those wrongs that occur within the jurisdiction.

Time limitations constitute a similar limiting of the scope of the intervention of the criminal law. The justification for limiting spatial intervention, that the capacity of the criminal law is finite, applies with equal force here. Resources available for the investigation and prosecution of crime are strained and must be used to best effect. For this reason a choice may have to be made between recent crimes and crimes of the past, and, as shall be discussed below, there are pragmatic grounds for preferring recent crimes. But this may not be the entire explanation: even where it is feasible to prosecute a crime of the distant past, it may be thought inappropriate to do so. This reluctance is the equivalent of the absence of moral *locus standi* identified in the discussion of spatial limitations: the case for prosecuting such crimes is simply weaker than it is in the case of recent crimes. Perhaps we should ask ourselves why this is so. If there is unease, as there often is, about prosecuting so-called *stale crimes*, we might try to identify what underlies this intuitive reluctance. Is guilt attenuated by the passage of time, or are there merely practical considerations (such as concern over the reliability of evidence) which advocates a doctrine of time limitations?

For the most part, criminal law looks backwards. In bringing an offender to trial, the criminal justice system initiates an enquiry into an act which that person has done, evaluating this act in the context of a system of rules which lays out the forms of punishable act and the mental state which must accompany them for criminal guilt to be established. At this stage, the focus is entirely on a past event and on a past actor (in the sense of the law's being concerned with the state of mind of the actor at the time of the commission of the act rather than with his or her state of mind at the time of the enquiry). At the sentencing stage the court may take into account the requirements of the present and the future; this happens, for example, when the future dangerousness of the defendant may be considered in order to determine the need for public protection.

A conclusion of criminal guilt, then, is a conclusion about the past. Every criminal conviction implicitly endorses the proposition that acts of the past have a current relevance. The criminal law understands that acts of the past have an effect on our current relationships because we see ourselves as historically situated actors: what I am today and how I relate to others is influenced by what happened to me in the past and what I myself did. My past acts continue to affect the present in that they are likely to determine a whole range of features of my current position. If I have obtained an unfair advantage over others through a wrongful act, that act resonates in my present. So too is my own present affected by the acts of others. If I was subjected to a wrong by another in the past—a serious assault, say—that may adversely affect my present well-being. The long-lasting distress of a person subjected to serious sexual abuse in childhood is an example of how the events of many years earlier may distort the emotional and social lives of those who survive them. All of our actions must be recognised, then, as having implications for an indefinite future. If we accept the principle of responsibility—as we must—for the immediate, foreseeable consequences of our acts, then this responsibility is logically extended to consequences which will manifest themselves in the longer term.

If guilt is tied to harm, then the continuation of the harm might be an important justification for the persistence of guilt. This might be tested on a few simple examples. Imagine that D1 commits a minor theft in 1990. Although not an inveterate thief, he responds to the temptation to steal a wallet which he sees protruding from the pocket of a fellow-passenger in a train. The wallet contains a small amount of money, not enough to cause the owner real inconvenience over its loss, but enough to deprive him of a purchase that he was intending to make. The harm which this single act of theft causes may be easily quantified as the irritation caused to the wallet's owner and his loss of the hoped-for purchase. After several weeks, however, the irritation has passed and the unbought purchase been forgotten about. To all intents and purposes the harm caused belongs to the past, in the sense that it has no *immediate* significance for the present. This is not to say that it has *no* significance; it has, for example, historical significance, and it may also be a matter that we could take into account in assessing the character of D1.

A contrasting case is where D2 subjects E, who is fourteen, to a serious sexual assault. E recovers from the physical injury of the assault, but suffers severe psychological damage as a result of the attack. She experiences bouts of depression and her ability to relate confidently to other people is compromised. At the age of thirty-four she is still unable to go out at night without feeling a certain amount of fear and she is incapable of entering into trusting relationships with men. This case involves persistent harm: the crime is still with us, in the sense that it continues to affect the life of its victim adversely. In E's view, the assault does not belong to the past, and if she were to confront D2, her relationship with him would still be one of assailant and victim, just as it was twenty years previously.

Let us imagine that in either of these cases we were to be invited to comment on the culpability of the wrongdoers some twenty years after the event. We would certainly have no difficulty in saying that both D1 and D2 are the authors of their acts. We would also say, one imagines, that they are both guilty of the acts in question. But if pressed to say whether they are still culpable, in the sense of being encumbered with guilt for the act, we might be inclined to distinguish between D1 and D2. In respect of the former, we might simply say: "It's too long ago". Metaphors abound in this context, and they tend to reveal the intuitions which underpin this attenuation of guilt. The crime belongs to *history*; it is *past business*; to bring it up would be *to rake over old coals*; and so on.

What is possibly occurring here is that forward-looking concerns, which dispose us to attend to the immediate future, prompt the making of a distinction between the relevant and the irrelevant past. The relevant part is that part of the past which has some bearing on future-affecting decisions; the irrelevant past is that which does not assist in this process. If the assessing of guilt is part of the business of making decisions which will have an impact on the future, then guilt which has little bearing on the future becomes irrelevant. It is an historical and academic enquiry, rather than an enquiry into something that matters for our current lives.

The making of this distinction between past and current lives leads naturally to a troubling point of personal identity. Every student of philosophy is familiar with the perennially popular topic of personal identity and with the arguments over what makes for continuity of identity between objects and persons. This debate can often be quite theoretical in tone, involving wildly-improbable thought experiments and colourful examples. However, the issue of responsibility for crimes of the past provides us with a very concrete example of how personal identity matters in the very practical setting of criminal liability.

When we contemplate the prosecution of an eighty-year-old war criminal for crimes alleged to have been committed in his early twenties, it would be surprising if it were not to cross our minds that the person being prosecuted is in a sense a different person from the person who committed the crimes. It would not be counter-intuitive to say that the person before the court is not the young man who committed the crimes. He may be the same physical person, of course, but the psychological and moral connection between the accused of fifty or so years earlier and the accused of the present may be attenuated, and possibly even lacking. In practical terms this is recognised in the way in which we deal with others, recognising that their tastes and interests may differ with the passage of time. In matters of responsibility, however, we assume continuity of identity, at least in the ordinary case, on the grounds that social relations are predicated upon the assumption that social actors will own up to their past actions and may be held to them. Even if on no other basis, this is a necessity if we are to enforce contracts: life would be uncertain and unpredictable if people were to be allowed to claim that the person who entered into an undertaking at time 1 is different from the person faced with a request to perform at time 2. The same applies with blame. In so far as we have to be able to attribute blame in order to regulate future conduct, we must be able to assume that actions will be owned by current persons rather than laid at the door of historical actors who have now been replaced by new persons.

Yet there is surely something in the claim that at a certain point the gap between the past actor and the current person seems sufficiently wide to justify treating the former as in some senses being no longer present.[6] This seems especially true in those cases where the psychological continuity between states of being is interrupted by a condition such as that of dementia, where not only is memory lost but the personality itself may be radically changed. In such cases, relatives and friends often complain that the person they knew is no longer there. In an extreme case, where a prosecution is launched in respect of a crime committed many decades earlier, there may be loss of memory of the acts in question as well as substantial changes in personality.[7] In the light of these we might be inclined to question whether there are sufficient links between the states to justify our holding the individual responsible for what was done by what appears to be a radically different person located in the distant past. A credible argument may be made out in such cases for holding that punishing the "current person" for wrongs committed by the "earlier person" is oppressive. This argument, however, must be considered in the light of the possibly overriding requirement that continuity of personal identity be presumed, on the grounds that without it notions of responsibility are just too seriously weakened.

REACTIVE ATTITUDES IN THE LAW

Wrongs that are done to us as individuals may be forgiven by us as individuals. If, after the passage of time, I fail to forgive one who has wronged me, I may be accused of harbouring undue resentment. I should know better than to nurse an ancient grievance. An act of forgiveness in these circumstances may even be regarded as a duty on my part, a point which we have already considered. But can we extrapolate from the requirements of individual morality to the moral requirements of the criminal justice system? Criminal justice, after all, is a social institution which, like the state, cannot credibly be personified. Criminal justice has no *feelings*; it has no memory and no emotions. We use it as a vehicle to express human emotions such as anger, but we must remember that the institutional needs of the system may make requirements which are quite distinct from the human feelings that lie behind it. Thus it is that formal justice operates according to a set of rules which have their own logic and which may make demands that are at odds with particular human aspirations (although it is argued below that there is at least some common ground between the institutional and the human spheres in this context). This is an important factor in assessing the law's response to old wrongs. It may be then that human

---

[6] The literature on the subject of personal identity is vast, and very well known. A useful recent contribution, however, is W Glannon, "Moral Responsibility and Personal Identity", (1998) 35 *American Philosophical Quarterly*, 231.

[7] The implications of this for identity are discussed by T Hope, "Personal Identity and Psychological Illnesses", (1994) 37 (suppl) *Philosophy* 131.

virtues call for a forgiving response, but the formal requirements of the law require a different outcome. We shall now explore the justification for this.

In his influential essay, "Freedom and Resentment", Peter Strawson draws our attention to the crucial role which reactive attitudes play in our moral life.[8] When a wrong is done, we resent the wrongdoer; when, by contrast, we are the objects of a benevolent act, we experience feelings of gratitude towards and approbation of the other. These feelings are a matter of human psychology, rooted, no doubt, in our most fundamental instincts to value and preserve the self against external harm. By reacting with hostility against a wrong which is done us we not only hope to deter future harms but we also express our sense of outrage that our interests have been wrongly infringed. In so far as they express anger, reactive attitudes constitute a primitive response to wrongdoing. Anger is often seen as a crude emotion, which should yield, on mature reflection, to a more considered, understanding view of events. Anger perpetuates conflict by giving rise to further reactive attitudes in others; by contrast, the suppression of anger allows room for negotiation and conciliation. Anger achieves nothing: it adds heat to a situation, and it increases the sum total of pain which the original wrongful act has initiated: it is unproductive. This seems to suggest that in a morally sophisticated world there would be very little room for anger. Wrongs would be viewed calmly and would give rise not to calls for the punishment of the wrongdoer but to the negotiating of reconciliation and, if necessary, recompense. While such a response may represent a Stoic ideal, can it be translated from the realm of private virtue to the arena of criminal justice? The answer is probably no, given the very particular functions which the criminal justice system has to fulfil in the recognition of wrongs done to people.

When a crime is committed, the typical (non-Stoic) victim experiences anger at the wrong which he or she has suffered. This wrong may also be sensed as a wrong to a community in general—the assault, for example, of one resident of a street may be seen by the other residents as a wrong against all of them. When the criminal justice system intervenes, it takes the part of the wronged party and exacts punishment on that person's behalf. The state effectively takes from the offender what the victim, or his family and community, would have taken in earlier society. The state "buys off" the desire for vengeance and exercises this vengeance exclusively—and it is vengeance, even if it is not described as such by the criminal justice system. If the state fails to do this, then individuals would claim this right themselves and would seek to exact punishment themselves. There are many examples of this in the form of vigilante movements, lynch mobs and the rest. This is anathema to civil society, with the result that the doing of

---

[8] P Strawson, *Studies in the Philosophy of Thought and Action* (Oxford, Oxford University Press, 1968), p. 71.

justice on wrongdoers is the jealously-projected preserve of the organs of the state.

Whatever the moral imperative may be for the wronged individual to control and conquer anger, the state must assume that most people, falling far short of the forgiving ideal, will have a strong desire for the punishment of those who wrong them. This means that the state must respond to the reactive feelings of victims, even if to do so is troublesome and expensive. In most cases, this will be uncomplicated. The state will prosecute the offender when he is found and may, moreover, make some effort to ensure that the victim or the victim's family are made aware of the action which has been taken. There are limits, however, to the response that is expected of the state, and one of these may be that there will be no duty to act when such action could be considered unreasonable. The victim may not expect that the State devote an undue share of criminal justice resources to the pursuit of the offender. Nor may he or she expect that the state will resort to illegal action in order to apprehend the victim. All that is required is that a reasonable effort be made.

Is it reasonable to investigate and prosecute old crimes? If we consider this in terms of reactive attitudes, it is obvious that in some cases it would be reasonable for the criminal law to assume that the feelings of the victim have been assuaged by the passage of the years. Thus there is no need to assume that the victim of a minor theft is going to continue to experience reactive attitudes ten years after the crime; to do so would, in many cases, demonstrate some psycho-pathology. But this conclusion might not be valid in every case. Some crimes may engender reactive attitudes which do persist over many years, and in these cases, if it is legitimate for the criminal law to respond to reactive attitudes, then it will be legitimate— and perhaps necessary—for the criminal law to respond to the wrong. Again, the justification might be that if the criminal law does not do this, then it is failing to forestall private anger and calls for private revenge.

The most common cases in which a sense of wrong may persist over the years are those of sexual assaults and homicide. In the case of sexual assault, although individual reactions will vary, the adverse psychological sequelae may continue to be felt many decades after the event. It is not uncommon for children who are sexually abused to feel anger over the abuse throughout their adult lives. If the criminal law fails to address these feelings, then it may be seen as denying their validity. Similarly, with homicide, the loss here is something that the relatives of the victim tend to feel indefinitely, as witnessed by parents who sometimes continue over many years to search for the killer of their child, or by the insistence of relatives that homicide of many years before be explained and acted upon. Such feelings are the raw stuff of the lives of ordinary people; if the criminal law claims the right to act on the behalf of victims, it must recognise the strength of these persistent feelings of wrong.

This, of course, all presupposes that we consider that the psychological role of the criminal law as a channel for reactive feelings is a defensible one. The contrary position may be argued, and the criminal law might be encouraged to promote forgiveness and conciliation. The existence of reactive feelings, however, is a fact and has to be acknowledged. Not everybody appreciates the benefits of forgiveness and reconciliation, and the criminal law cannot be too in advance of the moral reality of the society it serves. If the concordance between the criminal law and actual social and moral conditions is lost, the efficacy of the law will be weakened and the claims of the state to the exclusive right to punish may be weakened and ignored. There is a limit, then, to the extent to which the criminal law can realistically occupy the moral high ground. In many cases it must simply acknowledge that people want and expect the punishment of wrongdoers and that popular acceptance of the rule of law will be conditional upon the legal system's giving voice to the moral demands of the public. One implication of this is that when it comes to the issue of limitations, the criminal law will have to take into account what the community actually wants the law to do. If the moral sense of the community is that those who commit serious offences should be punished even if they have escaped prosecution for many years, then the criminal justice system ignores such sentiments at its peril.

FORGIVENESS

The political reality, then, is that the criminal law, being a practical human institution, rooted in the everyday world, simply has to recognise the psychological realities of how people feel. This means that the formal punishment by society of those who commit wrongs against others is an inescapable necessity of an any criminal justice system if it is to maintain public confidence and to prevent people from exacting personal vengeance. This, however, seems a bleak conclusion; it is particularly bleak if it implies that the criminal law cannot embody anything but crude retributive attitudes. The criminal law, of course, must do more than this: it must defend the link between criminal law and our moral sense. It must ensure that defensible moral positions dominate the law, rather than reactive antagonism towards the wrongdoer.

The way that the criminal law frames its rules of culpability and determines the scope of its interventions is a matter for moral debate. At the heart of a morally sensitive criminal justice system is a recognition that criminal punishment should be imposed only on those who deserve it, and this issue of desert is determined according to those moral principles that command broad acceptance.[9] The courts, therefore, tend to reflect the

---

[9] For a useful discussion of desert, see G Sher, *Desert* (Princeton, Princeton University Press, 1987).

moral attitudes of the society they serve: a system of criminal justice which failed to do so would be politically unstable and could survive only if the state were prepared, for whatever reason, to support it. It is true that criminal justice systems can survive in the face of popular moral rejection, but such systems exist only in authoritarian or totalitarian states. In a democratic society, the courts must show sensitivity to the moral views of society in general. For this reason, courts in democracies tend to appreciate the need for a moral "fit" between the shape of the criminal law and the way in which the public at large perceives crime and related issues of culpability. Unfortunately, public views are frequently shaped, and exploited, by the media and by politicians keen to play upon anxieties. Moral panics, whether large- or small-scale, demonstrate this process. In the face of this, it is important for the courts to give a moral lead in matters of crime and punishment and to resist, if necessary, the simplistic calls for retribution. An example of this process of moral engagement is the debate over mandatory sentences. These are often disliked by judges, who see them not only as a limitation of judicial power, but who appreciate that they remove the opportunity which the court may have to reach a more understanding and constructive disposal of complex cases. Judges who have resisted the calls of politicians for mandatory sentences have demonstrated their interest not only in doing justice in particular cases but also in using their position to make a moral stand. This amounts to a rejection of a limited view of the criminal courts as a means only of applying arbitrary rules laid down by the legislature.

If the judiciary can demonstrate to the public in that context that the task of the criminal justice system is to respond to crime in a morally responsible way, then it can, in the same context, recognise and proclaim the virtue of forgiveness. A criminal justice system in which forgiveness played no role would not therefore reflect the full range of moral principles which are accepted in society at large. If the criminal law is capable of exercising forgiveness, then it is merely conforming to the moral expectations of society in general.[10] There is thus no reason for the criminal law to be mechanistically applied, with no room for discretion. Obviously this discretion cannot be exercised in an arbitrary or whimsical way: *as a general rule* the commission of a criminal offence must be followed by punishment, as the consistent application of the rules is essential if the system is to be seen as fair and impartial. What room can there be, then, for forgiveness?

---

[10] There has been considerable recent philosophical interest in forgiveness and its potential for social and personal healing. General accounts include R Roberts, "Forgiveness", (1995) 32 *American Philosophical Quarterly* 289 and the illuminating exchange between J Murphy and J Hampton in their *Forgiveness and Mercy* (Cambridge, Cambridge University Press, 1988). See also the remarkable collection of essays edited by R Enright and J North, *Exploring Forgiveness* (Madison, Wisconsin University Press, 1998).

The criminal justice system cannot mirror in every respect the possibilities of forgiveness in the private moral life. What it can do, though, is to exercise forgiveness in those circumstances where its exercise—were the context to be a purely private one—would not be seen as unduly supererogatory or surprising, but which would be considered appropriate. There are some personal situations in which it would be widely accepted that forgiveness should be exercised. Our task, then, is to identify those cases where a failure to forgive would be seen as amounting to a moral failure. In such cases, the criminal law should be forgiving too, because the application of criminal justice is judged by the same moral standards as apply to individuals in the conduct of their moral lives. The court is a human institution which can, and should, embody human virtues.

It may be easy to identify those egregious cases in which forgiveness is clearly required. Usually these are cases where the offence is slight and the passage of time has rendered the wrong less relevant to the present. It is less easy to establish a moral requirement for forgiveness where the offence is a major one, for here the law may be required to respond to the wrong in order to avoid being seen either to connive in the offence or to fail to recognise the gravity of the wrong.[11] Forgiveness must not be too rapid, or it will suggest that what has been done is simply not serious. A criminal justice system which applied very short limitation periods could stand accused of exactly this. If a serious wrong is ignored by the courts after an unduly short period, this may be seen as a statement that the law no longer cares about the wrong in question, that the wrongdoer has been forgiven prematurely.

Forgiveness has to be restrained, too, by an awareness of the political context of the act of forgiving. There are some acts which should not be forgiven too readily because this will weaken the prohibition by which the wrong is defined. This applies most strongly in the case of war crimes, where there is a very good reason why the law may wish to emphasise that forgiveness will not be too readily granted. Indeed, there is a case for saying that with crimes of a particularly abhorrent nature—of which war crimes usually represent an example—the law should be shown to be prepared to act no matter how lengthy a period elapses between the commission of the crime and the prosecution of the offender. The aim of this approach is to underline the message that those who offend in this way will find no sanctuary, either territorially or temporally. It may be that individual victims may forgive, and indeed acts of forgiveness in such circumstances will probably strike us as being particularly meritorious, but formal justice may, for reasons of general deterrence, either decline to forgive at all or exercise forgiveness very sparingly.

---

[11] A point made by M Holmgren in "Forgiveness and the Intrinsic Value of Persons", (1993) 30 *American Philosophical Quarterly* 341.

The continued prosecution into the late twentieth century of crimes committed over fifty years ago in the course of the Second World War illustrates an unwillingness to forgive of those states bringing such prosecutions. Such prosecutions have to surmount all the usual hurdles that are faced by late proceedings: inadequate recollection on the part of witnesses, missing documentary evidence, and even difficulties of identifying the accused. Yet they have been brought and continue to be demanded in the case of offenders who are well into their eighties. Those who pursue such matters, either organisations or individuals, do not forgive the perpetrators, although they might be prepared to do so in the case of a perpetrator who has accepted his guilt and the necessity of punishment and who makes a full apology.[12] This desire to seek justice even after such a long period of time has tended to be recognised by states, which implicitly acknowledge the depth of feeling involved and the widespread feeling that forgiveness in such cases is precluded by the lack of repentance of the accused, the immensity of the crime, and the demands of deterrence.

Similar considerations apply in the case of some sexual offences. In the United Kingdom, where there is no statute of limitations affecting the prosecution of sexual assault, the criminal justice system appears unforgiving of those whose crimes lie undiscovered or unpunished for decades. Again there is a political factor in the decision not to forgive: prosecutors do not wish to be seen as stating that such sexual assaults are treated lightly, and there is also a desire to demonstrate that the criminal law will discover concealed crimes of this nature even if it has to wait some time to do so. This consideration becomes of particular importance when the victim is a child. Such crimes are likely to be concealed because of pressure brought to bear on the child, and so by the very nature of the crime some time may be required to pass before the crime comes to light. A child may not be in a position to complain until he or she is an adult, and even then the courage to take action may be slow to accumulate.[13]

Forgiveness, then, although a virtue and indeed a moral duty, may have to be exercised with great caution by the criminal justice system. The law can be forgiving—and statutes of limitation demonstrate just that—but there are reasons for distinguishing between expectations of individual forgiveness and expectations of forgiveness by the criminal law. The balance between the competing considerations will be a delicate one. We are unwilling to accept a system of formal justice that is harsh and

---

[12] Whether the Holocaust, for example, can be forgiven has been a matter of particular debate. For a recent intervention, see T Govier, "Forgiveness and the Unforgivable", (1999) 36 *American Philosophical Quarterly* 59.

[13] There has been extensive discussion of possible ways round limitation periods in the case of child sexual abuse cases. See, for example, J E Mindlin "Child Sexual Abuse and Criminal Statutes of Limitation: a Model for Reform", (1990) 65 *Washington Law Review* 189.

pedantic, that is incapable of understanding the ordinary human institution of forgiveness. At the same time, we recognize that the law cannot forgive in circumstances where an individual might do so. The real challenge for the criminal law is to determine the balance and to know just when the line can be drawn above the past and when the backward-looking focus of the law should yield to a concern with future relations. The criminal law has a healing power, but for it to achieve this healing it must be used with the lightest of touches.

This chapter began with a reference to the similarity between the personal and the public past. Whether we are dealing with a small, local wrong against an individual, or a major wrong against a whole nation, the moral issues are very similar. In each case, collective and individual emotions have a very similar face, and the demands which they make appear to be very much the same. What is important is to recognise that in dealing with both sorts of claim, the law can, and indeed should, refer to the moral issue of forgiveness. Admittedly the processes of the law must be formal, and there will often need to be a very calculated response to a past wrong, but in each sort of case, the public and the private, therapeutic considerations must be taken into account and the process of forgiving and release from the past must be given the room that it requires.

Part II

Justice Between Past and Future

5

"With the Benefit of Hindsight": Dilemmas of Legality in the Face of Injustice

DAVID DYZENHAUS[1]

In October 1997 South Africa's Truth and Reconciliation Commission (TRC) held a three-day hearing into the role of the "legal community"—the role of law and lawyers during apartheid. This was but one of the hearings into the role of professions and institutions during apartheid; the others included hearings into the role of the media, the health sector, business and labour, the "faith community" or religious organisations, and the prisons. These hearings were set up by the TRC in terms of its understanding of its broad mandate to establish "as complete a picture as possible of the causes, nature and extent of the gross violations of human rights . . . including the antecedents, circumstances, factors and context of such violations".[2] What made these professional and institutional hearings different from the other hearings which the TRC held is that their purpose was not to establish who is a victim or who may get amnesty. Rather, they were inquiries into how professions and institutions which on the face of it seemed no different from their counterparts in Europe or North America were deeply implicated in apartheid.[3]

[1] This chapter draws together and develops various arguments from my book, *Judging the Judges, Judging Ourselves: Truth, Reconciliation and the Apartheid Legal Order* (Oxford, Hart Publishing, 1998), published in South Africa as *Truth, Reconciliation and the Apartheid Legal Order* (Cape Town, Juta & Co., 1998). The transcript and submissions referred to here are on file with the author. I thank all the participants in the discussions that followed my presentations based on this essay: the School of Law at the University of Warwick, the Cambridge Southern African Students' Society, the British South African Law Association (London), the 1999 Conference on Transitional Justice at the Central European University, Budapest, the 1999 conference on Commissioning the Past at the University of the Witwatersrand, and the McGill Legal Theory Workshop. I also thank the participants in the Edinburgh Conference on Forgiveness and Mercy (convened by the editors of this collection) for an exceptionally stimulating series of discussions and Guy Davidov, Zvi Kahane, and Amnon Reichman for comments on the penultimate draft.

[2] Promotion of National Unity and Reconciliation Act 1995, s. 3(1)(a).

[3] See *Truth and Reconciliation Commission of South Africa Report* (Cape Town, Juta & Co., 1998), vol. 4, ch. 4.

Much of the focus of debate during the legal hearing was on the role of judges. This came about partly because judges singled themselves out from those invited to attend the legal hearing by refusing to attend, though quite a few made written submissions.[4] But this absence merely intensified and made rather rancorous an inevitable concentration on the judicial role, since it is in what judges do that the central question about the rule of law—the relationship between law and justice—is manifested. Indeed, the question of that relationship was the first issue on the list of items the TRC asked its invitees to consider.

Perhaps the most powerful testimony of the Hearing was given by Paula McBride, a human rights activist, who delivered an indictment of judges for having imposed the death penalty on soldiers of the liberation movements even when they had the option of finding that there were mitigating circumstances. She dwelt on the case of Andrew Zondo, a nineteen year-old soldier of the African National Congress (ANC), convicted of planting a mine in 1985 which killed five people in a South African shopping centre. Youth was among the factors a judge could take into account in avoiding imposing the otherwise mandatory death penalty for a crime of this nature. And one of the arguments put to the court was that it should take into account that Zondo had enlisted in the military wing of the ANC because his circumstances as a young black boy growing up in apartheid South Africa gave him reason to suppose that political activity within the confines of the law was futile.

But Zondo was sentenced to death by Raymon Leon, a liberal judge of the most liberal bench—Natal—in South Africa. After sentence was passed Zondo said:

> "I listened to the Prosecutor and I saw that he did not have any ideas about us. He was ignorant of our ways and feelings. I looked at the Judge and the prosecutor and the thought came to me that they were ants and in engaging with them we were dwarfing ourselves. It is a curse to be a Judge when you believe that you hold the life of a person in your hand. Only God holds our lives in his hands. He gives it and He alone can take it".[5]

The question about whether judges can be more than ants is, in my view, the same as the central question about the rule of law—whether there is an intrinsic relationship between law and justice. That there is such a relationship was assumed by many of the central figures at the Hearing. For example, in his opening address Archbishop Desmond Tutu said that the Legal Hearing was the "most important of the professional hearings", almost as important as the "victim/survivor hearings".[6] And he excoriated the judges for their failure to attend. Judges, he said, were faced with

---

[4] In addition, magistrates from the old order neither attended nor made written submissions.

[5] McBride Submission, p. 11.

[6] Transcript, p. 2.

moral choices under apartheid and generally they had made the wrong ones. They had been faced with another choice, whether to appear before the TRC, and again they had made the wrong choice. This showed, he said, that they "had not yet changed a mindset that properly belongs to the old dispensation".[7]

There is a legitimate question about both the Legal Hearing's and my own focus on judges. After all, judges are but a small part of any legal order; indeed, they are a small part of any legal order's judicial system if we conceive such a system as including all those officials charged with making authoritative determinations of the legal rights of those subject to the law. The cutting edge of any legal order—the place where subject meets the law—is going for the most part to be in the enforcement of the law by the police and in the adjudication of disputes about the law by magistrates and administrative officials. For this reason, some thought that the focus on judges at the Hearing distracted the TRC's inquiry from more important issues.

However, I believe such a focus to be productive. Robert Cover, an American Professor of Law, showed why this is the case in his pioneering work on a group of judges in antebellum USA who, despite their commitment to the abolitionist cause, almost relentlessly interpreted laws enforcing slavery in such a way as to shore up the institution of slavery.[8]

Cover pointed out that studies of the relationship between law and justice, a relationship highlighted when one studies the role of law in implementing and sustaining injustice, for the most part accepted "the perspective of the established order".[9] For such studies took the drama of the "disobedient" as exemplary of the problem—the stories of those who appeal to a "juster justice" beyond the law to justify disobedience.[10]

Such disobedients, and any study which makes them exemplary of the relationship between law and justice, take the perspective of the established order because they assume that the law is what the powerful in that order suppose it to be. Such disobedients make their moral stand on the basis of the utter injustice of the law, an injustice created by the arbitrary will of a powerful and unjust ruler. And they therefore exclude the possibility that the law is more than the static embodiment of some ruler's will, determinable as a matter of plain fact.

It is important, Cover thought, that a study of law and justice canvass that excluded possibility by asking whether the law provides opportunities to do justice which rulers, no matter how powerful they are, cannot completely control. Only that possibility allows that the relationship

---

[7] Transcript, pp. 8–9.

[8] R Cover, *Justice Accused: Antislavery and the Judicial Process* (New Haven, Conn., Yale University Press, 1975).

[9] *Ibid.*, p. 1.

[10] *Ibid.*

between law and justice might be an intrinsic one, one which creates tensions within the law when the powerful use the law as an instrument of oppression.

Cover argued that it is adjudication by judges which best manifests the tensions which arise out of that intrinsic relationship when law is put in the service of injustice. For judges everywhere claim that their duty is not simply to administer the law, but to administer justice. Indeed, the oath of office which South African judges swore during apartheid stated that they would "administer justice to all persons alike without without fear, favour or prejudice, and, as the circumstances of any particular case may require, in accordance with the law and customs of the Republic of South Africa".[11]

As I pointed out in my own submission to the Legal Hearing, one can adopt the view that the justice of the law mentioned in the oath is simply the conception of justice which, as a matter of fact, the powerful have used the law to implement.[12] Alternatively, one can read some significance into the word justice, for example, by noting that the oath would look rather odd if one substituted for "justice" the phrase "ideology of the powerful".

Encapsulated in these two ways of viewing the relationship between law and justice is the age-old debate in the philosophy of law between legal positivists and natural law theory. Positivists argue that the relationship between law and "juster justice" or true justice is purely contingent on political circumstance, while the natural lawyers argue that there is some intrinsic relationship. The complexity of that debate, especially in its more technical aspects, goes well beyond the confines of this chapter.

But an important, and I would argue the principal, aspect of that debate is illuminated by a focus on the role of judges at the TRC, even though their role was confined to some written submissions. For if we are concerned with the relationship between law and justice, then, as Cover says, we cannot study that relationship without maintaining the possibility that it is an intrinsic one. The relationship has to be intrinsic if law is to provide a place where those subject to it can contest it when it is used as an instrument of brute and arbitrary power. Only if the relationship is intrinsic can law provide the basis for judges to be more than the ants whom young Andrew Zondo encountered in the trial which culminated in his judicially-ordered death.

I will suggest that the conclusion one should reach is a heartening one—there is an intrinsic relationship between law and justice demonstrated by the few South African lawyers who committed themselves to finding justice within the law. Moreover, their commitment laid the basis for a significant role for law and lawyers in South Africa's inevitably difficult transition to becoming a fully functioning and stable democracy.

[11] Supreme Court Act 1959, s. 10(2)(a).
[12] Dyzenhaus Submission, p. 1.

However, the path to that conclusion is often a difficult one. I have already mentioned that the judge whom McBride condemned for his failure to find mitigating circumstances for Andrew Zondo was a liberal judge on South Africa's most liberal bench. And one of the peculiarities of the Hearing was that those few lawyers—I will refer to them as liberal lawyers—who did commit themselves to the cause of justice often came in for harsh criticism. At times it seemed that those who did most got judged most harshly.

I will start by exploring that issue through the perspective of one of South Africa's most prominent disobedients, the advocate Abram ("Bram") Fischer. As I will show, the dilemma he faced required his fellow lawyers to decide for themselves whether to be ants or to live up to some more exacting standard of fidelity to law. And through seeing that dilemma we will be in a position to appreciate the full range of dilemmas that faced other actors in the South African legal order, especially the judges.

THE CASE OF BRAM FISCHER

Fischer's case was brought to the attention of the TRC through the written and oral submissions made by the federal body of South African advocates, the General Council of the Bar (GCB). (The legal profession in South Africa is split between advocates (barristers) and attorneys (solicitors).)

At issue was the striking off of Fischer from the roll of advocates, a move initiated by his own Bar, the Johannesburg Bar, the most liberal component of the GCB. Fischer, as the GCB's submission notes, was son of the Judge President of the Orange Free State and the grandson of the Prime Minister of the Orange River Colony, the political entity which came into being between the end of the Boer War and the establishment of the Union of South Africa in 1910. He became one of South Africa's leading advocates, a position he maintained in the 1950s and early 1960s despite the fact that he was a prominent member of the South African Communist Party. In 1964 he was charged with various offences under the Suppression of Communism Act 1950, in reaction to which the Communist Party had dissolved itself and gone underground. Fischer was permitted to leave South Africa on bail to argue a case before the Privy Council in London since the court accepted that a man of his integrity would not estreat (break the conditions of) his bail. Fischer returned to stand trial, which commenced in November 1964. In January of 1965 he failed to attend his trial, leaving a letter for his legal representative explaining his reasons. Here are some extracts:

> "I wish you to inform the court that my absence, though deliberate, is not intended in any way to be disrespectful . . . I have not taken this step lightly. As

you will no doubt understand, I have experienced great conflict between my desire to stay with my fellow accused and, on the other hand, to try to continue the political work I believe to be essential. My decision was made only because I believe that it is the duty of every true opponent of this government to remain in this country and to oppose its monstrous policy of apartheid with every means in its power. That is what I shall do for as long as I can . . . Cruel, discriminatory laws multiply each year, bitterness and hatred of the government and its laws are growing daily. No outlet for this hatred is permitted because political rights have been removed. National organisations have been outlawed and leaders not in gaol have been banned from speaking and meeting. People are hounded by Pass Laws and by Group Areas Controls. Torture by solitary confinement, and worse, has been legalised by an elected parliament—surely an event unique in history . . . Unless this whole intolerable system is changed radically and rapidly disaster must follow. Appalling bloodshed and civil war will become inevitable because, as long as there is oppression of a majority such oppression will be fought with increasing hatred . . . These are my reasons for absenting myself from court. If by my fight I can encourage even some people to think about, to understand and to abandon the policies they now so blindly follow, I shall not regret any punishment I may incur. I can no longer serve justice in the way I have attempted to do during the past thirty years. I can only do so in the way I have now chosen".[13]

Just two days later, the Johannesburg Bar Council instructed its attorneys to prepare an application to court for the removal of Fischer's name from the roll of advocates. Shortly afterwards Fischer wrote another letter to his legal representative, expressing his dismay at the haste with which the Johannesburg Bar Council had acted. He was also distressed by the fact that the decision had been taken without any attempt to get his side heard.[14]

In his letter, Fischer strongly defended himself against the charge of conduct "unbefitting that of an advocate" entailed in an application to strike off:

"The principle upon which I rely is a simple one, firmly established in South African legal tradition. Since the days of the South African War,[15] if not since the Jameson Raid,[16] it has been recognised that political offences, committed because of a belief in the overriding moral validity of a political principle, do not in themselves justify the disbarring of a person from practising the profession of the law. Presumably this is so because it is assumed that the commission of such offences has no bearing on the professional integrity of the person concerned.

---

[13]   GCB Submission, vol. 2, pp. 190–1.

[14]   See S Clingman, *Bram Fischer: Afrikaner Revolutionary* (Amherst, Mass., University of Massachussets Press, 1998).

[15]   The war between Britain and the Boer Republics.

[16]   A raid into the Transvaal Republic in December 1895, instigated by Cecil John Rhodes in a botched attempt to get rid of President Paul Kruger.

When an advocate does what I have done, his conduct is not determined by any disrespect for the law nor because he hopes to benefit personally by 'any offence' he may commit. On the contrary, it requires an act of will to overcome his deeply rooted respect of legality, and he takes the step only when he feels that, whatever the consequences to himself, his political conscience no longer permits him to do otherwise. He does it not because of a desire to be immoral, but because to do otherwise would, for him, be immoral".

Fischer went on to say that he had returned to South Africa determined to see his trial through. But his experience of facing trial on evidence extracted from detainees held in solitary confinement under a 90-day detention law—the "gross injustice (apart from the cruelty) of this barbaric law"—convinced him that no prosecution which depended on evidence "extracted" during such detention could be considered fair. In addition, he thought he might be facing the kind of "indeterminate sentence" which the Minister of Justice had discretion to impose and of which he said "we have already seen how European [i.e. white] public opinion has failed to register any protest against this arbitrary, indefinite incarceration and has complacently accepted this total abolition of the rule of law". He thus found himself compelled, he said, into a stance of:

"open defiance, whatever the consequences might be, of a process of law which has become a travesty of all civilised tradition: A political belief is outlawed, then torture is applied to gather evidence and finally the Executive decides whether you serve a life sentence or not.

I cannot believe that any genuine protest made against this system which has been constructed solely to further apartheid can be regarded as immoral or as justifying the disbarment of a member of our profession".[17]

However, the Johannesburg Bar went ahead with its application to have him struck off. The court held that he should be struck off: he had been guilty of dishonest conduct because he had used his status as senior counsel to get bail and someone who took an attitude of defiance to the law could not serve the law.[18]

The GCB comments:

"Those who took the decision to apply for the striking of Fischer's name from the roll of advocates must have been confronted with an invidious problem. They namely recognised that Fischer had been 'regarded by the Courts of the Republic, by the members of the Johannesburg Bar and by other legal practitioners as a most honourable and trustworthy member of the Bar' who had at all times 'observed the highest ethical standards of legal practice' and had been 'in every respect a worthy and distinguished member of the legal profession'.[19] They believed that notwithstanding the esteem in which Fischer was held by all,

---

[17] GCB Submission, vol. 2, pp. 193–7.

[18] *Society of Advocates of SA (Witwatersrand Division)* v. *Fischer* 1966 (1) SA 133 (T).

[19] The quotations within this quote are from the founding affidavit supporting the striking off.

the deception to the Court, coming as it did from a senior practitioner, justified the striking off. There is no doubt that even in 1965, the issue was painful and divisive for those involved. Many of the leaders of the Johannesburg Bar felt that their personal relationship with Fischer was such that they would not be willing to appear in the application for his striking off. Thus it was that the then chairman of the GCB who practises in Durban, was approached to move the application. For him, the task was a distressing one, since he too had a great respect and liking for Fischer . . .

Today, with the benefit of hindsight, there is a different perspective. Fischer was confronted with an acute dilemma. He was torn between his fidelity to law, which he had served faithfully for many years and his profound commitment to opposing the injustices of apartheid. He acted not out of self-interest but from political and moral conviction. Far from securing any personal advantage, he realised that his actions would result in increased punishment".

The GCB then reported that the Johannesburg Bar Council believes now that "a grave injustice" was done to Fischer and it apologised to his family.[20]

The full presentation of the record here is to the credit of the GCB for it shows just how difficult memory's struggle is and how great is the temptation to manage it.[21] Unexplained in the GCB's submission is the phrase "with the benefit of hindsight". That phrase does not mean that one is engaging in a simple act of memory. Rather, it means that one can see things now that one was not able to see earlier. But since Fischer made the situation crystal clear at the time, hindsight is not required for gaining the "different perspective", but for understanding why the Bar chose to evade the issues presented by Fischer. And this perspective was not unique to Fischer—Leslie Blackwell QC, a former judge of the Supreme Court, published an article in the *Sunday Times* sympathetic to Fischer's case.[22]

The GCB not only invited the question of how hindsight was relevant when Fischer, whose moral stature it recognised both in 1965 and at the Hearing, had presented the moral complexity of his situation fully at the time. It also failed to deal with the fact that Fischer's situation was morally complex in part because of legal factors. Although Fischer had estreated bail, he had not clearly estreated the conditions imposed on him when he was initially granted bail. He had come back to stand trial and, as he explained, it was his experience on his return which had led him to view his situation in a different light.

More important, however, the argument he made based on that experience was one about the absence of the rule of law in South Africa. Not only were his concerns related to the fact that the majority of South Africa's population had no political rights and to the fact that legal polit-

[20] GCB Submission, vol. 2, pp. 201–04.

[21] The GCB closed its submission with a quotation from Milan Kundera: "The struggle against the abuse of power is the struggle of memory against forgetting"; *ibid.*, pp. 209–11.

[22] See Clingman, above n. 14, p. 371.

ical opposition had been closed to them, but also to the fact that his trial, as well as the sentence he might face, were in violation of his understanding of the rule of the law. Even if it were the case, as he was prepared to grant, that his decision to go underground was in violation of his initial undertaking, the reasons for his decision could not reflect negatively on his integrity as an advocate. In sum, at stake for him was not only his professional commitment to abiding by the bail conditions set by the court but also his professional commitment to the rule of law.

The "invidiousness" of the Johannesburg Bar's situation was one entirely of their own making. Their "indecent haste", as Fischer's daughters termed it,[23] to get Fischer struck off meant that the Bar took the initiative from the government in discrediting Fischer, thus helping to obscure the message he hoped to send his fellow white South Africans. As Fischer himself said in his letter, though the GCB did not quote this particular sentence, his "contention" was that "if in the year 1965 I have to be removed from the roll of practising advocates, the Minister himself and not the Bar Council should do the dirty work".[24] While it is true that, technically speaking, the application for striking off referred only to Fischer's decision to break the conditions of his bail, the Bar's narrowing of the issue to one about the personal integrity of an advocate, entirely abstracted from the political context of South Africa, was a deeply political act. It was and is a way of refusing to confront the wider political and rule of law implications of Fischer's decision, implications which were intimately connected to the charges he was facing and the "legal" process of a political trial.

In my view, Bram Fischer's story is central to any account of the choices South African lawyers faced during apartheid. The history of apartheid law can be roughly divided into ten-year periods. In the 1950s, the apartheid divide was legislated; in the 1960s, the security apparatus to repress opposition to apartheid was legislated and eventually consolidated. In the 1970s, cracks in the ideology behind the divide and in the law which maintained it started to appear but were patched over by ruthless use of the force licensed by security legislation. In the 1980s, the divide fractured, was maintained for ten or so years by force, but was eventually destroyed, a feat in which lawyers played a significant role.

As the Legal Hearing showed, lawyers when looking back over this period like to dwell on the period of the 1980s, when some of their number were most active in opposing apartheid. At the same time, they often claimed that opposition to apartheid through the law was usually futile, as demonstrated by the fruitless representations to the government which the professional associations on occasion made.

In the case of the professional associations, the tension is most exposed by the attorneys since in the 1960s they were almost totally silent about the

---

[23] Transcript, p. 243.
[24] Clingman, above n. 14, p. 371.

74   *David Dyzenhaus*

erosion of the rule of law. For the advocates, the tension comes about because at this time the most liberal of the Bars took part in the repression of one of its own, Bram Fischer. Moreover, it took that part in the face of an explicit and powerful challenge which Fischer threw down to South African lawyers.

Fischer did not simply ask these lawyers to confront their role in sustaining the injustice of the law. He tried to get them to see that there was more wrong with the law than that it was being used in the cause of unjust policies. He argued that any lawyer who wished to maintain respect for the rule of law had to question whether the ideal of the rule of law was not in fact better served by violating the law.

Fischer clearly regarded this question as an open one, to be decided by each individual. As we know, he decided that the only way he could participate in building a society founded on respect for the rule of law was to go underground in order to join the illegal armed struggle. But we also know that he hoped that his example, the example of an Afrikaner aristocrat who had established himself as one of the leaders of the legal profession, would make other lawyers rethink their role *within* the legal order. And that was, I think, because he regarded himself as in a genuine dilemma. However repugnant he found the apartheid legal order, it remained a legal order—an order in which there were still the vestiges of the rule of law—and his respect for the law still exerted a pull on him which he found difficult to resist.

As Stephen Clingman shows in his excellent biography of Fischer, Fischer's decision to return from England to stand trial in the face of considerable pressure from his comrades in exile abroad, his courtesy to his legal representative and to the judicial officers presiding at his trial, and his great concern about the uncomfortable situation he had created for his legal representative, were all occasioned by his continuing respect for the law, even as he planned to go underground. And as we have seen, it was the complete lack of understanding of most of his colleagues at the Johannesburg Bar of his position, evidenced by their haste to join in the government's attack on him as a political dissident, which so distressed him.[25]

The rule of law dilemma which Fischer faced casts into sharp relief all the other dilemmas which South African lawyers faced. The best description of Fischer's kind of rule of law dilemma is found in an essay by the distinguished philosopher Christine Korsgaard in an attempt to make sense of Kant's apparent ambivalence in regard to revolutionary action.[26]

[25] Clingman, above n. 14, pp. 344–56, 368–72, 389–91, 400–16.
[26] C M Korsgaard, "Taking the Law into Our Own Hands: Kant on the Right to Revolution", in A Reath, B Herman, C M Korsgaard (eds), *Reclaiming the History of Ethics: Essays for John Rawls* (Cambridge, Cambridge University Press, 1997), p. 297.

Korsgaard says the following of a morally upstanding citizen who contemplates joining a revolution against the established order:

> "When the very institution whose purpose is to realize human rights is used to trample them, when justice is turned against itself, the virtue of justice will be turned against itself too. Concern for human rights leads the virtuous person to accept the authority of the law, but in such circumstances adherence to the law will lead her to support institutions that systematically violate human rights. The person with the virtue of justice, the lover of human rights, unable to turn to the actual laws for their enforcement, has nowhere else to turn. She may come to feel that there is nothing for it but to take human rights under her own protection, and so to take the law into her own hands".[27]

Korsgaard suggests that such a decision is ethically different from most decisions we make. It is not the "imperfection" of justice—justice which fails to measure up to our sense of right and wrong—which is the basis for our decision. Rather, the basis is the "perversion" of justice, the sense that it is injustice disguised as justice. But given the consequences that likely attend overthrowing an established order, the revolutionary cannot, she thinks, claim that he is justified in resorting to revolution. "That consolation is denied him. It is as if a kind of gap opens up in the moral world in which the moral agent must stand alone".[28] Korsgaard thus maintains that justification in such matters is always retrospective—everything depends on whether the revolutionary is successful in establishing a stable government.[29]

Where Korsgaard goes wrong, however, is in suggesting that the decision has to be made in a moral gap or void. Fischer had no doubt that whatever the future would in fact say, he was at the time justified in taking his step. The difference between his own understanding of his situation and Korsgaard's is that he does not quite adopt the perspective which we saw Robert Cover term the "perspective of the disobedient", "the perspective of the established order". For although Fischer appealed, like Cover's disobedient, to a "juster justice" beyond the law to justify his disobedience, his perspective on the law was not entirely external. As we have seen, his appeal was also meant to awaken South African lawyers to the possibility for them of the pursuit of the ideal of juster justice within the law. In contrast, Korsgaard's analysis seems to suggest that for the disobedient revolutionary only the external "disobedient" perspective is available. But that would mean that there was no real dilemma, at least no moral dilemma.

Clingman also seems to rely on the external disobedient perspective in his exploration of the nature of Fischer's choice in 1965. He rejects the view that Fischer's life was a tragedy in the classical sense in which a great individual contributes to his fall "through some crucial error or flaw",

---

[27] *Ibid.*, pp. 318–19, footnote omitted.   [28] *Ibid.*, p. 315.   [29] *Ibid.*

preferring the idea that Fischer had to pay the price of an uncompromising stand on the side of right against the "unregenerate force of apartheid".[30] Here Clingman suggests that for Fischer the situation was one of a clash between opposites—evil might and total right.

Fischer's choice had of course tragic consequences for him personally. He died in 1975 when those involved in the struggle against apartheid had few grounds for hope. And that choice committed him to an armed struggle which had tragic consequences for others, consequences which, as Korsgaard suggests, attend any decision to engage in revolution. Even if one considers the turn to armed struggle by the ANC in the early 1960s as a completely justified reaction to government repression, one has to admit that the ANC's decision gave the apartheid government the excuse to engage in a no-holds barred war which escalated into the tale of human cruelty with which the TRC had to deal. And one can give the ANC the moral high ground in this war and still hold the ANC responsible, as the TRC has, for its own gross human rights abuses.[31] Indeed, the idea for the TRC was born in an ANC initiative in the early 1990s to appoint commissions to inquire into its record of brutality to its own soldiers in ANC training camps. In other words, the decision to engage in armed struggle was one whose human consequences could be predicted without having been able to predict the ultimate result. And it is unimaginable that someone as far-sighted and ethically rigorous as Fischer took his decision without accepting responsibility for these consequences.

However, at least from the institutional perspective of the rule of law, the idea of a clash between two opposites, and of a decision in a moral void, does not get exactly right the tragic nature of Fischer's choice in 1965.

We can think of a morally tragic situation as being one in which no choice can be made without ignoring the legitimate pull of important moral considerations. We have nevertheless to choose in such situations. And we have to try to make the best choice without the comfort, however the choice turns out, that the ignored considerations will cease to be legitimate. Even when one seems vindicated in retrospect, all one can say is that one did the best one could and that one is deeply sorry about one's complicity in the moral wrongs that resulted from one's choice.

Recall that at the same time as Fischer made his choice to go underground, he hoped by it to encourage others to take a different decision. And it is worth noting that Nelson Mandela seems to have been occupied by the same issue in the 1960s. He says that at the time of the trial which resulted in his own sentence to life imprisonment, he urged Fischer, leader of the defence team, who was already considering going underground, not to take this route. Mandela says that he stressed that Fischer "served the

[30] Clingman, above n. 14, pp. 449–51.
[31] See *Truth and Reconciliation Commission of South Africa Report*, vol. 2, ch. 4.

struggle best in the courtroom, where people could see this Afrikaner son of a judge president fighting for the rights of the powerless".[32]

In other words, Fischer and Mandela did not adopt a simple strategy of fighting an illegal war against an unjust state in order to establish a just one.[33] They thought that it was important that at the same time war be fought by legal means in order to keep alive an idea put to the Legal Hearing by Vincent Saldanha, leader of the delegation from the National Association of Democratic Lawyers which had been formed in order to provide a home for lawyers determined to use the law to resist apartheid. Saldanha had this to say about the lawyers involved in the radical opposition to apartheid:

> "[While we] took an oath of allegiance to the state, we certainly did not take an oath of allegiance to the apartheid state. If anything, we took an oath of allegiance to undermine the apartheid state, and I think a distinction must be drawn. That's why we distinguish ourselves from the establishment lawyers or the lawyers who operated within the Law Societies under the particular milieu and ideological context they did. We worked with these lawyers, we used the law as a terrain of struggle, unashamedly, and to that extent would continue to use the law as a terrain presently in furtherance of the principles and the values of the new Constitution".[34]

In order for that distinction—one between the government which brings about the enactment of the law and the law of the state to which the government itself is subject—to have any basis, right can never be entirely on the side of one who decides to overthrow an order which still contains vestiges of the rule of law. Indeed, besides the costs to human beings that follow a decision to overthrow an established order, the revolutionary has to take into account the costs armed struggle imposes on respect for the rule of law, a respect which might prove important during the period of instability which inevitably follows the overthrow of the old order. But the revolutionary can seek to justify his actions here and now in making his decision, as long as he recognises the pull of competing considerations and thus the moral worth of the other decision.

In South Africa that other decision, the decision to use the law to oppose the law, had almost as momentous a result as the decision to turn to armed struggle. In this regard, Clingman takes care to note that lawyers who worked with Fischer and who represented him, most notably Arthur Chaskalson, continued and even extended his work in the courts. Clingman points in particular to Chaskalson's co-founding of the Legal Resources Centre in 1978, the most important base of legal challenges to apartheid, and to his recent appointment to the Presidency of South Africa's Constitutional Court.[35]

---

[32] Nelson Mandela, *Long Walk to Freedom* (Boston, Little, Brown and Company, 1995), p. 472.

[33] See Clingman, above n. 14, pp. 310–11.   [34] Transcript, p. 450.   [35] *Ibid.*, p. 455.

Thus, while Fischer was a South African of altogether exceptional moral stature, the way he lived his life set an example for all other white South Africans, particularly lawyers. His choice, while tragic, was one which could be justified even at the time he made it, whatever the result. For the manner of its making opened up moral space for those who did not want to follow him, preferring to make their stand against apartheid from within the law. And, while they cannot be condemned for having decided to opt for the politics of legal opposition, they can and should be judged by how they behaved within that space.

However, those who took that stand had to cope with the moral question mark raised by the fact that one could with justification claim that the rule of law was best served by the politics of armed struggle. This was especially true for lawyers whose path of legal resistance to the law involved using the law against the law. Not only did they make themselves vulnerable to being judged by their own standards, in contrast to the vast majority of lawyers who either actively supported apartheid or who were merely content to ignore oppression while reaping the benefits of legal practice. It was also the case that the more successful they were at using the law to challenge the law, the more they legitimated the legal order by helping to vindicate the government's claim to be part of the family of states committed to such fundamental Western values as the rule of law.

In the next section, I explore the question about why that situation could arise at all—why it was the case that the space existed for law to be used to resist law.

DILEMMAS OF THE RULE OF LAW

In nearly all the cases which are regarded as landmark decisions for human rights by the South African courts during the apartheid era, the basic question the judges had to answer concerned whether they should impose constraints of legality on executive decisions. And such cases are regarded as landmark cases precisely because, as in the decision about whether to find mitigating circumstances for Zondo, the judge's decision turned on his judgment about how best to interpret the law.

These cases included decisions about how to implement apartheid policy, decisions about the suppression of political opposition and the detention of opponents, and decisions about the content of regulations made under statutory powers. Examples of the legal principles at issue included the following: the principle that policy should be implemented in a reasonable or non-discriminatory fashion; the principle that someone whose rights are affected by an official decision has a right to be heard before that decision is made; the principle that, when a statute says that an official must have reason to believe that X is the case before he acts, the court should require that reasons be produced sufficient to justify that belief; the principle that no executive decision can encroach on a fundamental right, for example, the right to have access to a court and to legal advice, unless the empowering statute specifically authorises that encroachment; the principle that regulations made under vast discretionary powers, for example, the power to make regulations declaring and dealing with a state of emergency, must be capable of being defended in a court of law by a demonstration that there are genuine circumstances of the kind which justify invoking the power and that the powers actually invoked are demonstrably related to the purpose of the empowering statute.

It is very important to understand why such principles are *fundamental* principles of *legality*. Take the principle that no executive decision can encroach on the fundamental right to have access to a court and to legal advice, unless the empowering statute specifically authorises that encroachment. That principle became particularly important in the period after 1960 in South Africa because the government sought to insulate detention from the scrutiny of the courts by barring in its legislation access by the courts or any other person to detainees. That meant it became almost impossible to challenge the legality of a particular detention which in turn meant that the violence of the administration could be exercised without any legal control. In such circumstances, the courts cannot be said to be administering "the law" because there is no law to which one can hold public officials to account.

Moreover, the law which the courts are failing to enforce does not primarily consist of rules which owe their existence to positive enactment by a legislature or explicit recognition by a court. Rather, this law consists of the principles which make sense of the idea of government under the rule of law, the idea that such government is subject to the constraints of principles such as fairness, reasonableness, and equality of treatment. One will expect such principles to be manifested in statutes and in judgments, but for the reason that it is only in making these principles manifest that legislatures and courts can give some content to the idea of the rule of law, of the accountability of public officials to the law.

In a legal order such as the apartheid one where the legislature is supreme, judicial scrutiny of official conduct for its legality is of course to some extent conditional on the legislature not saying explicitly that it wishes its administration to act illegally. The qualification is necessary because judges, in meeting their duty to administer the justice of the law, should take pains to find their legislature not guilty of wanting to subvert the rule of law. That duty explains why judges should require very explicit expressions by the legislature of an intention to evade the constraints of legality.

Had the majority of judges applied the law in a way that made best sense of their judicial oath, the government would have had to choose one of two options. It could have openly announced that it could not both abide by the rule of law and maintain apartheid as it wanted, thus explicitly choosing a lawless course, or it could have subjected its administration to the constraint of the fundamental legal principles sketched earlier. The first option would have significantly decreased support for the government both in the international community and at home. And had the government taken this option, judges faithful to their duty could have denounced such statutes for illegality—not for lack of compliance with some extra-legal ideal of justice, but for failing to be law. In other words, judges could then condemn the law not simply because they disagreed with it, but because the law profaned principles fundamental to maintaining legal order. In contrast, the second option—government submission to the rule of law—would have opened up precious space for opposition to apartheid from within.

In either case, the judges would have confronted the government with a rule of law dilemma. We saw that dilemma manifest itself for Bram Fischer as he contemplated taking his fight against apartheid underground. In his case, the dilemma was a genuinely moral one. His commitment to the rule of law required him to recognise that the values which he decided to pursue by revolutionary means were put at risk by a revolutionary course, and, more important, could still be fought for by legal means. In other words, the moral quality of his dilemma stems from the fact that a commitment to the rule of law informs both of its options. In the case of the South African government, however, the rule of law dilemma was not moral but strategic. It was a dilemma between accepting the costs as well as the benefits of operation under the rule of law or doing without the legitimacy which attaches to government under the rule of law.

In confronting the government with the strategic rule of law dilemma, judges would have affirmed their commitment to a process that "does not defer to the violence of administration";[36] rather, the process seeks to impose the constraints of legality on a state which licenses that imposition by its claim to be a *Rechtsstaat*—to be a state which governs in accordance with the rule of law. Such a commitment exhibits fidelity to the law because it shows that the rationale for having courts is their potential to articulate and maintain a "constitutional vision",[37] one informed by an understanding that the duty judges undertook in their oath to administer the law was one to "administer justice to all persons alike without fear, favour or prejudice".

The South African judiciary let the government escape from that rule of law dilemma and for that the judges are accountable, and not only for

---

[36] R Cover, "Nomos and Narrative", in M Minow, M Ryan and A Sarat (eds), *Narrative, Violence and the Law: The Essays of Robert Cover* (Ann Arbor, Michigan, Michigan University Press, 1995), pp. 95, 162.

[37] Cover, *ibid.*, pp. 162–3.

dereliction of duty. They are also accountable for having facilitated the shadows and secrecy of the world in which the security forces operated and for permitting the unrestrained implementation of apartheid policy. They thus bear some responsibility for the bitter legacy of hurt which was the main focus of the TRC.

To place the government in that dilemma would have been a deeply political act and judges do not like to be seen to be engaging in politics. But, as I argued in my submission,[38] when the politics in which judges engage amount to upholding the rule of law, requiring of a government that it live up to ideals which it itself, however cynically, professes, then judges are simply doing the duty undertaken in their oath of office. They are demonstrating their accountability to the law to which governments, who wish to claim the legitimacy of government through the medium of the rule of law, are also accountable.

Judges who assume that a legislature must be taken to intend to respect the rule of law do so in order to make sense of their role as one faithful to the duty to administer the law. And that tells us that the judges' duty is to moral ideals which play a role in constituting what they should take to be the positive law, even in the absence of a written constitution which gives them such authority. If judges fail to do that, the South African example shows that they fail in their duty as judges.

One must be careful here not to err on the side of over- or underestimation. Liberal judges could not have stopped apartheid and one can safely say that any significant act of judicial resistance would have been overridden by the government. But we should note that any particular act of resistance by the internal opposition to apartheid or by the liberation organisations was likely to be, and in fact usually was, overridden. Further, many white South Africans did not find it entirely easy to think of themselves as on the beneficiary side of the apartheid divide. Even when they were not enthusiastic supporters of apartheid, they needed to think that they were living in, and helping to maintain, a basically civilised society. Each time a person from within the ranks of the white establishment broke those ranks to point out how uncivilised their society was, the others were threatened with being forced to rethink their position.

Bram Fischer's example is the most striking here. And there is no doubt that a mass resignation of the few liberal judges, judges who condemned apartheid not only as a repugnant ideology but because of its subversion of the rule of law, would have rocked the government and white South Africans.

However, I believe—perhaps with the benefit of hindsight—that the few liberal judges were right to remain in office despite the fact that once in office a liberal judge confronted a rule of law dilemma in a particularly painful way. Even the most liberal judge who took office under apartheid

---

[38] Dyzenhaus Submission, p. 17.

could not avoid implementing its law. He had often to accept that even laws whose content he found abhorrent and whose provenance he regarded as illegitimate had a claim on his duty to administer the law. He therefore not only made himself complicit in an injustice he recognised as such, but gave to that injustice the aura of legitimacy.

In other words, what made a liberal judge different from other judges was not his complicity in apartheid but his conception of fidelity to the law. His presence could help to keep alive the idea that the law provides opportunities to judges to make the law meet its aspiration to treat all its subjects fairly, equally, reasonably, and so on. However, in keeping that idea alive, he also helped to legitimate the apartheid government by giving some genuine substance to the claim that the rule of law did exist in South Africa.

For the liberal judges, then, it was very much a case of "damned if you do, damned if you don't". But without them, there would have been little, perhaps no, point to the efforts of those few lawyers in the academy in the 1960s and 1970s who sought to provide their students with a critical perspective on the apartheid legal order, or to the efforts of those few lawyers in practice, attorneys and advocates, who were prepared to use the law against the law in the fight against apartheid. The distinction between the apartheid state and the ideal state which we saw Vincent Saldanha draw depended on the efforts of all of these lawyers, but most importantly on the liberal judges, simply because without an occasional victory in the courts no such distinction could have been drawn. And without a basis for that distinction during apartheid, there would have been precious little reason for the ANC to take law seriously both during the negotiations about the new order and in the transition to democracy.

Nevertheless, there is a salient difference between academic critics and human rights lawyers, on the one hand, and liberal judges, on the other. It is not that one legitimates while the other does not, for it is clear that the participation of all serves to legitimate. Rather, the difference is that liberal judges often could not help but allow the injustice of the law to speak through them. Further, this feature of their role was not confined to occasions when they had no choice but to interpret the law as the government wanted it interpreted. Even when a liberal judge had some room for interpretative manoeuvre it was usually the case that he could only mitigate to some extent the injustice of the law.

TRUTH, MEMORY AND THE RULE OF LAW

I have noted that no South African judge accepted the TRC's invitation to testify at the Legal Hearing. Two reasons seemed paramount in this judicial boycott, a claim that judicial independence would be compromised and the thought that such testimony would endanger the fragile bond of collegiality that exists between judges from the old order who have kept their jobs and judges appointed under the new order.

However, the claim for immunity because of the need to protect judicial independence is hollow once one sees that judicial independence is itself an instrumental virtue: it is instrumental to ensuring the accountability of judges to the law. And the majority of old order judges had failed to show fidelity to the law, had failed to take seriously a judicial oath which required them "to administer justice". As a Canadian judge once put it when judges in Canada raised a defence of total immunity to a summons to testify before a commission of inquiry: "[w]hen there is a real risk that judicial immunity may be perceived by the public as being advanced for the protection of the judiciary rather than for the protection of the justice system, the public interest . . . requires that the question be asked and answered".[39] And in regard to collegiality, one has to take into account the possibility that the kind of collegiality bought at the expense of an open and honest debate about the substance of judicial independence might be a very shallow one, unlikely to sustain a judiciary which carries the burden of huge expectations.[40]

Further, judges, in exempting themselves from the process of discussion at the TRC while in a few cases making written submissions, provoked a discussion from which they then held themselves aloof, thus demonstrating their sense that judges are not accountable like other citizens. Had even a few judges accepted the TRC's invitation, not only would this have imparted a different tone to the Hearing as a whole, but it would have done more for respect for the law and for the judiciary than any attempts to present their record in its best possible light. Accepting the invitation would have shown that judges acknowledged that they are not above the legal process that seeks to bridge South Africa's awful past to a democratic future. And only such an acknowledgment could have demonstrated a proper awareness that one of the things that made that past so singular was that the injustice of apartheid was implemented through what judges like to consider the vehicle for justice, the law.

In particular, such an appearance would have demonstrated that judges understand that they too are citizens in a democracy, citizens with special responsibilities, of course. But the weight of those responsibilities in the context of a fraught transition to democracy argued for their appearance. By appearing, judges would have accepted their commitment to a practice, well described by Paul W Kahn in an essay on judicial independence during

---

[39] Judge Bertha Wilson in her partial dissent in *MacKeigan* v. *Hickman* [1989] 2 SCR 796, at 808–9. I discuss the case in detail in *Judging the Judges, Judging Ourselves*, above n. 1, ch. 4.

[40] See on these issues *Truth and Reconciliation Commission of South Africa Final Report*, vol. 4, pp. 106–8.

transitions to democracy as the practice of the "morality of citizenship". They would have seen themselves as part of an attempt to articulate in public a sense of responsibility for the past and the future which makes sense of the relationship between state, court, and individual.[41]

Kahn argues that the courtroom is a "political theatre" but that does not make it the "theatre of politics". There is a distinction between law and politics, which is the distinction we have already encountered between the state and government, or the state as an ideal and the state in practice. At the moment that a court accepts jurisdiction over a controversy between government and an individual, government is demoted, it loses its claim to be the exclusive representative of the state. At the same time, the individual is promoted into a public role, to one with an equal claim to represent the state. The court, then, in deciding between these claims articulates a vision of what the state is and publicly draws the line between law and politics.[42]

In order to articulate this vision, the court needs to be independent. But Kahn plausibly suggests that what matters is not the formal structures of independence, which might differ from country to country, but "the informal tradition of norms and expectations that develop around political and legal institutions".[43] In a functioning democracy, courts and political institutions support each other: the "courts provide a kind of legitimacy to the political institutions and the political institutions return the favor to the courts".[44]

Now South Africa under apartheid was not a functioning democracy, though the courts had a kind of formal independence and were engaged in the reciprocal relationship of legitimacy with political institutions which Kahn describes. The enforced divide between racial groups in the service of white supremacy meant that it was impossible to develop an "informal tradition of norms and expectations . . . around political and legal institutions" common to most South Africans.

In a fraught transition a tradition of judicial independence can at best be said to be in the process of being forged. Hence, it was incumbent on judges committed to a democratic future fully to take part in the opportunity offered them to debate both their past and their future. The judges could have initiated a more general discussion which would have set the stage for sketching the legitimate role of judges in the new South African legal order, one in which the Constitution gives them enormous scope for shaping the moral direction of government. That discussion could then have framed more particular discussions about the role of the magistracy, the role of the legal profession—advocates, attorneys and public law advocacy centres—the kind of independence required by the Attorneys-

---

[41] P Kahn, "Independence and Responsibility in the Judicial Role", in I Stotzky (ed), *Transition to Democracy in Latin America: The Role of the Judiciary* (Boulder, Colorado, Westview Press, 1993), pp. 73, 85.
[42] *Ibid.*, p. 77.   [43] *Ibid.*, p. 84.   [44] *Ibid.*, p. 85.

General, and the type of legal education required in the new South Africa.

For the difference the new legal order of South Africa will make to South Africa's future does not so much depend on the formal differences between a legal order based on legislative supremacy and one based on a liberal democratic constitution. It depends much more on how those who staff the legal order do their jobs. And when a body is set up to bridge the old and the new in the service of constructing democracy, it is the democratic duty of all citizens, including judges, fully to assist the deliberations of that body.

Here I have suggested that Bram Fischer's story is exemplary for understanding these issues. It tells us that the authority of law depends ultimately on whether law serves justice. To use Korsgaard's terms, it is not that we should ever expect that the justice of the law will be better than imperfect—perhaps highly imperfect—justice. But when the law is used to pervert justice, used in the service of injustice, one who is truly committed to the ideal of law may justifiably decide to rebel against the law for the sake of the law.

But Fischer's story also tells us that that decision is more complex than Korsgaard supposes. She sees a dilemma there, but not that in order for there to be a dilemma the possibility of seeking justice within the law can never be wholly exhausted. Law has to maintain some link with justice in order to maintain even the barest claim to be law, to be the kind of thing that makes sense of the idea of the rule of law.

Of course, there is no necessity that a ruler will choose to rule through law. He might decide to rule by arbitrary power. But even a cynical ruler who wishes to maintain the facade of the rule of law will find, as long as there are lawyers who understand and are committed to the relationship between law and justice, that the facade cannot be had without the potential of substance. That potential is the redemptive promise of the law; and it was that promise which was the impulse of the Legal Hearing's inquiry into the legal community of apartheid.

It is no surprise that lawyers who had been complicit in apartheid were often reluctant to admit or even discuss the extent to which they failed to redeem law's potential. But the Legal Hearing will have done its task if Fischer's example hangs over the present as a constant reminder—the reminder that accountability to the law is also accountability to principles of justice that together make up the ideal of the rule of law.

POSTCRIPT

Since I wrote this chapter, the Supreme Court of Israel has handed down a unanimous decision which in my view illustrates my argument about the rule of law.[45]

The issue was the legality of the regulations which permitted certain interrogation practices of the General Security Service (GSS). Several applicants, including human rights groups, brought an application to have declared illegal certain interrogation methods of the GSS. Under secret directives, the GSS was allegedly authorised to use physical means to obtain information from detainees when such methods were deemed necessary for saving human lives threatened by acts of terror.[46] These included: "forceful shaking" which, according to expert evidence, was likely to cause brain damage, harm the spinal cord, cause the suspect to lose consciousness, vomit and urinate uncontrollably, and suffer serious headaches;[47] waiting in the "Shabach" position, which involved hooding a suspect and tying his hands so that he is secured to a small chair, which is then tilted forward while he waits for a prolonged period for his turn to be interrogated; the "frog crouch", where the suspect is forced to crouch on the tips of his toes for five minutes at a time; excessive tightening of hand or leg cuffs; and sleep deprivation.[48]

The state argued that that the GSS was generally authorised to interrogate suspects by the general prerogative powers of government, that the authority of each investigator to interrogate is bestowed on him by Israel's Criminal Procedure Act, that the practices did not amount to torture by international law standards, and that the defence of "necessity" made legitimate the "moderate pressure" used by investigators as a last resort to prevent real injury to human life and well-being.[49]

The Court accepted that GSS investigators had the authority to conduct oral interrogations of suspects but that such an interrogation had to be "reasonable", which meant free of torture, cruel or inhuman treatment of the suspect, and free of "any degrading handling whatsoever".[50] And it

---

[45] Judgment of the Supreme Court of Israel, sitting as the High Court of Justice, September 6th 1999, concerning the Legality of the GSS' Interrogation Methods. The reasons were given by Chief Justice Barak. Of the eight judges who concurred in his reasons, one, Justice Kedmi, dissented not on the substance, but on the issue of timing. In his view, the order made by the Court should be suspended from coming into force for a year in order to give the Israeli Parliament an opportunity to consider producing legislation that would deal with the problem before the Court.

[46] The state offered to provide evidence of these means *in camera*, but the applicants' attorneys were opposed. Hence the Court had to rely on the evidence revealed in each particular application, which, as it happens, the state did not seek to deny.

[47] This evidence was contested by the state, which also claimed that the one suspect who had died after having been shaken was a rare exception.

[48] See the judgment at paras 8–13.   [49] See para. 15.   [50] See para. 23.

found that all of the above means of interrogation were by one or other of these criteria unreasonable. Nor, the Court reasoned, could these means be authorised by the defence of necessity. Even if one accepted in principle that a necessity defence might be available in a particular "ticking time bomb" situation, it could not provide an advance legal authorisation to investigators:

"The very fact that a particular act does not constitute a criminal act (due to the 'necessity' defence) does not in itself authorise the administration to carry out this deed, and in doing so infringe upon human rights. The Rule of Law (both as a formal and substantive principle) requires that an infringement on a human right be prescribed by statute, authorising the administration to this effect. The lifting of criminal responsibility does not imply authorisation to infringe upon a human right".[51]

The Court also emphasised that it was not ruling out in principle legislation that might give the appropriate authorisation:

"In other words, general directives governing the use of physical means during interrogations must be rooted in an authorisation prescribed by law and not in defences to criminal liability . . . The power to enact rules and to act according to them requires legislative authorisation, by legislation whose object is the power to conduct interrogations. Within the boundaries of this legislation, the Legislator, if he so desires, may express his views on the social, ethical and political problems connected to authorising the use of physical means in an interrogation. These considerations did not, naturally, arise before the Legislature at the time when the 'necessity' defence was enacted . . . The 'necessity' defence is not an appropriate place for laying out such considerations . . . Endowing GSS investigators with the authority to apply physical force during the interrogation of suspects suspected of involvement in hostile terrorist activities, thereby harming the latters' dignity and liberty, raises basic questions of law and society, of ethics and policy, and of the Rule of Law and security. These questions and the corresponding answers must be determined by the legislative branch. This is required by the principle of the Separation of Powers and the Rule of Law, under our very understanding of democracy".[52]

The Court concluded in a strikingly unique fashion, at least for readers outside of Israel, by making explicit the personal tensions of the judges about their resolution of this case:

"Deciding these applications weighed heavily on this Court. True, from the legal perspective, the road before it is smooth. We are, however, part of Israeli society. Its problems are known to us and we live its history. We are not isolated in an ivory tower. We live the life of this country. We are aware of the harsh reality of terrorism in which we are, at times, immersed. Our apprehension . . . that this decision will hamper the ability to properly deal with terrorists and terrorism disturbs us. We are, however, judges. Our brethren require us to act according to the law. This is equally the standard we set for ourselves.

[51] See para. 36.   [52] See para. 37.

When we sit to judge, we are being judged. Therefore, we must act according to our purest conscience when we decide the law".[53]

In adopting this stance, the Israeli Supreme Court showed how on purely administrative law grounds, that is, without benefit of a written constitution, a court can require of a government that it abide by the constraints of the rule of law. And its stance reflects very poorly on the way in which South African courts, including the highest court, connived at torture during the apartheid era.[54]

Of course, in a legal order where ultimately the legislature is supreme, the legislature may respond, as the Israeli Supreme Court suggested, by legislating an explicit authorisation for torture. It is, however, a matter of some difficulty to decide whether that suggestion is meant as a challenge or an invitation. If the threshold of legal validity set by the Court in its reasons is extremely high, then it is a challenge. And, on my interpretation, it is set high.

The Court seems to assume that a legally authorised interrogation is not a blank cheque for torture, but a statute carefully crafted to recognise the "extraordinary" nature of the situation it seeks to regulate. And it clearly supposed that the criteria for a defence of necessity in criminal law would have to play a fundamental role in the crafting exercise.

In other words, the statute would have to turn the defence of necessity into a prior authorisation. It would have to set out what constituted necessitous circumstances, what methods of interrogation were permissible in such circumstances, and to give prior legal authority to GSS investigators to use such methods. In addition, the legislature would have to decide whether to put the decision as to when such circumstances existed in the discretion of GSS investigators, or in the discretion of an administrative (perhaps quasi-judicial) tribunal, or in the discretion of a judge or panel of judges.

Most important of all, unless the legislature was willing to override explicitly Israel's Basic Law: Human Dignity and Liberty, the legislation would be subject to judicial testing. Judges would ask whether the legislation, which clearly permits violations of fundamental human rights, nevertheless sets out a legitimate objective which can be implemented in a reasonable or proportional fashion. The Court seems to assume that the legislature would not be willing to override the Basic Law, but it also relied in its judgment on the very same analysis which it would adopt were the Basic Law in issue.

Assume, however, that the Court's invitation to the legislature to craft a law was a genuine one—that a statute could provide for the interrogation practices and be consistent with the Basic Law. Or even assume that what

[53] See para. 40.
[54] I deal with this issue in *Judging the Judges, Judging Ourselves*, above n. 1, pp. 62–74.

the Court seemed to think of as a politically impossible option in fact was adopted, that the legislature explicitly overrode the Basic Law.

In these situations, the Court could attempt to claim for itself a substantive review power, arguing that this legislation violated the substance of the rule of law to such an extent that it is *ultra vires* the legislature. But such a claim would look, in my view rightly, like an illegitimate power grab.

There is fortunately another option, one which is consistent with, even required by, the understanding of the ideal of the rule of law to which my arguments lead. The Court could simply point out that the legislature had issued an authorisation to torture, an authorisation which is in violation of the rule of law, and which will signal that it and the society on behalf of whom it acts lack a genuine commitment to the rule of law. And that option would effectively and clearly proclaim the judges' own fidelity to the ideal of the rule of law.

6

"Nothing but the Truth": the South African Alternative to Corrective Justice in Transitions to Democracy

FRANÇOIS DU BOIS

"[I]n the event, this very *certainty* proves itself the most abstract and poorest *truth*."

G W F Hegel, The Phenomenology of Spirit[1]

The spectacle of an apparently successful transition to democracy after more than 300 years of violent conflict, sporadically quelled only by ruthless oppression, has excited much interest in the process whereby South Africa harnessed the past in service of the future through the creation of a Truth and Reconciliation Commission. Is all this interest justified? Does the TRC provide a signpost for the path from liberation to liberty? Or is it merely another of those curios we offer to gullible foreign tourists on our street-markets, cheap wood turned into ebony by the energetic application of shoe polish and distressed to antique perfection with the aid of a screwdriver? This question is important for several reasons. One is that, just as the architects of the South African strategy drew on experiences elsewhere,[2] others have looked expectantly towards South Africa for a precedent on dealing with past injustice in the transition to democracy.[3] Another, equally fundamental, reason is that South Africa

---

[1] Translated by A V Miller (Oxford, Oxford University Press, 1977), p. 58.

[2] In 1994, during and after the run-up to the first democratic elections, two conferences were held in Cape Town on justice in transitions, both involving participants from Latin America, East and Central Europe. They resulted in the publication of two books co-edited by Alex Boraine, who was to become vice-chair of the TRC: A Boraine, J Levy and R Scheffer (eds), *Dealing with the Past: Truth and Reconciliation in South Africa* (Cape Town, IDASA, 1994) and A Boraine, J Levy (eds), *Healing of a Nation?* (Cape Town, Justice in Transition, 1995).

[3] See e.g. A J McAdams (ed), *Transitional Justice and the Rule of Law in New Democracies* (Notre Dame & London, University of Notre Dame Press, 1997), in which several contributors refer to South Africa.

has provided us with a sort of legal theorists' laboratory. Because of the seriousness, rigour and sincerity with which it embarked on this attempt, South Africa's experiment enables us to explore whether there is a "third way"[4] between giving free rein to the rulers of the future—victor's justice—and leaving intact the claims to right made by rulers in the past—impunity. It allows us to ask whether the phrase "transitional justice" signifies not only a problem, but also a solution; a form of justice attuned to the special exigencies of transitions to democracy.

TRUTH AND JUSTICE

"Reconciliation through truth"[5] was the lodestar of the South African vision of transitional justice. This would, in the words of the Constitution that was in force between 1994 and 1996, provide an "historic bridge between the past of a deeply divided society characterised by strife, conflict, untold suffering and injustice, and a future founded on the recognition of human rights, democracy and peaceful co-existence and development opportunities for all South Africans".[6] Truth was to mediate between the demise of the old moral order and the birth of the new, providing the foundations for a new "rainbow nation". It would help to reconcile past adversaries and so reconstruct South African society.

The search for, and official establishment of, the truth of past events was carefully and deliberately selected as an alternative to corrective justice by way of civil and criminal legal liability. Attempts to come to terms with past injustices by means of the latter were seen as compelling a choice between two sets of equally unpalatable alternatives: between victor's justice and impunity; and between individual and collective justice.[7] The

---

[4] Like Kader Asmal in his recent Chorley Lecture published as "Truth, Reconciliation and Justice: The South African Experience in Perspective", in (2000) 63:1 *Modern Law Review* 5. I must remark that after settling on the use of this phrase, popularised in another context by A Giddens, *The Third Way: The Renewal of Social Democracy* (Cambridge, Polity Press, 1999), I noticed that others have also used it to describe the topic discussed in this chapter. In addition to Asmal, see D Tutu, *No Future Without Forgiveness* (London, Rider Books, 1999).

[5] This phrase was selected as its motto by the Truth and Reconciliation Commission, and was prominently displayed on its website as well as on banners whenever it held a meeting or press conference.

[6] Epilogue to the 'Interim Constitution', the Constitution of the Republic of South Africa Act 200 of 1993.

[7] This was articulated clearly by K Asmal "Victims, Survivors and Citizens—Human Rights, Reparations and Reconciliation", in (1992) 8 *S.A. Jnl on Human Rights* 491, and the Minister of Justice, Dullah Omar, in an interview published in (1994) 7 *RSA Review* 1, a government publication. He said, "We do not want Nuremberg type trials to take place . . . We cannot and do not have the right to forgive on behalf of a victim . . . Reconciliation is not simply a question of letting bygones be bygones".

official establishment of the truth was thought to provide an escape from this apparent dilemma: revealing what was done by whom would establish responsibility for past injustices and give recognition to individuals who had been wronged, without simultaneously allowing those who now commanded the resources of the legal system to use it to further their own ends, or tying up scarce resources desperately needed for social development. To overcome this dilemma the focus had to shift from a concern with corrective justice to reconciliation, from a paradigm in which justice determined what was to count as the relevant truth, to one in which justice was to be the product of truth.[8]

Selective amnesty was the keystone of the structure designed to bring this about. In authorising the granting of amnesty, the Promotion of National Unity and Reconciliation Act 34, of 1995 created a mechanism for channelling the task of dealing with the past away from the courts, the central institutions of corrective justice. By tying the granting of amnesty to the condition that full disclosure "of all the relevant facts relating to acts associated with a political objective"[9] be made to the satisfaction of a body charged with "establishing as complete a picture as possible of the causes, nature and extent of the gross violations of human rights which were committed" as well as "establishing and making known the fate or whereabouts of victims and. . .restoring the[ir] . . . human and civil dignity . . ., and . . . recommending reparation measures in respect of them",[10] the Act directed that task to an institution empowered to tell the truth, and no more.

Thus amnesty would avoid victor's justice and the primacy of the individual over the collectivity, while the requirement of "full disclosure" would prevent both impunity and disregard of the individual. Selective amnesty would allow truth to finesse what other transitional societies had found to be an intractable dilemma.

It is easy to see why this should have appeared attractive at the time. South Africa's liberation from apartheid was a triumph of right over power—to have opted for either of the two alternatives might have subverted the very transition that was taking place. Both an unconstrained discretion to prosecute[11] and a blanket amnesty—impunity—would have amounted to a continuation of the primacy of power over right, albeit that each of these alternatives would have placed the power to control the past

---

[8] See the speeches of the Ministers of Justice (Omar) and Water Affairs (Asmal) in the Promotion of National Unity and Reconciliation Bill Second Reading Debate, *Debates of the National Assembly (Hansard)* 17 May 1995.

[9] The Act also set further requirements: see s. 20.

[10] See s. 3(1).

[11] South Africa adheres to the principle of prosecutorial discretion and there is accordingly no duty on the relevant authorities to prosecute. See the Constitution of the Republic of South Africa Act 108 of 1996, s. 9, and the National Prosecuting Authority Act 32 of 1998, Chapter Four.

in different hands. Little wonder then, that the question of the treatment of the past was one which nearly scuppered the negotiations that led to South Africa's democratic transition, with neither the representatives of the past nor those of the future being prepared to accept the other's preferred option, until the amnesty-plus-truth formula yielded a solution that proved acceptable to both.[12] Born of compromise, and precisely for that reason, this formula symbolised the movement from a society notable for the naked exercise of power to one in which the constraints of democracy would hold sway; from separation to a search for common ground. Although it cannot be denied that this compromise was vital in preparing the way for the first democratic elections in 1994, there was more to it than mere expediency. The adoption of this formula was based on the conviction that it was in accordance with, not in derogation of, the pursuit of justice.[13]

In retrospect it is difficult to be quite so convinced of the appeal of South Africa's "third way". True, the TRC ensured that neither the past nor the present holders of political power could freely mould the past to their own ends: both the National Party and the African National Congress rushed to court in 1998 to prevent the publication of its *Report*, and afterwards roundly condemned it.[14] True it is also that the TRC process, sometimes through hearings and investigations linked to amnesty applications, did uncover hitherto hidden facts and establish the identity and whereabouts of victims, that it provided to victims an opportunity to relate their own accounts of the violations of human rights suffered by them, and that it ensured that all this received wide media coverage. Yet, as

[12] See L Berat, "South Africa: Negotiating Change?", in N Roht-Arriaza (ed), *Impunity and Human Rights in International Law and Practice* (New York, Oxford University Press, 1995), for an account of the negotiations that led up to the decision in favour of selective amnesty. The adoption of this formula was finally settled by the post-1994 Government of National Unity, in which all parties were represented.

[13] Asmal, above n. 4, p. 14. This is argued at some length in K Asmal, L Asmal & R Roberts, *Reconciliation Through Truth* (Cape Town, David Philip, 1996) (Kader Asmal is a current government minister and played an early and crucial role in setting up the TRC) and is also stressed in various statements contained in the two books edited by Alex Boraine, above n. 2. See also the speeches during the parliamentary debate above n. 8, Villa-Vicencio C, "Restorative Justice: Dealing with the Past Differently", in C Villa-Vicencio and W Verwoerd (eds), *Looking Back, Reaching Forward: Reflections on the Truth and Reconciliation Commission of South Africa* (Cape Town, UCT Press, 2000) and the judgment of the Constitutional Court in *Azanian Peoples Organisation (AZAPO) and others* v. *President of the Republic of South Africa and others* 1996 (4) SA 671 (CC).

[14] See "FW acts to block report", *Sunday Times* (Johannesburg), 25 October 1998 and "ANC in 11th-hour bid to silence TRC", *Cape Times* (Cape Town) 29 October 1998 regarding the court actions; and "Verbatim", *Mail & Guardian* (Johannesburg) 29 October 1998, "FW has own reconciliation plan", *Saturday Argus* (Cape Town), 31 October 1998, and "Submission of the African National Congress to the Truth and Reconciliation Commission" October 1998 (http//www.anc.org.za/ancdocs/misc/trcreply.html) for the criticisms by these two parties.

I am writing this, the final draft of my contribution to this book, nearly two years after the publication of the TRC *Report*, South African newspapers are being held in thrall by two themes that are difficult to square with a positive assessment of the TRC's legacy: shocking confessions in a criminal trial by apartheid henchmen of poisoning campaigns and other gruesome killings of political opponents,[15] and the fears of whites, treated with evident concern by the government, that the escalating campaign against white farmers in Zimbabwe is a harbinger of South Africa's future. In the background are rumblings of hints of further amnesties (perhaps even a blanket amnesty), debates about whether whites can claim to be South *Africans*, and threats of legal proceedings against the state by some of apartheid's victims.[16]

How could this be? Was the TRC not supposed to ferret out the truth about the past in exchange for amnesty? Why, then, is a criminal trial now such a prominent instrument for uncovering the truth? Why has talk of a further amnesty not died down? And was the choice exercised in favour of accountability-through-truth and against impunity—the latter having been Zimbabwe's choice at independence—not meant to contribute to the forging of a new "rainbow nation" and to satisfy victims' claims? Why, then, do the prejudices that animated South Africa's past still haunt expectations regarding its future? Why does the pain persist and why do apartheid's victims feel betrayed by the democratic state? Did "reconciliation through truth" turn out to be a chimera, leaving important truths uncovered and the historic bridge out of the past still to be constructed?

The obvious answer to questions such as these (and hence the stock reply of defenders of the TRC) is that reconciliation is a long-term process, of which the TRC could only be the beginning, not the end, and that much needs to be done apart from what the TRC itself was able to accomplish.[17] This is indeed a good answer, but only up to a point. Clearly only the most naïve would expect that the TRC process or, indeed, either of its two alternatives, could fully come to terms with the past and fashion solidarity out

---

[15] *S* v. *Wouter Basson*, unreported criminal trial in the High Court, Pretoria. Dr. Basson, a brigadier in the SA Defence Force who headed South Africa's chemical and biological warfare programme has been charged with murder, conspiracy to murder, fraud and drug offences. The Centre for Conflict Resolution at the University of Cape Town has been publishing weekly reports monitoring the progress of the trial since its commencement on 4 October 1999. These can be accessed at http://ccrweb.ccr.uct.ac.za

[16] See below n. 78, and "Court action considered; NGOs to pressure govt on reparations", *Cape Times* (Cape Town) 27 March 2000.

[17] This was repeatedly stressed by the TRC itself. See *Truth and Reconciliation Commission of South Africa Report*, 5 Vols (Cape Town, Truth and Reconciliation Commission, 1998) (cited hereafter as "*Report*"), especially vol. 1, ch. 1 and vol. 5 *passim*. To similar effect was the speech of President Mandela during the parliamentary debate on the TRC "Subject for Discussion: National Response to TRC Report", *Joint Sittings of Both Houses of Parliament (Hansard)* 25 February 1999, cols. 34–5.

of animosity. But there are limits to the extent to which this reply affords an answer to the concerns expressed by questions such as these. The more vehemently the inevitable limitations of the TRC are insisted on, the less compelling becomes the case for accepting "reconciliation through truth" as a viable alternative to corrective justice. After all, this "third way" was conceived of as a means for improving on the ability of the alternatives offered by the corrective justice paradigm to deliver justice in South Africa's transition. Underlying questions such as those raised in the previous paragraph, is the suspicion that the search for truth does *not* provide a way out of the dilemma of having to choose between, and deal with the draw-backs of, impunity—allowing the past to rule the future— and victor's justice—allowing the future to harness the past to its own ends. If the continued elusiveness of both truth and reconciliation is indeed inevitable, then it is surely appropriate to ask whether South Africa's "third way" amounted to anything more profound than an evasion of the responsibility of choosing between the only true alternatives.

The stock reply in fact seems more appropriate to a defence of the manner in which the actual institution itself, the women and men who acted as (and assisted) Truth Commissioners, carried out the tasks entrusted to the TRC. It *is* an appropriate defence, and may even be an effective one, of the work done by the Commissioners to point out the institutional limitations under which they laboured, and to remind their critics of the fallibility of all human institutions. It will not do, however, as a defence of the idea—the principle of opting for the TRC approach, for the very considerations that may exculpate the Commissioners of charges of dereliction of duty, may indicate that this duty should never have been entrusted to anyone.

My assessment of the South African experiment focuses on this last issue. I aim to examine the idea of "reconciliation through truth" that received its institutional expression in the TRC, rather than the TRC as concrete embodiment of this idea. I seek neither to criticise the weaknesses of its operations or conclusions, nor to praise the strengths and virtues of the manner in which the Commissioners acquitted themselves of their tasks. Instead, I seek to explore the general viability of this "third way" in political transitions by using this deliberate institutional crystallisation of the idea to throw light on the idea itself. I thus take seriously, and adopt as my point of departure, the claim by its supporters that the TRC was capable of ensuring justice in South Africa's transition, and therefore truly an institution of transitional justice.

I do so by way of an investigation into the capacity of a search for the truth to produce justice. In doing this, I take justice to refer to a situation in which fundamental social questions, those concerning the assignment of basic rights and duties and the distribution of social benefits and burdens, are not settled by force alone, and thus are not left entirely at the mercy of the balance of power among the élite.[18] In the sections that follow, I first attend to the general relationship between the assertion of the truth about past injustices and the transitional political process. This is followed by two sections in which I consider in turn the lessons to be learnt first from the TRC's own search for the truth, and secondly from the product generated by that search. In uniting these explorations, the final section offers a general conclusion about the viability of this "third way" as a form of transitional justice.

TRUTH AND POLITICS

Gadamer observed that, "understanding is not playing, in the sense that the person understanding holds himself back playfully and withholds a committed attitude to the claim made upon him . . . Someone who understands is already drawn into an event through which meaning asserts itself".[19] To this may be added: nor is the initial decision to engage in understanding "playing", for someone who seeks to understand is already committed to the possibility of meaning. To engage in the search for understanding is therefore to express a commitment to the possibility of meaning. Hence, before the search can begin, that possibility must be established.

The TRC was alive to this and, in the first volume of its *Report*, sought to delineate the "truth" it understood itself as being charged with establishing.[20] The *Report* distinguishes between "four notions of truth: factual or forensic truth; personal or narrative truth; social or 'dialogue' truth and healing and restorative truth".[21] The first is said to constitute the "familiar legal or scientific notion" and to have "featured prominently in the Commission's findings process";[22] the second, to have been "a distinctive and unique feature of the legislation governing the Commission, setting it apart from the mandates of truth commissions elsewhere";[23] and the third to have provided "the closest connection between the Commission's process and its goal".[24] But it is the fourth that appears to have been truly central to the Commission's concerns and to have guided its pursuit of the other three "notions" of truth.

The TRC itself discounted the value of the "forensic notion" of truth,

---

[18] This is a deliberately abstract formulation, intended to be broad enough to encompass any meaningful conception of justice. It can accommodate not only liberal and communitarian theories of justice, but also, I believe, Ruti Teitel's notion of "transitional justice" as existing where "law maintains order, even as it enables transformation", set out in Teitel, "Transitional Jurisprudence: The Role of Law in Political Transformation", (1997) 106 *Yale Law Journal* 2009, 2014.

[19] Gadamer, *Truth and Method* (London, Stead & Ward, 1975), p. 446.

[20] *Report* above n. 17, pp. 110–14.

[21] *Report*, p. 110.   [22] *Report*, p. 111.   [23] *Report*, p. 112.   [24] *Report*,p. 113.

claiming only, after quoting Michael Ignatieff's well-known remarks about the limitations of truth commissions, for this aspect of its work that "disinformation about the past . . . had lost much of its credibility". "Narrative" and "social" truth again, were both explicitly tied to healing and the restoration of human dignity and integrity. In the words of the *Report*, the TRC:

> "was required to help establish a truth that would contribute to the reparation of the damage inflicted in the past and to the prevention of the recurrence of serious abuses in the future. It was not enough simply to determine what had happened. Truth as factual, objective information cannot be divorced from the way in which this information is acquired; nor can such information be separated from the purposes it is required to serve . . . What is critical is that these facts be fully and publicly acknowledged. Acknowledgement is an affirmation that a person's pain is real and worthy of attention. It is thus central to the restoration of the dignity of victims".[25]

Thus the meaning—the truth—which the TRC saw as possible and towards which it directed the processes of understanding under its control, was to be therapeutic in character. "Forensic", "narrative" and "dialogic" drew their value from the role they played in making "acknowledgement" possible.

It is difficult to see how the TRC could have concluded otherwise. As we have seen, its creation was predicated on the idea that establishing the truth was a viable alternative to the choice which would otherwise have to be made between the twin dichotomies of victor's justice/impunity and collective/individual justice. It was meant to be neither a court nor a promoter of impunity. Its task was not to establish guilt, but to establish responsibility. Since it could not judge and punish, it had to diagnose and heal.

Establishing a "healing truth", however, requires a correct diagnosis and that, in turn, presupposes an understanding of the disease. The crucial dependence of the TRC's truth on a prior judgement about the pathology of South Africa's past became evident in the immediate aftermath of the publication of its *Report*. The responses of the major "losers" and "winners" under the democratic transition, the National Party and the African National Congress respectively, were neatly symmetrical. The National Party claimed that the *Report* was "a mess. It has been compromised so many times . . . that it has no credibility left".[26] Its former leader, FW De Klerk, accused the TRC of vengeance, retaliation and victimisation and said it had "failed lamentably to carry out its mandate to establish the truth concerning the conflict of the past and to promote reconciliation."[27] The ANC objected that the TRC "in effect delegitimise[s] the struggle

---

[25] *Report*, p. 114.

[26] "Verbatim", *Mail & Guardian* (Johannesburg) 29 October 1998.

[27] "FW has own reconciliation plan", *Saturday Argus* (Cape Town) 31 October 1998.

against Apartheid [and] . . . wittingly or unwittingly, accords legitimacy to real gross human rights violations committed under apartheid" and "has shown scant regard for the truth it was supposed to establish". In its view, the *Report* failed to reflect "*the truth* that the struggle we waged helped our country to avoid the death of millions of civilians and radically reduced the hostility of the majority of our people towards those who belonged to the 'oppressor nation', as well as their black partners".[28] The TRC is guilty of pursuing the worst form of victor's justice, the National Party seemed to say;[29] the TRC promoted impunity and was in thrall to the past, appears to have been the charge levelled by the ANC.

The importance of this controversy, for those who are interested in the TRC as an experiment in adopting a "third way" in dealing with a repressive past, lies not in whether the TRC diagnosis was correct or not. It resides rather in how this contest over the truth illuminates the viability of the idea embodied in the TRC, since it has been said that "the real value of truth commissions lies in their impact on the social consensus".[30]

Most obviously, it highlights that the truth identified by an institution meant to transcend the division between winners and losers in a democratic transition, jostles for space with their competing interpretations. The TRC's truth existed within, not outside, the arena of political conflict: as in all other situations, "to advance an interpretation is to insert it into a network of power relations".[31] These disagreements consequently draw attention to a further question: does a TRC process contribute something distinctive to the arena of political conflict, does it insert something into the network of power relations that would have been absent but for this official search for a therapeutic truth?

"Acknowledgement" was said to be the mechanism whereby truth heals, and for this reason I explore this question in the following two sections by looking in turn at each of the two dimensions of acknowledgement identified in the TRC *Report*: the process whereby the truth was reached, and the actual outcome or findings of its investigations.

[28] "Submission of the African National Congress to the Truth and Reconciliation Commission" October 1998 (http//www.anc.org.za/ancdocs/misc/trcreply.html). This accusation was repeated by Thabo Mbeki, the current South African President, during the parliamentary debate, above n. 17, at cols. 48–50.

[29] The Inkatha Freedom Party, found by the TRC to have been in league with the apartheid state, took a similar line in the parliamentary debate, above n. 17, with one of its MPs describing the TRC as "clueless" and "futile" and rejecting its findings as "legally obscene and repugnant"—see cols. 68–78.

[30] Asmal, above n. 4, p. 16.

[31] M J Pratt, "Interpretive Strategies/Strategic Interpretations", in J Arac (ed) *Postmodernism and Politics* (University of Minnesota Press, 1986) p.52, quoted in Coombe, "Same As It Ever Was": Rethinking the Politics of Legal Interpretation', (1989) 34 *McGill LJ* 604, 633.

TRUTH AS PROCESS

The TRC was meant to function as a distinctive institution. It was said to have:

> "a specific function beyond the ordinary norms and procedures of crime and punishment. It must not become ensnared in . . . the narrow business of determining individual guilt or innocence. We already have courts that can do that".[32]

Did the pursuit of "truth" as an alternative to punishment create the space for it to do so? Could it function as a distinctive institution by following a distinctive procedure? The TRC believed it did and that it could. It took the view that it was not bound by the same rules of procedure and evidence as the courts, being convinced that, "if the full array of legal technicalities and nuances had been introduced into its work and decision-making function" the fulfilment of its task would have been jeopardised.[33]

This issue was raised directly by two separate legal challenges to the work of the TRC's Human Rights Violations Committee.[34] Both were brought by members of the police, and arose from notifications they had received from the TRC that unnamed witnesses would testify at forthcoming hearings that they had been involved in, or had knowledge of, human rights violations. They objected to the notices on the basis that they were "vague in the extreme" and sought court orders prohibiting the hearing of evidence before they had been provided with "such relevant facts and information as might be reasonably necessary" to enable them to exercise and protect their rights. The TRC's response was that it was entitled to hold the hearings without prior notice or the prior furnishing of witness statements.

The judges before whom these two applications were brought, came to opposite conclusions. King J issued the order applied for, ruling that the Commission had to give the applicants proper, reasonable and timeous notice of its intention to hear evidence which might detrimentally implicate or prejudicially affect them, and of the time and place of the proposed hearings. He also ruled that the Commission had to furnish the applicants with the facts and information reasonably needed to identify the events, incidents and persons concerning which it was proposed to present the evidence.[35] To this, Buchannan J, who heard the second application, responded as follows:

---

[32] Asmal *et al*, above n.13, p. 26.

[33] *Report*, above n. 17, vol. 5, p. 212.

[34] These events are recounted in the *Report*, vol. 1, ch. 7.

[35] *Du Preez and another* v. *Truth and Reconciliation Commission* (Unreported decision of the Cape Provincial Division of the Supreme Court, 30 April 1996), appeal upheld by a Full Bench in *Truth and Reconciliation Commission* v. *Du Preez and another* 1996 (3) SA 997 (C).

"The Act envisages rather a procedure which is unique and which, in the national interest, is designed to investigate and establish as complete a picture as possible of the nature, causes and extent of gross violations of human rights . . . There exists no *lis*, in the true sense of the word, between the witnesses and the persons who may be implicated by them during the course of any hearing . . . It seems to me undesirable, except to the extent absolutely necessary, that procedural obstacles should be placed before witnesses who wish to make full disclosure of all relevant facts before the Committee on Human Rights Violations. That this may result, in some cases, in prejudice to persons who may be implicated may be unfortunate. Such prejudice, however, should, in my view, nevertheless be weighed against the laudable and important objectives which the Act seeks to achieve".[36]

The contrast between these two approaches identifies crisply the issue raised by the two applications: should the TRC, in view of having an objective which sets it apart from administrative, judicial and quasi-judicial institutions, be recognised as a unique institution entitled to follow a unique procedure which need not fully comply with, for example, the *audi alteram partem* rule? Should its pursuit of truth as a means towards reconciliation be seen as distinct from enquiries which may prejudice an individual and therefore automatically attract the application of this rule and other familiar principles of legal procedure?

The final answer was given by the Appellate Division of the Supreme Court (now the Supreme Court of Appeal.) Agreeing with King J, this Court held that the TRC was "under a duty to act fairly towards persons implicated to their detriment by evidence or information coming before the Committee in the course of its investigations and/or hearings . . . [and] might well be under a duty to hear the rebutting evidence forthwith or to permit immediate cross-examination". Corbett CJ reasoned that:

"the subject-matter of inquiries conducted by the Committee is 'gross violations of human rights'. Many of such violations would have constituted criminal conduct of a serious nature, or at any rate very reprehensible conduct. The Committee is charged with the duty of establishing, *inter alia*, whether such violations took place and the identity of persons involved therein. The Committee's findings in this regard and its report to the Commission may accuse or condemn persons in the position of appellants. Subject to the grant of amnesty, the ultimate result may be criminal or civil proceedings against such persons. Clearly the whole process is potentially prejudicial to them and their rights of personality".[37]

Truth is not without consequences. At least, it cannot be if truth is pursued as an alternative to impunity, for then the relevant truth is one that is *meant* to have consequences. This, after all, is why the Promotion of National Unity and Reconciliation Act provided for the identification of

---

[36] *Nieuwoudt* v. *Truth and Reconciliation Commission* 1997 (2) SA 70 (SE) at 75A–E.

[37] *Du Preez and another* v. *Truth and Reconciliation Commission* 1997 (3) SA 204 (A) at 233C–E.

individual perpetrators, and the TRC concluded that it had to do more than establishing "forensic truth". The outcome of this decision appears to fit neatly with the objective of creating the TRC: "reconciliation"—turning one's back on "victor's justice" but also refusing to succumb to "past oppressor's justice"—implied impartiality and attention to both sides of the story, whilst "reconstruction"—providing a new moral point of departure for society—required that brute facts be clothed with meaning. The TRC, it seems, was meant to have an impact and to be impartial. Thus the very task entrusted to the TRC appears to have imposed certain constraints on its operation, preventing it from operating as an entirely distinctive institution applying a unique procedure.

Yet the TRC's own view of the matter cannot lightly be dismissed as mistaken. The application of established legal principles did affect the work of the TRC. The TRC reported that, after complying with the Appellate Division's ruling, it came to be seen as too "perpetrator-friendly", the environment of the hearings risked causing further trauma to many victims who had finally found the courage to testify, and an unspecified large number of people identified as perpetrators (including, most spectacularly, the last apartheid president, FW de Klerk)[38] could not be mentioned in the *Report*.[39] If the pursuit of the truth were to heal through the acknowledgement provided to victims by officially recounting what happened to them, and by providing a forum in which they could experience the catharsis of voicing their suffering, then a procedure which hampered the TRC in these ways was indeed difficult to square with the TRC's task. To require of the TRC, in the words of counsel who appeared on its behalf before the Appellate Division, to "have approached the matter as if it entailed a judicial proceeding based on the adversarial format",[40] does seem strange in the light of the creation of this body as an alternative to leaving the exploration of the past in the hands of the courts.[41]

---

[38] He succeeded in having the Commission's only, and very modest, finding implicating him personally blacked out after the *Report* had already been sent to the printers—see "TRC forced to cut its finding on FW", *Cape Argus* (Cape Town) 28 October 1998, which also reports that some names had been omitted because the notices had not been served, others because of representations made after notification and yet others because the alleged perpetrator had been incorrectly identified.

[39] *Report*, above n. 17, vol. 1, pp. 185–6 and vol. 5, pp. 205–6.

[40] *Du Preez and another* v. *Truth and Reconciliation Commission* 1997 (3) SA 204 (A) at 218 . This comment was made in respect of the decision of the court of first instance.

[41] It should therefore come as no surprise that the TRC in its actual operations, according to a critique as controversial as it is fierce, "in practice exempted itself" from "established legal principles"—see the "Foreword" of John Kane-Berman in A Jeffery, *The Truth about the Truth Commission* (Johannesburg, South African Institute of Race Relations, 1999), p. 2. Jeffery accuses the TRC of having failed to verify the evidence before it, to ensure that it took all relevant information into account, to give reasons for its findings and of having shielded important parts of the evidence on which it relied from public scrutiny: see especially ch. IX.

There is, of course, a contradiction between the preceding two paragraphs. That, however, is precisely the point: the duty entrusted to the TRC was impossible to fulfil. The task of pursuing reconciliation through truth pulled the Commission's operations in two, opposed, directions. Reconciliation signifies the bringing together of adversaries, the creation of some commonality, the transcending of at least some differences. It also requires equality between the adversaries, since it would otherwise amount to no more than a coerced acceptance of the past. Hence the truth required for reconciliation is one that restores to victims the dignity needed to face perpetrators as equals, and accordingly, as the TRC realised, acknowledges victims as *victims*. This, however, implies that the distinction between victims and perpetrators should be kept alive, emphasised even. Thus arose a tension between process (the search for truth) and outcome (reconciliation): the truth necessary for reconciliation also threatened its achievement. This paradox to which the TRC was subjected flowed directly from its quest for "reconciliation through truth".

There was nothing new or unique about the idea that simply establishing the truth about past injustices is not enough in itself, but must have a restorative, or healing, aim. This, after all, underlies well-known classical theories about the corrective, or retributive, justice role of courts. Nor was it a dramatic revelation that the pursuit of this objective does not involve a search for "ultimate verities". Judges have recognised this in respect of their own procedures too.[42] The notion that official searches for the truth can, and should, provide an opportunity for catharsis was also hardly alien to understandings of court proceedings. What *was* different about the idea embodied in the TRC, and distinguished this body from a court, was the specific notion of healing or restoration to which it gave expression— reconciliation instead of the correction of injustice. And it is this difference that gave rise to the tension between process and outcome that marked the work of the TRC.

Reconciliation, in contrast with corrective justice, has an inescapable subjective mental element. It is perfectly coherent to maintain in the face of vehement denials by a victim of past injustice that justice has now finally been done. However, one can only meaningfully say that reconciliation has been achieved if erstwhile adversaries indeed believe that at least some differences between them have been transcended. The tension between process and outcome observable in the controversy regarding the TRC's operation is a product of this contrast between reconciliation and corrective justice. The mental constituent of reconciliation means that process

---

[42] "A court of law . . . is not engaged in ascertaining ultimate verities: it is engaged in determining what is the proper result to be arrived at": Viscount Simon in *Hickman* v. *Peacey* [1945] AC 304 at 318; "Now the first and most striking feature of the common law is that it puts justice before truth."—Viscount Kilmuir, "Introduction" (1960) 76 *Law Quarterly Review* 41, 42–3.

and outcome cannot be separated from one another and assigned to different dimensions as they are in the case of the distinction between procedural justice and substantive justice. Substantive (corrective) justice may be achieved despite procedural injustice, and procedures may be just even though their outcomes are not, but the sense of reconciliation, the actual belief that divisions have been transcended, is always at the mercy of how someone experiences the reconciliation process.

How victims are treated during the process, particularly whether the authenticity of their identity as victims is acknowledged, is therefore uniquely decisive to reconciliation. This militates against the treatment of victims and perpetrators as mere adversaries. On the other hand, the achievement of reconciliation also depends on the participation and beliefs of perpetrators, and this counsels against a process that might alienate them by evoking doubts on their part about its even-handedness.[43] The result is that whereas healing in the form of corrective justice can combine the elision of difference in the procedures (*audi alteram partem*) with the assertion of difference in the outcome (the guilty must be found and made to pay), healing as reconciliation is hostage to a conflict between process and outcome, between stressing difference and commonality. The latter detracts from the distinction between victim and perpetrator, while the former risks maintaining the schism reconciliation is meant to bridge.

In the circumstances of transitional justice, where the coincidence between the victim/perpetrator and ruled/ruler dichotomies is no longer stable, this tension reproduces the main contours of political conflict. Because the importance of "acknowledgement" lies in its according to victims the dignity denied to them whilst the perpetrators held sway, thus reversing the effects of the past, and the promotion of even a limited common ground among former adversaries avoids a straight exchange of roles between past victim/ruled and past perpetrator/ruler, thereby inhibiting this reversal, this tension coincides with transitional political struggles between those who aim to transform society and those who seek to impose constraints thereon. And so the search for "reconciliation through truth" is ineluctably drawn into and made part of contemporary politics, and, as acknowledgement and commonality each renders succour to one of the opposing sides in the transitional political contest between the rulers of the future and of the past, the institution entrusted with this mission is forced to exercise a choice within the political arena.

The conflict between the TRC and the courts also brought to the fore that "reconciliation through truth" does not create a space to escape to

[43] The impact of such doubts, whether justified or not, is there for all to see in the *Report*: vol. 3, pp. 162–3, for example, discusses the striking disparity between the number of victim statements made respectively by UDF/ANC supporters, and Inkatha (IFP) and former "security force" members, saying about the latter groups: "These victims and their families did not come forward to tell their stories".

from what Asmal called "the narrow business of determining guilt or innocence". The TRC's objection against *audi alteram partem* as understood by the courts stemmed from its fear that full compliance with this maxim would undermine reconciliation through its public truth-telling processes by inhibiting participation and adding secondary victimisation. That is, it was convinced that reconciliation required that victims be treated as victims and perpetrators as perpetrators, and not as mere adversaries. But designation as "perpetrator" and "victim" is, of course, merely another way of expressing a determination of guilt or innocence. Seen in this light, the struggle of the TRC to operate as a distinctive institution involved the Commission in some of the hottest debates of South Africa's transitional politics, for the question whether the identities of victims and perpetrators have already been settled, has remained a point of contention, not least between the ANC and the Inkatha Freedom Party in respect of the conflict in Natal.[44]

In settling on the procedures it wished to follow in investigating the past, South Africa's TRC opted for the acknowledgement of difference and therefore also for its prerequisite, the identification of victims and perpetrators, as a *starting point* for its operations. In doing so it inevitably echoed the position of one side in South Africa's transitional political debates.[45] It is therefore not surprising that the TRC has been accused of systematic bias.[46] Such accusations must, however, be placed in perspective by taking account of the dilemma in which the TRC was placed by the task of pursuing "reconciliation through truth". To have chosen the other available option, a failure to differentiate among adversaries, would have been no less biased and is likely to have elicited a symmetrical response from the opposite political corner. What is evident, then, is that the TRC could not insert anything distinctive into the network of power relations, but merely provided a further forum in which the politics of South Africa's transition were enacted according to a well-worn script, albeit by a broader cast of characters.

---

[44] Thus an IFP MP stated during the parliamentary debate, above n. 17, cols. 69–70, that, "The TRC Report has failed to understand, expose and reconcile the most significant aspects of the armed struggle which, . . . was mainly waged against black communities. The armed struggle was used as a tool of political action to achieve political hegemony within the liberation movement which was divided into competing and equally deserving segments". The leader of Inkatha, Mangosutu Buthelezi, insisted that he played an important role in the liberation struggle and that "the armed struggle. . . necklaced black people to subjugate entire communities in fear, and destroyed the black education system causing an entire generation to be lost": *Business Day* (Johannesburg), 27 March 2000.

[45] Of course neither fully, nor always the same side, as is shown by the fact that the *Report* was criticised from all sides. This does not, however, detract from the point made in the text.

[46] This is the general theme of Jeffery, above n. 41.

TRUTH AS PRODUCT

How different was the product of "reconciliation through truth" from that which corrective justice through adjudication might have produced? The structure of the *Report* in which the TRC presented its findings does not suggest that its brand of healing truth was fundamentally different from the healing truth that a court might have delivered. In the first volume of its *Report*, the TRC derives norms for decision-making from its founding statute and interpreted these. In subsequent volumes it relates events and their context, and then characterises these events in terms of those norms in order to make findings in the final volume about responsibility for gross violations of human rights and entitlement to reparations. This does not differ materially from what a court would have done in the pursuit of corrective justice, except, of course, for the fact that a court could have *ordered* the implementation of its findings.

The TRC itself saw things differently, remarking that "[j]udicial enquiries into politically-sensitive matters rarely satisfy the need for truth and closure", and contrasting its own *modus operandi* with that of the judicial system.[47] However, while it is true that courts might have come to different conclusions, as one court did in respect of former Defence Minister Magnus Malan,[48] and another did about police participation in the Boipatong massacre,[49] it is a mistake to think that actual and potential discrepancies between judicial verdicts and the TRC's findings show that it was capable of establishing truths not accessible to courts. Not only did the TRC's own investigations, by its own admission, suffer under the same constraints of lack of money and skilled personnel that its *Report* lays at the door of the judicial system,[50] but such divergences from the outcomes of judicial proceedings might well have been absent if different judges had

[47] *Report*, above n. 17, vol. 1, pp. 122–3.

[48] In *S v. Msane and 19 others* (unreported, October 1996, Durban and Coast Local Division of the Supreme Court of SA) General Malan was found not guilty in a criminal trial concerning his alleged involvement in Operation Marion, which involved the training of hit squads. The TRC *Report* declares him guilty of gross human rights violations in consequence of this operation: vol. 5, p. 235.

[49] *S v. Zulu and others* (unreported, 30 March 1994, Transvaal Provincial Division of the Supreme Court of SA). The TRC, unlike the court, found the police co-responsible for the massacre, and concluded on this basis that the Commissioner of Police and Minister of Law and Order were responsible for the gross violations of human rights: *Report*, vol. 3, pp. 686–7.

[50] "National economic challenges and priorities meant that the Commission operated under strained financial conditions virtually all the time.": *Report*, vol. 1, p. 300 and see vol. 5, p. 205. For descriptions of the impact of limited resources and the need to prioritise them on the gathering and processing of information, see especially *Report*, vol. 1, pp. 141 n.2, 155–7, 173 and 329–30. The description of the resource-constraints affecting the judicial system are to be found at *Report*, vol. 1, pp. 122–3.

presided over these trials, or if different people had been appointed to the TRC. Judges also disagree about factual findings and display varying degrees of rigour, and, as the reservations expressed about the *Report* in Commissioner Malan's minority report make clear, the TRC's approach was a matter of choice, not compulsion.[51] Moreover, law reports everywhere contain judgments of which it could be said, as the TRC said of its own decisions, that they "endeavoured to reach positive findings whenever the circumstances allowed this, even where the available information was extremely scanty"[52] and that "some remain value-laden and can be defended only as judgements by people of integrity".[53]

More importantly, the TRC's truth was as conditioned by the network of power relationships that existed during the transition as criminal trials would have been. To begin with, the primary source of information on which the TRC's findings were based, appears to have been statements by people identifying themselves (and, at times, others as well) as victims of human rights violations.[54] To the extent that the makers of these statements were self-selected,[55] the information yielded by this source was liable to be shaped by attitudes to the state, and the TRC itself, as well as factors such as fear of reprisals, literacy, access to the media, and the urban-rural divide, all of which play a not insignificant role in moulding the interaction between the courts and society in South Africa. The importance hereof to the truth told by the TRC is intimated in the *Report* itself, in a section that deals with the regional conflict which involved the largest number of recorded gross human rights violations nationwide and generated nearly 50 per cent of all victim statements.[56] After stating that the "antagonism of the provincial majority IFP [Inkatha Freedom Party] to the work of the Commission inhibited many IFP supporters from coming forward to tell their stories" about this conflict, the TRC observes that the "Commission received many more accounts of the political violence from UDF/ANC supporters, creating the impression that the violations suffered by the UDF/ANC outnumbered those suffered by Inkatha by five to one".[57]

---

[51] The scathing critique in Jeffery, above n. 41, of the TRC's approach to the admissibility, testing and assessment of evidence does not detract from this.

[52] *Report*, vol. 5, p. 10.   [53] *Report*, vol. 1, p. 253.

[54] "Statement taking . . . was the primary information-gathering activity of the Commission": *Report*, vol. 1, p. 439; "[T]he primary data of the Commission (including the hand-written statements) were given priority attention by researchers in the drafting of the report.": *Report*, vol. 1, p. 377. The impact of these statements was enhanced by the fact that at most 10 per cent of deponents testified at a public hearing, very few of these were subjected to cross-examination, and corroboration was haphazard and limited. See on this, Jeffery, above n. 41, pp. 27–41.

[55] The Commission indicates that this was the principal method through which statements were obtained: see *Report*, vol. 1, p. 165.

[56] *Report*, vol. 3, p. 157.

[57] *Report*, vol. 3, pp. 162–3. This assessment of the accuracy of this source of information did not restrain the TRC from finding that "the most devastating indictment of the role of

The TRC indeed recognised the role of such factors in shaping the information provided by such statements, [58] and accordingly also sought out victims through a more pro-active strategy of sending out statement-takers to canvass victim statements.[59] This, inevitably, involved an important element of "pre-selection" of deponents, no less vulnerable to being influenced by configurations of power. The TRC's Research Department had to "familiarise statement-takers with political events and with the people involved in these events", and did so on the basis of assistance from (unnamed) organisations and individuals invited to workshops, research into newspaper reports and information supplied by (again unnamed) community-based organisations.[60] Clearly, the identification in this way of whom to seek out for interviews would have been affected by factors influencing enthusiasm about the TRC, ability to participate, and those shaping news and research agendas.[61] Moreover, much of this canvassing of deponents appears to have been carried out by community-based organisations on behalf of the Commission and this, in turn, brought the effects of local "differences between rival groups" to bear on the *Report*.[62]

It is even harder to maintain, as the TRC Report does, that "trials would probably have contributed far less than did the amnesty process towards revealing the truth about what had happened to many victims and their loved ones".[63] Where the amnesty process managed to uncover facts that had not already become a matter of public record as result of press investigations,[64] judicial inquiries[65] and NGO activities[66], this was

the IFP in political violence during the Commission's mandate period is to be found in the statistics compiled by the Commission directly from submissions by victims of gross human rights violations. These established the IFP as the foremost perpetrator of gross human rights violations in KwaZulu and Natal during the 1990-94 period". Indeed, IFP violations constituted "over one-third of the total number of gross human rights violations committed during the thirty-four year period of the Commission's mandate.": *Report*, vol. 5, p. 232.

[58] *Report*, vol. 1, p. 163.

[59] *Report*, vol. 1, p. 397 (Cape Town Office); p. 427 (East London Office); p. 447 (Johannesburg Office).

[60] *Report*, vol. 1, pp. 396–7.

[61] This is emphasised by Jeffery, cited above n. 41, pp. 41–3.

[62] *Report*, vol. 1, p. 141, where it is also stated that this participation by external bodies increased the number of statements taken by the Commission by almost 50 per cent.

[63] *Report*, vol. 1, p. 121.

[64] As early as 17 November 1989, the *Vrye Weekblad*, an Afrikaans newspaper, carried an interview in which the police officer Dirk Coetzee stated: "I was the commander of the South African Police's Death Squad".

[65] The Harms Commission of Enquiry, appointed in 1990, while largely unsuccessful, did confirm the existence of the Civil Co-operation Bureau, a covert military body. More successful was the Goldstone Commission of Enquiry, which reported in 1993 that there was every justification for the perception that the South African Police were working with Inkatha-aligned groups.

[66] The work of the Human Rights Commission was particularly significant. The information collected by this body was provided to the TRC, which made extensive use thereof.

due to the continued existence in the background of the ordinary criminal justice system. By far the majority of amnesty applications were submitted by prisoners.[67] The *Report* attributes the large number of security police members who came forward to apply for amnesty, to disclosures made in an amnesty application by Eugene De Kock (one of the most infamous of the apartheid henchmen) launched *after* the start of his criminal trial.[68] Thus the truth revealed through the TRC's distinctive process—the provision of amnesty—depended largely on the credibility of the threat of prosecution. Truly obscure events and those which proved intractable to the criminal process were not the subject of amnesty applications,[69] and where *esprit de corps* or organisational distance between decisions and their implementation could be counted on, no amnesty applications were made: according to the *Report*, not a single application was received from members of the National Intelligence Service,[70] and neither former Presidents Botha and De Klerk, nor former Defence Minister General Magnus Malan applied for amnesty. As far as those who emerged victorious in the transition are concerned, the complaint in the *Report* that the TRC was denied "the kind of rich and specific detail . . . that it gleaned, for example, from Security Branch operatives" because "not all MK [the ANC's armed wing] operatives applied for individual amnesty"[71] suggests that estimations regarding the likelihood of being prosecuted by one's "own side" might, perhaps, also have influenced the truth harvested by the amnesty process. Amnesty applications at any rate played only a modest role in the truth told in the *Report*, as it was published at a time when the great majority still remained to be heard.[72]

There is nevertheless one respect in which the TRC's truth *does* appear to differ from a court's truth. The TRC was able to venture beyond the boundaries of victim-perpetrator relationships into the realm of social structures where courts rarely go. Its conclusions were not limited to naming victims and perpetrators and recommending prosecutions and reparations. It also concerned itself with matters such as the closing of the poverty gap, creation of job opportunities, affirmative action, the elimination of corruption, encouragement of the non-governmental sector, and the holding of regular and fair elections.[73] In exercising its mandate, the TRC, it therefore appears, could speak a "broader" truth than the courts would

---

It has also been published as M Coleman (ed), *A Crime Against Humanity. Analysing the Repression of the Apartheid State* (Cape Town, David Philip, 1998).

[67] *Report*, vol. 5, p. 112.

[68] *Report*, vol. 5, p. 202. His trial having concluded before the verdict of the Amnesty Committee, he was sentenced to 121 years in jail.

[69] Perhaps the most important gaps relate to the political violence in KwaZulu-Natal.

[70] *Report*, vol. 5, pp. 202–3.   [71] *Report*, vol. 5, pp. 202–3.

[72] See Jeffery, above n. 41, p. 76.   [73] *Report*, vol. 5, ch. 8.

have been able to, one which not only identified the requirements of corrective justice, but also pointed out the measures of social justice needed for
reconciliation.[74]

This appearance is misleading, however, for if there is one feature that
characterises these recommendations, then it is their banality. They are in
truth no more than broad statements of what has become political ortho-
doxy after 1994. Virtually every recommendation in the *Report* merely
restates commitments already contained in the Constitution and post-1994
legislation. It was hardly a revelation to South Africans generally, or to the
post-apartheid government specifically, to read that prison officers had to
receive adequate training, that children needed adequate housing and education, that the judiciary should be more representative of the population, that
the independence of the central bank had to be protected and that environmental protection ought to be a key ingredient of economic growth strategies. Besides, these were but recommendations, their implementation being
dependent on their acceptance by government. Consequently, although the
TRC seems to have ranged wider than a court might have felt able to, this
did not make its truth any more significant or powerful than that which a
court could have spoken.[75] What is more, far from settling the clash between
individual and social justice that was thought to be characteristic of the
corrective justice approach, the truth spoken by the TRC has prolonged and
emphasised this conflict. Nearly two years after the publication of the TRC
Report, the recommended individual reparation grants remain unpaid, and
government ministers downplay their significance and cast doubt on their
feasibility.[76] In this respect, too, the TRC's truth failed to insert anything
distinctive into the network of power relations: the treatment of the past and
the way of the future both remained to be decided within constraints and
upon priorities stemming in large measure from the balance of power
among South Africa's political and economic élite. The latter will determine
what is to be done to escape from the past, as surely as it would have done
had the TRC remained no more than a twinkle in its champions' eyes.

Is this merely a contingent feature of the South African Act or was this
unavoidable, a structural inevitability flowing from the idea on which the
TRC was founded? In my view it was the latter. Reconciliation, being
directed towards the establishment of the community of the future, a
"rainbow nation", rather than the mere correction of the past, demands

[74] This is emphasised by the *Report*, vol. 1, pp. 121–2, 129.

[75] The black-letter lawyer in me asks: how do these recommendations differ from the
occasional *obiter dictum* urging law reform?

[76] See especially the speech of the Minister of Justice in the parliamentary debate of 25
February 1999, above n. 17 ("we will also bear in mind that our gallant sons and daughters
did not participate in the struggle . . . for monetary compensation . . . reparation measures
must help to proclaim before history the nobility of the struggle for freedom in our country
and that the privilege of participating in that struggle is its own reward"); and the Chorley
Lecture by the current Minister of Education, Kader Asmal, above n. 4.

the making of myriad choices, eloquently captured by South Africa's current Chief Justice in the following sentences from his judgment in the Constitutional Court decision sanctioning the TRC's amnesty process:[77]

> "Generations of children born and yet to be born will suffer the consequences of poverty, of malnutrition, of homelessness, of illiteracy and disempowerment generated and sustained by the institutions of apartheid and its manifest effects on life and living for so many. The country has neither the resources nor the skills to reverse fully these massive wrongs ... The resources of the state have to be deployed imaginatively, wisely, efficiently and equitably, to facilitate the reconstruction process in a manner which best brings relief and hope to the widest sections of the community, developing for the benefit of the entire nation the latent human potential and resources of every person who has directly or indirectly been burdened with the heritage of the shame and the pain of our racist past".

This can only be achieved by a complex, polycentric, and enduring process of raising and distributing resources. That is underscored by the broad sweep of the TRC recommendations that were referred to above, and by the fact that they amount to little more than a restatement of the general political, social and economic policy already being pursued by the South African government. Truly to entrust reconciliation to an unelected body such as the TRC would amount to handing over the reins of government, thereby defeating the very process of democratisation it is supposed to accompany. The consequences of opting for corrective justice, on the other hand, are different and less dramatic, even though the rigorous provision of compensation would clearly constrain the scope of action of a democratically elected government. Determining guilt and liability may be difficult, but it does not require of the relevant unelected body (the court, in this case) to engage in the kind of forward-looking policy-making necessitated by the pursuit of "the benefit of the entire nation", and leaves this instead to the nation's elected representatives. Hence the specific task the TRC was meant to accomplish condemned it to failure in this respect as well. Nothing shows this more clearly than the continuing debate about further amnesties despite the TRC's implacable opposition thereto,[78] and the government's reluctance to give effect to the reparations recommended by the TRC.[79] National reconciliation is the stuff of government, not of appointed commissions.

---

[77] *Azanian Peoples Organisation (AZAPO) and others* v. *President of the Republic of South Africa and others* 1996 (4) SA 671 (CC).

[78] See e.g. "Amnesty battle looms: Anger as Mbeki urges deal for parties and security forces", *Cape Argus* (Cape Town) 26 May 1999; and "TRC left unfinished business", *Sunday Independent* (Johannesburg) 25 July 1999, in which the chair of the Human Rights Commission urged that "those who escaped the net of the commission must receive forgiveness by the nation".

[79] See the text below at nn. 89 and 90.

CONCLUSION

The TRC process was the outcome of careful reflection on the challenge of ensuring justice in South Africa's transition. It was justified by its proponents as opening up a "third way" between punishment and impunity for "the age-old quest for a better life for all".[80] Hence it was not an alternative mechanism for achieving corrective justice, but was instead meant to allow South Africa to break free from the seemingly intractable choice, imposed by an emphasis on corrective justice, between these two alternatives. It had to implement transitional justice by pursuing "reconciliation through truth".

The TRC's own assessment of its success in establishing the truth and promoting reconciliation was modest. "We will never know exactly how many people suffered during the mandate period",[81] "the Commission's capacity to provide the 'full and complete' picture that the Act demands" was "severely constrained" by the lack of co-operation from key individuals and organisations on *all* sides as well as the TRC's own failings and limitations,[82] and the account given of the causes, motives and perspectives of perpetrators provides only "partial understandings [that] may be better than none",[83] is how the TRC summed up the results of its enquiries. The *Report* likewise claims no more in its chapter on "Reconciliation" than that "it underlines the vital importance of the multi-layered healing of human relationships in post-Apartheid South Africa" and admits frankly that "[c]learly, everyone who came before the Commission did not experience healing and reconciliation".[84]

This chapter has emphasised that the TRC indeed had much to be modest about. If "transitional justice" is anything more than an excuse for allowing power to trump right by giving *carte blanche* to the balance of political forces among the élite during a transitional period, then it must involve some constraint on political actors beyond that which derives from their own objectives, one which forces them to moderate their actions in the interest of those who have little or no say in the restructuring of society. Legal responses to a past marked by exploitation and oppression must "attempt to supervene and transcend prevailing politics" if they are to "help to construct the transition".[85] Otherwise, those who suffered most in the past, and are thus least well-equipped with the resources essential for effective political participation in the present, face the prospect of a future all too painfully familiar to them. South Africans have the dubious advantage of seeing proof of this not far beyond their own borders. Looked at in this light, the "historic bridge" built by the establishment of the TRC may

---

[80] Asmal, above n. 4, p. 2.   [81] *Report*, above n. 17, vol. 1, p. 173.
[82] *Report*, vol. 5, pp. 196–208.   [83] *Report*, vol. 5, p. 260.   [84] *Report*, vol. 5, p. 350.
[85] The quotations are from Teitel, above n. 18, p. 2079.

turn out to have been one by which the past was ensured continued access to the future, for while this "third way" was certainly constituted by South Africa's transition towards democracy, it cannot, I have argued, be regarded as constitutive thereof.[86]

This failure of "reconciliation through truth", I have tried to show, was not simply the result of contingent features of the South African Act or the human frailties of the individuals appointed as Commissioners, but was due to the idea embodied in the TRC. In fulfilling its mandate of telling the truth about past gross human rights violations, the TRC could not but become a participant in debates among those who sought to enhance, or protect, the political capital that is to be made by politicians of all persuasions during a transitional period out of tarring an opponent with the brush of human rights violations. Although the criticism of the *Report* from different sides in the apartheid struggle might tempt one to the satisfying conclusion that the TRC was impartial, it is vital to note that the common ground established by the symmetry of these reactions lies in a shared rejection of the TRC's truth.

That conclusion to the search for "reconciliation through truth" should not have come as a surprise. Already when it settled on a process through which to pursue "healing truth", the TRC was drawn into the politics of the transition by being faced with a choice between giving priority to the needs of victims or to those of perpetrators. That it was precluded by the courts from giving (full) effect to its choice, should not blind one to the impact this had on its ability to tell the truth and reconcile past adversaries: *not a single one* of the organisations singled out in the *Report* as responsible for human rights violations proved an enthusiastic participant in the TRC's enquiries and investigations.[87] Finally, the primary means whereby the TRC gathered the truth told in its *Report*, victim statements and amnesty applications, were subject to most of the institutional limitations and socio-political factors that would have moulded the search for truth through criminal and civil trials, and yielded a truth which ultimately failed to make a contribution to reconciliation that would not have been possible through judicial proceedings directed at corrective justice.

One is led to ask: how could it have been otherwise when the TRC was expected to "transcend the divisions of the past" and yet was spawned by a process which established—for the first time in South Africa's history— that those decisions of resource distribution that are essential for eradicating these divisions were to be made by the democratically elected representatives of the people? Nonetheless, Truth Commissioners, especially the chairperson Archbishop Desmond Tutu, have reacted with some vehemence at the treatment their *Report* has received at the hands of

---

[86] The allusion here is again to Teitel's article, above n. 18, where transitional justice is said on p. 2014 to be "alternately constituted by, and constitutive of, the transition".

[87] See above n. 82.

South Africa's first democratically elected governing party, the African National Congress. When the ANC criticised the *Report*, Tutu warned that "there is no way you can assume yesterday's oppressed won't become tomorrow's oppressor".[88] More recently, he accused government of failing the victims of apartheid,[89] and Ms Hlengiwe Mkhize, who chaired the TRC Reparation and Rehabilitation Committee, complained of the silence on the part of government regarding the Commission's proposals on reparations, and expressed the fear that "victims are being re-victimised again".[90] These reactions suggest a desire to have the TRC's findings and recommendations treated as if they were the verdict and order of a court, authoritative, final and merely to be executed. Perhaps, therefore, they can be read as hinting at a dawning realisation that there is no "third way" and that, however narrow in scope the concerns of trials may be, corrective justice is an indispensable element of transitional justice.

It appears then, that a choice *has* to be made between the past and the future, between impunity and punishment. In a transition to *democracy*, where an oppressed populace has emerged victorious, the only viable and legitimate option is to pursue victor's justice: correcting the injustices of the pre-democratic order by holding those liable who violated the human rights fought for. This undoubtedly imposes constraints on a newly elected government's ability to follow its own lights and to pursue social justice, but such constraints find their justification in their affirmation of the triumph of right over power. Corrective justice is also not easily, cheaply or perfectly attainable, and safeguards, possibly in the form of international supervision, may be needed to prevent its abuse by a new political élite. There is no escape from the fact that even if it is scrupulously upheld, transitional justice remains "limited and partial".[91] However, South Africa's experiment shows that when contemplating these limitations and costs, and balancing them against those of "reconciliation through truth", it is well to remember that, as Hegel suggests in the section from which the quotation at the start of this contribution was taken, sense-certainty, that is, mere truth unmediated by the values locked up in abstract, general categories of thought, is "nothingness".[92]

---

[88] "Freedom is eternal vigilance", *Saturday Argus* (Cape Town), 31 October 1998.
[89] *Cape Times* (Cape Town), 24 February 2000.
[90] "Red tape ruins reconciliation", *Saturday Argus* (Cape Town), 11 October 1999; "Reparations a logical conclusion", *Business Day* (Johannesburg), 13 March 2000
[91] Teitel, above n. 18, p. 2014.
[92] See above n. 1, p. 65.

7

Law as Mnemosyne and as Lethe: Quasi-Judicial Institutions and Collective Memories

ADAM CZARNOTA

INTRODUCTION

Is law in contemporary societies changing the past? This is the problem I will address in this chapter. It seems to me that a positive answer to such a question does not necessarily involve some form of regenerated Stalinist revisionism. During the process of state-building in particular, the modern nation-state has always been involved in re-designing the past. So the thesis is not new. What is new is the density of the process, and its depth, as well as the different legal strategies applied in re-designing the past. Such processes are happening not only in countries undergoing democratic transition such as Poland, the Czech Republic, Hungary, South Africa, Chile and Argentina: a similar process is taking place in democratic countries such as Australia and Canada, as well as, arguably, within the European Union.

Countries in the process of dealing with difficult pasts are choosing legal means in order to do so. In all these countries, we see examples of law expanding towards the past in order to control more efficiently the present and the future. In the contemporary world, to regulate the future it is not enough to control the present; it is necessary also to control the past. But since the past has already happened and it is impossible to undo or change what has been done, how can the past be controlled? The thesis that I put forward is that law tries to control the present and the future by expanding itself into the past through an attempt, if not actually to regulate collective memories, then at least to provide a legal framework that might allow the modification of collective memories. The question is to find out not only precisely *why* this is taking place but also *how*; which legal strategies have been applied in different countries, and what indeed are the characteristic features of the legal institutions which try to change the past?

In the accepted paradigm law draws on experiences from the past which are then directed towards the present and the future. In this paradigm law's function is located within a linear progression from past to present to future. Law's governance of present and future social relations is based on experiences from the past, and in this paradigm the past is unchangeable. On the one hand, it assigns individual responsibility for things done in the past on the basis of pre-existing law. On the other hand, its focus is on governing future human behaviour. The classical paradigm is expressed in such legal principles as *lex retro non agit* (the law does not act retrospectively), *nulla poena sine lege* (no penalty without a law), *nullum crimen sine lege* (no crime without a law), as well as mechanisms such as statutes of limitation. Such an approach is based on a principle similar to those in traditional historiography embodied in the idea of *historia magistra vitae est*.

When we examine the empirical facts in many contemporary uses of law, the situation is different. The recent phenomenon I perceive is that, rather than adopting the dominant historical narrative, law is attempting to reconstruct and to recreate it. In order to fulfil its role as regulator of the present and future, law is changing the past and thus including the past (not only the present and the future) within its objects of regulation. It is a striking development, with implications both practical and theoretical. In many countries there is a process—wrongly presented as a "return to history"—of "re-writing" the past through legal institutions. In the case of former communist countries this is done mainly via lustration, decommunisation and the restitution of property.[1] In South Africa it is through the Truth and Reconciliation Commission. In the former colonies such as Australia, law plays the role of generator of parameters of "proper" collective memories. The *Mabo* case is one example;[2] when the High Court in the *Mabo* case threw out the doctrine of *terra nullius*, it was playing a central role in changing society's perception of the past.

These new developments in various parts of the globe are based on the implementation of legal standards that are not necessarily generated through a community's on-going "internal" historical narrative but are taken from outside as transcendental. These are then absorbed into the narrative of the community and imposed upon the past in order to show continuity. So, it appears that the starting point is the present, if not the future, rather than the past. Whereas in the classical paradigm law's legitimacy was based on the past, today it is rather based on the future in the sense that law is being used to change and re-write collective memories for the sake of a future social order. It is important therefore to consider the degree to which, in the contemporary world, law is the main medium through which collective memories are being re-written. And also, therefore, to ask the question from the point of view of the sociology of law, to what degree is law successful and efficient in such a strategy?

[1] See the Symposium "Law and Lustration: Righting the Wrongs of the Past", (1995) 20:1 *Law and Social Inquiry* 1–276.
[2] *Mabo v. The State of Queensland (No. 2)* (1992) 175 CLR 1.

What I have just suggested is a broad working framework. In light of the work of Barbara Adam and her research on time and social theory,[3] I am convinced that time is an overlooked variable in the conceptualisation of law and its role, and that analysis of legal processes from this perspective will provide an opportunity to focus on currently fragmented discussions of globalisation, judicial activism, transitional justice, individual versus collective rights, the role of law in promoting social change, and the concept of the rule of law in the contemporary world.

Law is immersed in time, though this is usually only indirectly rather than explicitly spelt out. Law depends on time; yet it may also regulate and change time, not in the sense of physical time, but rather in terms of changing social time, the perception of time and of collective memories. And it is specifically, I will suggest, through an analysis of the role of "quasi-judicial institutions" that this phenomenon is most clearly visible today.

LAW'S TIME

In a decisive way our perception of time is always connected with movement and change. Traditionally time was interpreted as movement from that which had happened and is impossible to change, to the present experience of social relations, and then towards an uncontrolled, unknowable future. But individuals and groups try to control social time, and this immediately stresses the connection of time with power. The future is the least controllable, controllable only as the probability that one out of many possible futures will occur. Similarly we control the past as the probability that one reconstruction of social processes from the past will prevail. Between these two elements is the present in which the control of both sets of risks take place. Both elements in the spectrum of past and future inform processes in the present.

From the present we reflect upon an under-determined past and an undetermined future. Helga Novotny has described the phenomenon of extended present time which is characteristic of societies in late modernity.[4]

---

[3] B Adam, *Time and Social Theory* (Cambridge, Polity Press, 1990), and B Adam, *Timewatch. The Social Analysis of Time* (Cambridge, Polity Press, 1995). It is necessary to add that many recent publications on law and time focus mainly on different conceptualisations of time in law; they nevertheless represent a good starting point for an engagement with related works within social theory and contemporary sciences. See e.g., J Bjarup and M Blegvad (eds), "Time, Law and Society", (1995) 64 *Archiv fur Rechts-und Sozialphilosophie*, also F Ost and M Van Hoecke (eds), *Temps et Droit. Le Droit a-t-il pour vocation de durer?(Time and Law. Is it the Nature of Law to Last?)* (Bruxelles, Bruylant, 1999).

[4] H Novotny, "From the Future to Extended Present: Time in Social Systems" in G Kirsh, P Nijkamp and K Zimmerman (eds), *Time Preferences: An Interdisciplinary Theoretical and Empirical Approach* (Berlin, Wissenschaftzentrum, 1985), pp. 11–21.

Such an extension of the present, it seems to me, occurs simultaneously towards the future (in the sense of a present-future) and towards the past (in form of present-past). This new perception of time in developed societies is connected with our effort to control our life, to control social processes and to eliminate uncertainty as much as possible. It is the paradox of our situation that on the one hand we live in a risk society yet on the other we are consciously involved in a reduction of risk by extension of the present. This may be evidenced in the way we attempt to project ourselves towards immortality in a variety of different ways: in the continuity of the family and its legal manifestations, in our wills, foundations, legal limitations of disposal of our property etc.; in a word, in all those ways in which human beings attempt to overcome the limitation of biological time.

Traditionally, the perception of law and its function has been as the main tool of social control in dealing with the future, where the normative element of law—law's authority—has been based on a particular society's experience and understanding of its past. The past, and the longevity, of legal institutions provide legitimacy for their existence. Some layers of law are in long existence, something the famous French historian of the Annales School, F Braudel, termed the long duration (*longue durée*), and which W I Buhl called structural continuity.

Today we can perceive that law is facing a challenge from the past. More precisely, it is forced to deal with the past, and in that sense law's control of the past becomes equally important as a matter of controlling risk. This is not only the problem of restitutive justice, or retributive justice—the present regulation for harms done in the past—but goes to the very problem of the historical narrative which is adopted by law. It is in this sense that I speak of law's extended empire. For law must regulate not only for the future, but for the past as well. That is, it must change the nature and experience of the past as past.

This is indeed a striking power. But in this development the linear connections between past, present, and future, and the traditional need for law's authority to locate comfortably within this predictable sequence, is challenged. Law extends not only to what will be based on what has been (its justification for future regulation), but to what has been based on what is. In legal theory and sociology, and indeed for contemporary society in general, this is a remarkable transformation.

LAW AND COLLECTIVE MEMORIES

Law is actively involved in the social construction of different forms of social time. Law and legal institutions exist in time and shape time as well, and it is in this context that I suggest that law is involved in the re-designing of collective memories and not *tabula rasa* design. The degree of fixity of collective memories is unknown, but they also adapt to institutional rules. This is then a reflexive relation. In democratic and recently-democratic countries throughout the world, law or legal mechanisms are being used to re-conceptualise and re-write those countries' histories, to re-interpret them through the infusion of new normative elements. This is, I suggest, a novel phenomenon in its speed, depth and breadth.

The term "collective memory" was coined by Maurice Halbwachs.[5] He sees collective memories as definitive of (and peculiar to) a social group. The social group may use collective memories in consolidating an identity, or may even use collective memories in establishing itself as a social group. Halbwachs in his writing on collective memories tried to grasp a general phenomenon that structures all human societies: collective memories are part of their culture, tradition and social institutions.

Halbwachs focused on the problem of relations between collective memory and individual memory. Collective memory transcends individual memories, or memories of generations only: "The collective memory, for its part, encompasses the individual memories while remaining distinct from them. It evolves according to its own laws, and any individual remembrances that may penetrate are transformed within a totality having no personal consciousness".[6] Individual and collective memories are governed by different dynamics and operate in different time frames and spatial borders.

The question of time becomes particularly pertinent here, its meaning dependent upon the density of social interactions. To the extent to which law is involved in creating networks of social interactions it too is involved in the creation of social time. Halbwachs writes:

> "While the collective memory endures and draws strength from its base in a coherent body of people, it is individuals as group members who remember. While these remembrances are mutually supportive of each other and common to all, individual members still vary in the intensity with which they experience them. I would readily acknowledge that each memory is a viewpoint on the collective memory, that this viewpoint changes as my position changes, that this position itself changes as my relationships to other milieus change. Therefore, it is not surprising that everyone does not draw on the same part of this common instrument".[7]

Halbwachs also analysed relations between collective memory and historical memory. The phenomenon of remembering the events which we do not

---

[5] M Halbwachs, *Collective Memories* (New York, Harper & Row Publishers, 1980). Halbwachs was Bergson's pupil and was later influenced by Emile Durkheim. In current social science scholarship his work is, if not forgotten, then at least overlooked. Interestingly, Halbwachs' unfinished book on collective memories was an outcome of a controversy about time.

[6] *Ibid.*, p.51.   [7] *Ibid.*, p. 48.

experience but learn about is what he called "borrowed memory". We can increase that memory by education, reading or conversation but it is not generated by us.

> "During my life, my national society has been a theater for a number of events that I say 'I remember', events that I know about only from newspapers or testimony of those directly involved. These events occupy a place in the memory of the nation, but I myself did not witness them. In recalling them, I must rely entirely upon the memory of others, a memory that comes, not as corroborator or completer of my own, but as the very source of what I wish to repeat. I often know such events no better nor in any other manner than I know historical events that occurred before I was born. I carry a baggage load of historical remembrances that I can increase through conversation and reading. But it remains a borrowed memory, not my own. These events have deeply influenced national thought, not only because they have altered institutions, but also because their tradition endures, very much alive, in region, province, political party, occupation, class, even certain families or persons who experienced them firsthand. For me they are conceptions, symbols. I picture them pretty much as others do. I can imagine them, but I cannot remember them".[8]

"History indeed resembles a crowded cemetery, where room must constantly be made for new tombstones"[9] wrote Halbwachs. And it is "living history" which is the recall of events from the past that will furnish collective memories. "History is neither the whole nor even all that remains of the past. In addition to written history, there is living history that perpetuates and renews itself through time and permits the recovery of many old currents that have seemingly disappeared. If this were not so, what right would we have to speak of a 'collective memory'?"[10] "Collective memory", he adds, "differs from history in at least two respects. It is a current of continuous thought whose continuity is not at all artificial, for it retains from the past only what still lives or is capable of living in the consciousness of the groups keeping the memory alive. By definition it does not exceed the boundaries of this group".[11]

The second half of the twentieth century saw the particular importance of law in preserving and shaping the identity of groups that in turn determine the crucial position of the relationship between collective memories and the law. Surprisingly, in jurisprudence that process was largely overlooked, conceptualised only in a fragmented way, even although processes of conflict resolution, redress and coming to terms with the past are all related to collective memories and group identities. That omission is due to the fact that leading theories in jurisprudence still presuppose an abstract and a-historical concept of human nature and contract, and not a properly historicised one. Judith Shklar in her writings on the liberalism of fear[12]

---

[8] *Ibid.*, pp. 51–2.   [9] *Ibid.*, p. 52.   [10] *Ibid.*, p. 64.   [11] *Ibid.*, p.80.
[12] J Shklar, "The Liberalism of Fear", in N L Rosenblum (ed), *Liberalism and the Moral Life* (Cambridge, Harvard University Press, 1984).

criticised the founding fathers of modern liberalism for that mistake, and it would seem to apply to the leading trends in jurisprudence.

At the end of the century the memories of the most terrible atrocities—the Holocaust, the Cambodian genocide, and genocide in Rwanda—all put a stamp on collective memories and established bases for a global collective memory.[13] But collective memories are also at the core of violent conflicts, as between ethnic, religious and political groups, between oppressors and oppressed, and between the powerful and the powerless everywhere. Collective memories divide societies and polities and are vigorously contested between groups in society and also between nations.[14]

During the process of nation-building the nation has always been involved in engineering a particular type of official collective memory. Such memory will become embodied in the history textbooks, the historical monuments and rituals of the State. While official memory suppresses other memories, some survive and live through oral traditions that are transmitted from generation to generation. A good example of this is the survival of the collective memory about the Second Republic or about the Katyn massacre that was suppressed by the communist regime in Poland.

Collective memory is embodied in law, and experiences from the past are formalised in legal language. Sometimes the function of this will be to prevent future mistakes and it is possible to see developments of international law in the twentieth century in this light. We have witnessed the establishment of legal procedures and legal institutions in the broadest sense to deal with violence and atrocities, and to come to terms with guilt and shame. The Hague Conference in 1899 took the first step—the Hague Land Warfare Convention; the Nuremberg Trial took the next step leading, as is likely, to the establishment of a permanent International Criminal Court.

In international law, the way in which the law and legal institutions relate to and deal with collective memories seems to be particularly clear. But on the national level, and often less visibly, we might well include a much broader range: legal institutions that facilitate the coming to terms with the past; legal redress in civil wars; social movements which base their claims on collective memories; indigenous communities who base their claims for land rights on an oral tradition of collective memories. It is to explore these developments that we will need now to consider the range of institutions employed at the nation level.

---

[13] See J Balint, "Conflict Victimization, and Legal Redress, 1945–1996", (1996) 59:4 *Law and Contemporary Problems* 231–47.

[14] In this last case a good example is the so-called Transylvanian problem and contestation of historical memory between Hungarians and Romanians.

LEGAL INSTITUTIONS AND THEIR NEW TASKS

Legal institutions are involved more than ever before in processes that relate directly to collective memories. Most prominently, legal institutions have had to solve problems that arise out of the task of coming to terms with the consequences of the injustices committed in the past. Dealing with difficult pasts is at present not restricted to the Holocaust and Second World War crimes, or to large-scale transitions from authoritarian rule to democracy (including, here, the collapse of communism.[15]) Past injustices are now haunting well-established liberal-democratic regimes, exemplified again in Australian cases of Aboriginal land claims and the "stolen generations". We might say that what we are witnessing on the national and international levels is an impetus towards the uncovering of subterranean and suppressed collective memories. Official or state-sanctioned histories are coming under pressure from previously submerged memories. One of the most interesting elements in that process is the involvement of law in settling accounts with the past. In some cases groups look to law's authority to uphold their memories. In others, legal or quasi-legal institutions such as truth commissions, help to unveil facts. Perhaps, from a global point of view, this is connected with the creation of the New World Order after the Cold War. Nevertheless, in all these cases involving truth-finding and legal redress, procedures are employed that extend beyond the framework of traditional legal institutions.

In many countries the legal process has had to merge opposing collective memories into a common one, thereby redefining memories and identities of the groups in conflict or in potential conflict. Legal institutions are involved in the process of nation-building and establishing a common—and as such basically collective—memory that integrates those of different social groups. Here, legal procedures and institutions have to perform a balancing act between forging peace and redressing the justified claims of the victims, between retributive justice and mercy.

Post-communist states have begun their own processes of coming to terms with their past. Particular countries have dealt with the problem differently. Dealing with the past in East-central European countries is restricted to the national level, and mostly to a more recent past.[16] Ten years after the collapse of communism the problem is still there with social, political and legal repercussions. The political and social transformation reshaped power and authority relations between groups. It

---

[15] See R Brooks (ed), *When Sorry Isn't Enough. The Controversy over Apologies and Reparation for Human Injustice* (New York and London, New York University Press, 1999).

[16] Czarnota and Hofmanski, "Polish Law Deals with the Communist Past" in (1996) 22 *Review of Central and East European Law* pp. 521–34.

redefined group identities and established new lines of conflict between them. Because of the peculiar modes of negotiated transmissions of power, the legal procedures and institutions were based on the principle of legal continuity. They have not emerged from intense civil strife and there has been no break in the continuity of the system. On the one hand the "negotiated revolution" minimised social conflicts, but on the other if it did not contribute then it did at least open the way for the proliferation of social conflicts in other areas: due to the negotiated and legalised mode of the transmission of power, the law and legal institutions interfere with the process of reshuffling elites and bureaucracies, producing new conflicts or intensifying existing ones.

Another aspect of law's proliferation of conflict in these instances is related to its importing into the public realm previously suppressed collective memories. In post-communist East-central European politics, new political groups rose to the surface, their strong identities based not on interests but on shared memories. Those groups wanted to imprint their memories on law and also use law to vindicate their collective memories and sanction them in an authoritative way. In a sense, law became the battleground of memory. The concern is, of course, that this may contribute to a climate of distrust within the society, may damage the prestige of law and jeopardise the society's commitment to an already fragile rule of law.

So we are currently faced with two contradictory processes. On the one hand, we have regional unification connected with globalisation which undermines the nation-state and of course revitalises local collective memories (as in the examples of the EU and the devolution of power within formerly unitary states, such as the United Kingdom). The second process is the dismantling of some former political units and the creation of new nation-states as in the case of the disintegration of the USSR, Czechoslovakia and Yugoslavia. Legal institutions have played a role in re-establishing collective memories suppressed by the hegemony of the former strong states. These collective memories were inserted into the constitutions of the newly-built nations. Parliaments and courts also reached back to legal traditions and collective memories of a distant past, and tried to "revitalise" them in a legal system that was in the process of establishing itself. Claims on property rights have, in this regard, been particularly involved in the making and reshaping of collective memories.

Collective memories thus bear on present conflicts. They are part of the contested definitions and identities of groups. Collective memories play an important role in the empowerment as well as the disempowerment of groups. Legal institutions by their very nature support hegemonic collective memories, but they give room—increasingly so today—to those of minority groups, to suppressed or colonised peoples.

The problems law will be confronted with thus include the following: whose collective memories are to be dealt with? How are legal institutions to be made independent of the political processes of shaping and using collective memories? How far do we reach back into the past? These problems are directly related to two functions of the law: institutional remembering and forgetting.

<h2 style="text-align:center">REMEMBERING, FORGETTING AND
LEGAL INSTITUTIONS</h2>

In his story "Funes the Memorious", Borges described the situation of a man who mastered his memory and achieved a perfect state where he remembered everything. The effect of this is that he was unable to live a normal life. Remembering all events and situations is impossible. Human beings apply categories, classification, values and norms which select events and facts. We forget in order to remember. Individual and collective memories are based on such processes. Remembering and forgetting are, in other words, socially located and constituted activities, and this characterises both individual and collective memories. But collective memories have an institutional character on the basis of which selections of what is remembered are systematised and reproduced. Institutions are part of the collective memory and represent them by their specific tasks, functions and structural organisation. One such institution is law.

Law deals with conflicts and has developed impressive techniques in handling individual memory albeit less so when it comes to groups. If we analyse procedural law, such as the law of evidence we will find an impressive body of rules on how to prove the "truth" of contested memories, which kind of proofs are acceptable and justifiable, how far in the past memories should reach. Law is based on remembering but is also balanced by a machinery of systematic forgetting: cases are closed, offenders are rehabilitated, victims are compensated and conflicts are solved.

The law and legal institutions have always explicitly and intentionally dealt with the fact that memories of the past depend on conflicts in the present, and that systematic forgetting is part of what the future requires. Because law and legal institutions carry collective memories they become an integral part of the identity and integrity of a community. Embedded in constitutions, for example, are collective memories of the conflicts from which they emerged.

Dealing with collective memories poses challenges to the law and legal institutions. Two main problems can be identified. The first and crucial problem arises from the fact that the law and legal institutions mostly deal with individual rights. Modern law clearly gives individual rights priority over collective rights. Therefore, conventional law and legal institutions seem to have difficulty dealing with collective identities and their underlying collective memories. Despite the fact that international law deals mainly with collectivities, not individuals, it is still the case that group rights are very much in the process of creation and recognition.

The second problem emerges from the fact that collective memories and collective identities are established by and within the framework of discourse taking place in the public sphere. It is through social discourses that morally justifiable claims are constituted. The problem arises because legal discourse is, however, highly specialised and professionalised, which means that very often political claims are lost in the process of translation from social discourse to legal discourse. There is no guarantee that claims will cross the legal threshold without being compromised.

Finally, it should not be forgotten that the legal system is often itself thoroughly compromised by the past. Dealing with collective memories may require new ways of institutionalising forgetting and remembering within the legal system in order to deal with a whole set of questions such as the following: whose collective memories are valid, and what is constitutive of collective identities? Which time-frame is to be taken into consideration? Which kind of traditions establish claims in the present? What kind of compensation should be given to victims? Would not the legal procedure itself stir up and exacerbate new conflicts? In which way can legal procedures contribute to the imminent task of peace-making and redress, if collective memories of injustice and terror are attached to the legal system?

These issues are best addressed by institutions which are not within traditional law or the legal system—that is, by quasi-judicial institutions—since the very fact that legal institutions are part of the national hegemonic system, means they are restricted in dealing with processes of social transformation and the conflict of collective memories. Law in each country is based on a dominant or hegemonic historical narrative which provides not only narrative but more importantly normative coherence to legal systems. Alternative collective memories challenge not only the dominant historical narrative but also the normative structure and coherence of the legal system.

QUASI-JUDICIAL INSTITUTIONS AND TRANSITIONAL JUSTICE

One of the most striking features therefore of contemporary regulation of the past is that it is conducted mainly by quasi-judicial bodies such as constitutional tribunals, truth commissions, and lustration courts. Not all of them are very innovative but it is possible to identify a trend in contemporary approaches to the problems of dealing with the past. (Of course there are others which I do not want to touch on here, such as re-shaping the property rights by re-privatisation for instance. Mark Osiel in his book on Law and Collective Memories[17] tried to show that special criminal trials within existing criminal law systems could reshape collective memory

[17] M Osiel, *Mass Atrocity, Collective Memories and the Law* (Transaction Publishers, 1999).

and lay down the foundation for "liberal" collective memory. But what he really shows are the enormous difficulties faced by courts in such a process: those trials which succeeded were really special types of "show trials" designed to make an impact on social consciousness.)

The most visible and dense problems of "dealing with the past" are in societies in accelerated transformation from authoritarian or communist rule to new forms of society and politics. Because of the pressure of issues which have to be solved such societies can not leave it to normal legal procedures but show varying amounts of institutional creativity in coping with the problems. The "transition" is not merely a space between two well known and easily characterised resting points, but a journey with *sui generis* characteristics and no clearly identifiable destination. And as the problems of transition are specific problems, so some of the means of dealing with them are novel means, and some of the institutions developed in this period have been unique institutions. That is the case with the quasi-judicial institutions and practices that we can identify.

Such transitions may be understood to be governed by "transitional justice", which cannot be reduced to the so-called "normal" application of justice in polities with existing constitutional and political frameworks with settled laws and practices. For there is an in-built paradox in the contemporary transitions: they are "revolutionary" because they lead to a total change of existing constitutional, political and legal structures and also to the re-design of dominant collective memories and, underlying these, historical narratives (as for example with the Hungarian Constitutional Court's concept of the "invisible constitution"). At the same time they are "reformist" because they try to avoid dramatic upheaval, "evolutionary" because they follow a step by step gradualist approach, "legalistic" because they pay at least lip service to the rule of law, and "conservative" in that they include previously politically dominant social groups with their collective memories rather than excluding or even eliminating their representatives. The institutional manifestations of this are the quasi-judicial bodies—bodies which look and behave like normal courts but are not conventional courts. In their selection process, adversarial procedure, and relative independence from the government of the day they remind us of traditional courts, yet at the same time they have the powers of law-making traditionally reserved for representative bodies. They also possess some elements of executive bodies and traditional courts for vindication of grievances related to the past regime (for instance re-privatisation). These bodies are much more palatable to the society because they carry little of the stained baggage of traditional politico-legal institutions, and have greater room for manoeuvre and space for discretion than traditional courts. Yet they share the norm-fashioning role that courts do, and some of the prestige of an idealised vision of law, which has some popular resonance.

At present is too early to say if all of such quasi-judicial institutions are more capable of dealing with collective memories than traditional courts based on the individualistic approach to law deeply present in the Western legal tradition. Nevertheless it looks as if they possess institutional structures and characteristics which are able to respond at the same time both to the need for radical change and the need for substantive continuity in dealing with the complicated nature of collective memories. No other legal institutions are able to perform this role effectively. It may then be that this new type of legal institution is possibly the institution of the future for dealing with collective memories, particularly since the problem with the legal re-design of collective memories is not only a feature of "transitional justice" societies.

Ruti Teitel has emphasised this, pointing out, *inter alia,* that

> "theories of adjudication associated with understandings of the rule of law in ordinary times are inapposite to transitional periods. Our ordinary intuitions about the nature and role of adjudication relate to presumptions about the relative competence and capacities of judiciaries and legislatures in ordinary times that simply do not hold in unstable periods".[18]

In such circumstances, law is called upon to restrain arbitrariness and secure legitimate expectations while at the same time being a central instrument for bringing about change.

I agree with Teitel's claim, but it must be pushed further than she has done, to focus not merely on the distinctive problems which transitions pose, but more closely on some distinctive *institutional* innovations that occur in the process of transitional justice, and in the process of permanent transition. For, notwithstanding the many important differences between contexts, historical inheritances, directions of transition, and many other things, we can find in the institutional dimensions of transitions some common characteristics which may illuminate the role of and potential for institutional design in the contemporary time of permanent transitional justice. These characteristics have to do, briefly, with the surprising and puzzlingly powerful role of quasi-judicial bodies.

These bodies are crucial for dealing with collective memories. As I have said, the paradox of legal involvement in the "correction" or re-designing of collective memories requires reconciling the new, sometimes revolutionary, substance with the reformist-evolutionary-legalistic-conservative elements outlined above, in turn creating a demand for special institutional structures which would be able to respond at the same time to the need for radical change and substantial continuity. No *political* branches of the government (including parliamentary and executive bodies) can perform this role effectively, largely because of the dissatisfaction with or suspicion

---

[18] R Teitel, "Transitional Jurisprudence: The Role of law in Political Transformation", (1997) 106 *Yale Law Journal* 2009–80, at 2034.

towards politics and politicians in these periods. The combination of distrust in politics and a hunger for "justice" makes political branches particularly inadequate in overseeing processes of re-designing collective memories. On the other hand, regular courts are unable to perform this task either, due to restrictions of the existing legal tradition, and the traditional view that courts should only apply rather than transform the law. It is into this vacuum that quasi-judicial bodies enter.

Powerful and innovative constitutional courts on the one hand, and various bodies designed specifically for "coping with past" on the other, are most involved in "changing the past" in these societies. For all the differences between these two types of bodies, it is possible to perceive important similarities: in the selection procedures (usually, appointed by parliaments or presidents), relative independence from the executive branches, and quasi-judicial procedures. Most importantly, however, the common function of these bodies is to adjust both the normative structure in society, and the public narratives of past and future to new social expectations and values, without recourse to dramatic, revolutionary means. Constitutional courts do this by introducing major changes in the law through constitutional review which takes the form of "interpreting" the constitution (albeit by conjuring up what in Hungary is termed, by the Chief Justice, an "invisible constitution") rather than openly revising the law; on the other hand, bodies such as truth and reconciliation commissions and so-called lustration courts perform this role through implementing new concepts, and new standards of justice. Simultaneously then, they seek to assuage expectations of the public whilst, to a considerable extent, applying standards conformable to procedural justice.

CONCLUSION

This process of "legalising" collective memories is not only an increasingly visible phenomenon, but also provides one important key to understanding the nature of contemporary social and political transformations. In particular, the recent development of quasi-judicial institutions in the evolution of law is enormously significant since control of the past is always connected with power. The activity of these institutions is at the crossroads of different concepts of time and hold a potential for change and control which is not within the capacity of traditional judicial bodies. Quasi-judicial institutions thus become guardians of our present and also present-future and present-past. They therefore possess the power of two Goddesses from Ancient Greek mythology, Mnemosyne and Lethe, and require careful attention from legal theory and legal philosophy.

8

Law's Constitutive Possibilities: Reconstruction and Reconciliation in the Wake of Genocide and State Crime

JENNIFER BALINT

INTRODUCTION

The Security Council resolution that created the International Criminal Tribunal for Rwanda declared that prosecutions would contribute to "the process of national reconciliation and to the restoration and maintenance of peace".[1] Desmond Tutu, in his introductory statements at the "Mandela Football Club" hearings stated: "We seek again, may I emphasise, the truth, not for purposes of prosecution, but for the purpose of seeking to re-integrate people into our society".[2] A victim of apartheid praised the South African Truth and Reconciliation Commission for "helping us to restore our humanity". A member of the Aboriginal Tent Embassy in Australia avowed "I am sick of this reconciliation . . . There can be no reconciliation until there is cessation of hostilities".[3] Israeli poet and Holocaust survivor Dan Pagis, in the wake of the Holocaust, wrote of the farce that "[e]verything will be returned to its place".[4]

Reconciliation has been used both as an argument in favour of legal proceedings as well as an argument against them. When used as an argument in favour of legal proceedings, it is assumed that accountability and the attribution of responsibility are integral to reconciliation after a

---

[1] Statute of the International Criminal Tribunal for Rwanda, adopted at New York, 8 November 1994, S.C. Res. 955, U.N. SCOR, 49th Sess., 3453d mtg., U.N. DOC, S/RES/955 (1994).

[2] 24 November 1997. Transcript: South African Truth and Reconciliation Commission.

[3] Aboriginal Tent Embassy, Canberra, July 1998.

[4] Final paragraph, D Pagis, "Draft of a Reparations Agreement" in *Variable Directions. The Selected Poetry of Dan Pagis* Stephen Mitchell (trans.) (San Francisco, North Point Press, 1989), p. 35.

conflict.[5] When used as an argument against, it is that legal proceedings will hinder any prospect of reconciliation.[6] The assumption in both these arguments is that reconciliation is not only a desirable outcome, but the *primary* desirable outcome; and, that reconciliation and law are integrally linked. Thus it is not suggested that reconciliation is *not* a desirable outcome: what can be questioned, however, is whether reconciliation should always be assumed, or taken on as a specific goal, of the legal process.

It has been presumed that there is a certain relationship between reconciliation and law, that law can create conditions for reconciliation. The expectation, for instance, of the Security Council resolution is that law will occupy a central place in the reconciliation process in Rwanda. The expectation is that law, at this particular time, will have a role to play in societal transformation. The South African Truth and Reconciliation Commission also supported such an expectation. It is a perspective that suggests that legal proceedings initiated in the wake of regime transition and gross harm perpetrated by states can provide a broad working framework beyond the actual focus of trials or particular legislation, and that their role can go beyond prosecution and punishment, towards societal reconstruction. There is clear evidence that this happens. This chapter suggests, however, that it is not always the case.

Although law can initiate and stimulate broader societal processes in the wake of state crime, it does not always play this role. Moreover, even when such a process can be identifiably linked to law (for example, legislation which specifically bans the communist or the Nazi party, or lustration legislation), the impact of law, in each case, may be very different. No matter how central a role it may play, law does not always function in a broadly *constitutive* manner in all situations of transition.

This chapter investigates the constitutive function of law in the wake of genocide and other forms of state crime. These are crimes committed "in the name of the state": serious and systematic human rights abuses perpetrated by a state or state-like body, as part of state policy and using state institutions. The questions raised are: when and how do legal processes at such times stimulate or harness *broader* societal processes? and when is this transformative space opened and when is it blocked?[7] In the wake of

---

[5] The use of the term reconciliation as an unqualifiable "good" can be observed in the "trial" of Pol Pot in Anlong Veng: one of the charges read out was "destroying the policy of national reconciliation", a reference to the attempt to block the Funcinpec deal: N Thayer, "Brother Number Zero", *Far Eastern Economic Review*, 7 August 1997.

[6] This was the case in Haiti, in which amnesty was given to the military leaders. See M P Scharf, "Swapping Amnesty for Peace: Was There a Duty to Prosecute International Crimes in Haiti?", (1996) 31, *Texas International Law Journal* pp. 7–41, p. 9.

[7] It is interesting to compare here the relationship between such official law and what Leon Petrazycki and Eugene Ehrlich conceived of as "intuitive living law". Further developed by A Podgórecki, *A Sociological Theory of Law* (Milano, Dott. A. Giuffrè Editore, 1991).

such crime, law can play a role in the establishment of a "new reality", one which deliberately counters the old reality of the criminal state or criminal legislation, and the harm perpetrated. With reference therefore to a series of examples, the chapter will discuss the role of legal mechanisms in stimulating these societal processes, suggesting that the important role of law in the wake of state crime *is in its constituting spaces for societal reconstruction and reconciliation rather than pursuing these objectives as legal objectives.*

INSTITUTIONAL AND SOCIETAL RECONSTRUCTION

In the wake of violent conflict, particularly conflict directed at a particular group as in the case of genocide, there is generally not only societal division, but institutional fragility as well. The perpetration of state crime entails the harnessing, transformation, and sometimes destruction of state institutions. The destruction in 1994 of the legal profession (including many of the "law-bearers") in Rwanda, for example, meant that the rebuilding of the institution of law became a primary task for the country. It also meant that the potential for another "re-fashioning" existed—as can be seen by the fact that no Hutu judges have been appointed. In post-apartheid South Africa institutional fragility can be interpreted in part as the need to build a supportive institutional framework for the majority of South Africans: that is, a set of institutions geared, not to their separation and oppression, but to their constitutional well-being. It is another "institutional re-fashioning" that is required in terms of the establishment of new institutions, and the transformation of existing ones.

Reconstruction can be both societal and institutional. Institutional reconstruction is to be found on a number of levels: physical reconstruction, structural and political reconstruction, and economic reconstruction. Societal reconstruction also contains a number of dimensions: the establishment of ways of living together, as well as dimensions of reconciliation, healing, and forgiveness. If we consider institutional reconstruction as providing a dimension of breadth, and of societal reconciliation providing a depth to interpersonal social relations, then we see that the two are interdependent but distinguishable: for example, and specifically for the purpose of this discussion, one clear interdependence is the relationship between the restoration of rights, property and citizenship, and any potential reconciliation.

Law can play a role in reconstruction in a number of ways: through criminal trials, through investigative reports and other mechanisms which might include truth commissions. Its potentially constitutive role here in terms of societal reconstruction will be dependent upon a number of factors, such as political will, institutional design, the particular pasts being addressed, the manner in which the harm ended, the legitimacy that the legal system enjoys, and the prevailing socio-political context. Now some of these factors are locally contingent, some universal. The impact of even similar institutional solutions can in fact vary significantly. For example, not all truth commissions or criminal trials will contribute to reconciliation, as is clear if we compare the Truth Commission established by Idi Amin in June 1974 in Uganda after international pressure,[8] to the South African Truth and Reconciliation Commission.

Even when the local context provides optimum conditions for the contribution of the legal process to reconstruction, legal institutions and legal processes cannot do everything. Law is thus an important part of the picture, but not the only part. This chapter focuses then on law's contribution to reconstruction, its availing of channels—of a constitutive space—for reconstruction, and in particular, for reconciliation.

BEYOND ACCOUNTABILITY

When crimes have been committed by a state there are two options: to ignore them or to address them. Addressing such crimes can take a number of paths, and can vary in intensity and purpose. It can be said, however, that when genocide and other forms of state crime are addressed by state legal process, two things occur:

(1) there is official acknowledgement of the harm perpetrated, and
(2) a statement is produced of the facts of such harm and an attempt made to establish a common story of events.

Both provide substantial "building blocks" for any broader reconstructive role law may play. They are the basis for two further processes:

(3) A framework for societal debate,
(4) A "foundational moment" for the society.

In seeking to establish accountability, law provides official acknowledgement of the offences committed. On a first, pragmatic level, this provides a statement of the facts of what has happened. On the broader "constitutive" level, this official acknowledgement and statement of facts—in allowing for the harm to be accounted for in a "common language"—can provide a framework and baseline for societal debate, and thus potentially become a foundational moment for a society.

This term, "foundational moment" was introduced by Elizabeth Jelin in the context of the transition in Argentina in which she saw the law as an

---

[8] The Commission of Inquiry into "Disappearances" of People in Uganda since 25 January 1971. Its findings were ignored by Amin.

important basis for further societal healing and reconciliation.[9] The potential of the legal process at such a time can be as a reference point for the society, one which can provide a basis as well as a framework for wider restoration and reconstruction, both institutional and societal.

A "foundational moment" can be described as a break from the past, a basis for the transformation of state and society, a turning point for it, a reconfiguration of its normative framework. Law facilitates such a normative shift through the creation of new or alternative reference points for a particular society. Such a shift was evident, for example, in the recognition by the High Court of Australia of the claims of Torres Strait Islander, Eddie Mabo. The recognition in the 1992 *Mabo* case of indigenous title to land, and the recognition that the Australian continent was not *terra nullius* when Europeans arrived, institutionalised a normative shift in the Australian consciousness. Significantly, other fora had not been able to give legitimacy to Aboriginal and Torres Strait Islanders' claims of dispossession. Although it can be argued that *Mabo* did not go far enough, it can be said that it did provide a "foundational moment" for Australian society. Legal statements to do with the past are a key component in such normative shifts,[10] and are part of what Cass Sunstein termed the "expressive function of law": the function of law, that is, that consists in "making statements" as opposed to the function of law in directly controlling behaviour.[11] Law can possess a centrality of voice within societies which other institutions lack. As such, law can perform an important constitutive function in societies emerging from conflict and division. This is what is meant by "foundational moment".

Within law as "foundational moment" we can also include symbolic acts. Public statements of apology by political leaders as the legal and legitimate representatives of a society are key, as are public and official investigations of harm. In the first category we have the example of Willy Brandt kneeling before the memorial to the victims of the Warsaw Ghetto in the *Umschlagplatz* (the site of deportation of Jews from Warsaw to Auschwitz) in the 1970s in front of the national and world media in an apology to the Jewish people. Private communications of regret do not have the same impact.[12] (The converse "symbolic act" would be, for

---

[9] E Jelin, "The Politics of Memory: The Human Rights Movement and the Construction of Democracy in Argentina", (1994) 81:2 *Latin American Perspectives* pp. 38–58.

[10] These include the July 1993 (former Czechoslovakia) Law on the Illegality of the Communist Regime; the 1993 Hungarian Constitutional Court recognition of the 1956 Acts as war crimes and crimes against humanity, Procedures Concerning Certain Crimes Committed During the 1956 Revolution; the South African Promotion of National Unity and Reconciliation Act No. 34 of 1995 which established the Truth and Reconciliation Commission.

[11] C R Sunstein, "On the Expressive Function of Law", (1996) 5:1 *East European Constitutional Review* pp. 66–72.

[12] For example, the Chilean President's letters to victims after the findings of the Chilean

example, the absence of any form of official apology by Turkey for the crimes committed against the Armenians.) In the second category—of official investigation—we have the example of the Australian Royal Commission into Aboriginal Deaths in Custody, as well as the more recent Australian Human Rights and Equal Opportunity Commission *Report* which found that the forced separation and removal of indigenous children in Australia up until the 1950s constituted the crime of genocide.[13]

Of course, not all official investigations will come to play the same role.[14] Yet it is the public nature of such processes and acts which create the possibility for foundational moments, and act as potential generators of further reconstructive processes.

The decision to investigate publicly is nonetheless official acknowledgement that harm was or may have been perpetrated. The decision to make public what before was hidden can lead to a public statement of facts, which, in the framework of law, can become the "authoritatively interpreted truth". This public process can provide a framework for societal debate—for public discourse—in which law stimulates the potential for "(re)constitution" in that particular society.

The engagement of law constitutes the official, legitimate recognition of wrongs done, and their integration into the official history of the state. This has a potentially deep effect both on the psyche of the victim community (the lack of such official acknowledgement can be devastating to survivors)[15]

Truth Commission. The essentially private nature of this act, in combination with the Commission not having worked in an open and transparent manner, meant that public channels were not opened. In this we can also include the private nature of the opening up of security files in former communist countries such as Hungary and former East Germany. This has been a private, not a public process, and as such has not impacted in a more broadly societal way. There have been instances of public discussion arising out this process, but they have been fleeting rather than enduring discussions.

[13] See Sir R Wilson in *Bringing Them Home: Report of the National Inquiry into the Separation of Aboriginal and Torres Strait Islander Children from Their Families* (1997). The implementation of recommendations in such reports is, of course, the necessary next step, and one which too often is not forthcoming; the findings of the *Report* are in fact contested by the current government.

[14] Unlike the Australian *Stolen Generation Report* which stimulated wide public discussion, it can be argued that the 18 volume publication of the German Parliamentary Commission investigation into the former East German regime *Study Commission for the Assessment of History and Consequences of the SED Dictatorship in Germany*, did not have the same public effect.

[15] Denials include the scope and nature of killings of the Armenian community during the First World War. The termination of the Turkish Courts-Martial with the overthrow of the Sultan at the end of the First World War was the end of any reckoning of the Ottoman state, and the creation of an "alternate" history, one which suppressed the killing of the Armenians. The marginalisation and transformation of these legal proceedings into a message of Turkish martyrdom meant that the eventual role they played was not the intended one of accountability, but of reconstruction of the nationalist Kemalist Turkish party and the Ottoman State.

and in the broader society. It is in this vein that Justice Richard Goldstone noted that the importance of the South African Truth and Reconciliation Commission cannot be underestimated in terms of acknowledging what apartheid has meant: "If it were not for the Truth and Reconciliation Commission people who today are saying that they did not know about apartheid would be saying that it didn't happen. This is a fact, and it cannot be underestimated".[16] Official institutional knowledge provides the necessary foundation for any later societal reconstruction and institutional transformation. The authority of such legal statements provides a framework for other non-legal reconstructive processes.[17]

This is not to claim that legal process can tell the whole story. In providing one "collective memory" for those involved and establishing a common historical narrative, a memory is codified that may clearly not include all memories and all experiences.[18] Establishing an official version of the story can give the crime an element of one-dimensionality, a "flat plane" leaving unaddressed many facets of the crime. For there is no story there waiting to be "unveiled" as such.[19] The decision as to what to include is political and social. Historical scholarship has shown us this. A narration is never a passive reflection of a reality.[20]

The absence, for example, of women's stories in the telling of state crime is clear in the omission, until very recently, of the inclusion of gendered experiences. Rape has been an "untellable" story, left out of most "common" or "official" stories of genocide and state crime, just as it has so often been absent from the ordinary national courtroom. The including of charges of rape (and significantly, the finding of rape) as a tool of genocide,[21] and the

---

[16] Justice R Goldstone, "Justice or Reconciliation", paper presented in University of Chicago Law School, Center for International Studies Conference, University of Chicago, 26 April 1997.

[17] When the state does not take up this task, it is sometimes carried out in this way, yet to lesser effect. In the context of Australia, this can be observed through "bottom up" initiatives such as the Sea of Hands, and the national Sorry Day.

[18] This is not a problem unique to law. The telling of the story of the Holocaust, for example, for many years omitted the experiences of women. It is only in the last decade that the stories of women have been included in the Holocaust narrative.

[19] Elizabeth Jelin relates another type of "hidden story" in the context of resistance in Argentina. Jelin notes that in Argentina collective reactions to violations emerged outside the human rights organisations, in social spaces where group activities and organisations had existed beforehand. Such protests have persisted in the memory of the local participants and in a kind of "public silence", yet have not become part of the "official story" of the resistance to the dictatorial regime: E Jelin "The Politics of Memory. The Human Rights Movement and the Construction of Democracy in Argentina", (1994) 81:21 *Latin American Perspectives* p. 45.

[20] T T Minh-ha, "Cotton and Iron", in R Ferguson *et al.* (eds), *Out There. Marginalization and Popular Cultures* (New York, The MIT Press, 1990), p. 328.

[21] In the case at the International Criminal Tribunal for Rwanda against the former mayor of Taba commune, Akayesu, an important development in international law: Case No: ICTR-96-4-T.

inclusion of charges of rape and sexual assault in almost half of all indict-
ments brought in the International Criminal Tribunal for the former
Yugoslavia, signals some recognition. Further, the inclusion of rape as a war
crime and crime against humanity in the statute of the proposed
International Criminal Court is another crucial development: it is a further
guarantee that a fuller story will be told, and signals a meeting of legal
description and the reality of the kinds of gross harm perpetrated during
conflicts.

Yet there are hazards in relying on the institution of law as the only
vehicle for the telling of the story. Law cannot provide an all-encompassing
narrative framework. Rules about jurisdiction can leave much of the harm
perpetrated unaddressed;[22] rules of legal procedure can preclude much of
the telling. Significantly, the law will also of necessity define the kinds of
harm it investigates. This is not only a problem of mandate, but can be due
also to constraints of language and procedure. Law is a peculiar institution
with its own rules and procedures, and its own fact-finding mechanisms.
Even the South African Truth and Reconciliation Commission's reliance on
legal procedure undoubtedly impacted on the operation and findings of the
Commission.[23]

LAW'S CONSTITUTIVE FUNCTION AND ITS LIMITATIONS

Legal processes do not necessarily stimulate processes of reconciliation.
Law does not always provide the necessary constitutive space, nor is reconciliation always a feasible aim. The channels that facilitate the move from
official acknowledgement and statement of the facts to institutional and
intra-societal reconstruction and reconciliation are dependent upon a

---

[22] For example, the criminal activities of the Nazi Party began in 1933, if not earlier: this
is the starting point for many historians, and also the reference point for many German
Jews. The Nuremberg Tribunal, however, took 1939 as its starting date. Similarly, the South
African TRC has 1 March 1960 as its starting point (the date on which the apartheid policy
was drafted), yet similar atrocities occurred earlier as well. Another problem is when the
mandate does not include all *types* of harm perpetrated. For example, the mandate of the
Bolivian Truth and Reconciliation Commission did not include incidents of torture, illegal
and prolonged detention, and other abuses: P Hayner, "Fifteen Truth Commissions—1974
to 1994: A Comparative Study", (1994) 16:4 *Human Rights Quarterly* p. 614.

[23] The use of terms in the amnesty hearings such as "Evidence Leader" was a thin veil for
the role of the prosecutor in a court. The fact that those hearing the amnesty pleadings were
lawyers and judges, and those "leading the evidence" and "representing" those seeking
amnesty were lawyers, that terms such as "all rise" were used for the entrance of the
Amnesty Committee, and that terms such as "cross-examination" were also used for the
questioning of witnesses and applicants, meant that the boundaries maintained were essentially those of law, not any other institution: personal observation, Amnesty Hearings,
Durban Christian Centre, Durban, South Africa, 30 November–2 December 1998. See also
Du Bois in Chapter 6 above.

number of factors. While certain general observations can be made, these are contingent upon particular local realities which help to explain the different approaches adopted in the wake of state crime, and the differing impact of the legal processes. How is it that law plays a constitutive role? When is it "deep" and when "shallow"? The important factors in determining the type of impact any legal process may have will include how the harm was ended, who runs the legal process, and how this legal process is designed. Two general determinants will therefore be presented here: the manner of cessation of the conflict (the means of regime change) and the legal institutional approach taken in its aftermath.

Cessation: negotiated or non-negotiated?

A central distinction can be drawn between legal proceedings convened in the wake of negotiated transitions, and legal proceedings convened in the wake of non-negotiated transitions. That is, between conflicts[24] ended through negotiation, and conflicts ended through force, specifically, military overthrow. A further distinction can be drawn in those conflicts ended by military overthrow, namely whether this was by an internal or external player. Negotiated transitions are usually internal.

Conflicts ended through force include the Armenian genocide (which ceased with the defeat of the Ottoman State), the Holocaust (which ceased with the defeat of Germany), and the conflict in Rwanda (which ceased with the defeat of the Hutu government by the Tutsi exile army). In all these cases, the genocide ended only when there was an armed victory against the perpetrators. Into this category of non-negotiated transition can be added a number of situations of systematic killing by a State: Cambodia under Pol Pot (ceased with the defeat of the Khmer Rouge by Vietnam), Ethiopia under the military dictatorship of Mengistu and the Dergue (ceased with the defeat of Mengistu by the EPLF and EPRDF), and the former Yugoslavia 1992–1994 (ceased with the defeat by NATO forces).[25] As with genocide, these were ideological crimes, committed "in the name of the state".

Within the category of harm ended through negotiation can be placed other forms of state crime, in particular State oppression. We can include here most of the former military regimes in South America, most of the former communist countries, and South Africa under apartheid. These were negotiated and essentially non-violent transitions. It is in the negotiated

---

[24] Conflict is defined to include acts which include the perpetration of state crime and genocide, or acts which in themselves constitute the perpetration of state crime and genocide.

[25] Note that the conflict in the former Yugoslavia is a case of genocide as far as the attempted destruction of the Bosnian Muslim people is concerned. The conflict as a whole, however, includes both systematic killing and genocide.

transition that the possibility of an approach that identifies the perpetration as "State crime" becomes more likely. The cessation of harm meant the beginning of a new type of governance.

In light of this typology of cessation, a few further points can now be made with regard to the constitutive function of law we are considering.

External defeat

When the defeat is external and violent, then the main legal redress will be primarily external or externally run. When genocide or other forms of systematic killing have been addressed by law in any serious way, this has been done (i) by outsiders, (ii) generally outside the bounds of the nation-state (that is, in the international arena), and (iii) by criminal trial and no other legal mechanism.[26] All sustained "rule of law" legal redress for genocide has been external, with limited internal mechanisms deployed. The result has, generally, been fourfold: (a) the society is generally not witness to the proceedings and fails to participate in any meaningful way; (b) the group of people affected is relatively small; (c) the use of the criminal trial as the only tool means that law plays a fairly limited role: and (d) there may be a lack of "societal ownership" of the proceedings. As Michael Ignatieff emphasises, there are limits to the healing that outsiders can bring.[27]

This is not to argue that legal proceedings which are external play no constitutive role at all; rather, it is to argue that it is not a *truly* constitutive role.[28] For example, the legal proceedings in the Hague regarding the former Yugoslavia (namely the International Criminal Tribunal for former Yugoslavia and the case brought by Bosnia-Herzegovina at the International Court of Justice) do play a broader global role without this being either a truly societal or constitutive role. Thus while it could be argued that the Rwandan and Yugoslav Tribunals are functioning as a foundational moment for the international community—in terms of the visible successes of some kind of international legal order, which have in turn been crucial for the momentum towards the permanent International Criminal Court—it cannot as yet be argued that they play this role in the countries they are addressing.

[26] This is with the exception of the denazification process in the American zone of Germany post-Second World War.

[27] M Ignatieff, *The Warriors's Honour. Ethnic War and the Modern Conscience* (London, Chatto & Windus, 1998), p. 7.

[28] In post-War Germany, law was a tool of accountability, with the new Constitution providing probably a foundational moment, but not a framework for reconciliation, rather institutional reconstruction. However, legal process with regard to the specific atrocities committed against the Jews was in the hands of the Allies. It was only in the 1960s that German courts started dealing more systematically with the crimes committed, and it was arguably only with the end to a statute of limitations that the scope of the crimes committed during the Second World War was further absorbed by German society.

Internal defeat

A comparison of internal and external military defeat raises the issue of the intended purpose of any legal process. The overthrow of the Nazi regime in Germany by the Allies sought not control but defeat of the regime. So too the defeat of the Ottoman State in the First World War. This is substantially different to the internal defeat of Rwanda and Ethiopia. If the harm is ended through internal defeat—that is, if the "victor" gains control of the country—then the legal proceedings can be an extension of this control.[29] This has an impact on the nature and role of any subsequent legal proceedings, including their institutional design. Both Ethiopia and Rwanda were overthrown by forces seeking control of the country, comprised of nationals of that country, or, at least, who identified themselves as such.[30] In the case of Rwanda, although the military successes of the RPF put an end to the genocide, reports demonstrate that the main interest of the RPF was in the undisputed control of Rwanda, not the saving of Tutsi lives.[31] The purpose was thus defeat of the regime, not cessation of harm.

[29] See O Kirchheimer, *Political Justice. The Use of Legal Procedures for Political Ends* (Princeton, New Jersey, Princeton University Press, 1961).

[30] As in the case of the RPF in exile in Uganda, many of whom had been exiled from Rwanda in their early years, or who had been born outside Rwanda. Cambodia can also be included in this category. Although the overthrow of the Pol Pot regime by Vietnam was external, Vietnam did seek the military conquest of Cambodia, and subsequently put in its own government, the Vietnamese-backed Heng Samrin regime. Little effort was spent on bringing to justice those most responsible for the crimes committed. Those trials which were held—particularly the show trial of Pol Pot and Ieng Sary—served the political purpose of drawing a line between the old and the new regime, and the consolidation of control. The RPF (Rwandan Patriotic Front) was the Tutsi exile army at war with the FAR (Hutu-dominated Rwandan Army), who invaded Rwanda in 1990. Their primary interest was in control of the country. This was reflected in reports that in July 1994, when the FAR was in retreat yet the killings had not stopped, the RPF kept advancing, in order to gain absolute control over the country. They refused offers of American help, even though this would have stopped the killing: "*Leave None to Tell the Story: Genocide in Rwanda*", (Human Rights Watch (March 1999)). Further reports of massacres carried out in their passage through Rwanda confirm this. The EPLF and EPRDF overthrew the Mengistu regime in 1991.

[31] In an investigation into RPF "excesses", commissioned by UNHCR, undertaken by a senior US Government official, Robert Gersony, it was concluded that the RPF killed an estimated 30,000 civilians in their approach to Kigali. The inquiry, concluded in September 1994, was suppressed by the former UN Secretary-General Boutros-Boutros Ghali, although the findings had already been presented to members of the Rwandan Government by officials of UNHCR. These conclusions were later confirmed by Gérard Prunier, who testified at the Belgium Senate Inquiry into the Rwandan genocide that "je crois aujourd'hui que ce chiffre est une sous-estimation" ("I believe today that this figure is an undervaluation"): *Compte Rendu Analytique des Auditions*, Commission d'enquête parlementaire concernant les événtments du Rwanda. Bruxelles, Senat de Belgique, 11 June 1997, p. 717. I am grateful to Fiona Terry for this information. The later massacres in internal refugee camps (including that at Kibeho) confirm this too: an independent International Commission of

The state crime approach

Another significant distinction to be drawn is whether the harm is charac-terised broadly as "State crime" or whether an (often purely "scapegoat") retributive individualist approach is taken. It is suggested that a "State crime" approach has more chance of stimulating processes of societal reconstruction than a purely retributive individualist approach.

An approach taken which investigates crime as "State crime", that is, as acts which contain an institutional and political dimension different to individual murder or individual acts of harm, can have a different impact to one which highlights only individual responsibility. This is not to suggest that individual responsibility not be highlighted: what is suggested is that whereas the location of responsibility purely at the individual level will not stimulate societal reconstruction, the inclusion of responsibility at the political and institutional level may. The suggestion is that building into the legal process the investigation of such crime as *State crime* will allow communities and societies to develop their own transformative and constitutive spaces.

If a purely individual approach is taken, the effect can be the closing of channels, and the limitation of any foundational moment for that society. A more holistic approach, one which recognises the institutional dimension of the crime, has a greater chance of contributing to societal reconstruc-tion. The constitution of the society through legal proceedings for the purposes of societal reconstruction and possible reconciliation is absent in Rwanda and Ethiopia.[32] The purpose of legal process is, as I suggested earlier, the further consolidation of control: this is its constitutive function. It could be termed a backwards-looking foundational moment. This is in contrast with the South African Truth and Reconciliation Commission, an institution which was designed to address both individual and institutional responsibility.

Inquiry into the killings at the Kibeho camp (established in Kigali on 3 May 1995) for inter-nally displaced persons in April 1995 did confirm the killings, however concluded that "there is no evidence to suggest that the operation was intended to eliminate a certain category of people, especially those belonging to one ethnic group": M Brisset-Foucault *et al.*, *Report of the Independent International Commission of Inquiry on the Events at Kibeho April 1995* (Kigali, 18 May 1995), p. 7.

[32] In the case of the Ethiopian national trials (convened under Art. 281 of the 1957 Penal Code of the Empire of Ethiopia (Proclamation No. 158 of 1957)), public debate has been essentially forbidden. According to memoranda issued by the Office of the Special Prosecutor, the trials of the Dergue and other participants in the "Red Terror" have as their mandate the two-fold task of establishing for public knowledge and for posterity a historical record of the abuses of the Mengistu regime, as well as of bringing those criminally respon-sible for human rights violations and/or corruption to justice: yet it is a historical record the government is keeping a very tight reign on. A Chamber ruling prohibits critical commen-tary of these trials: the only reports are the daily ones given by government journalists.

An approach which locates responsibility purely at the individual level will freeze identities. In the context of Rwanda, the Hutu will remain killer and the Tutsi victim. In the Rwandan national legal proceedings, there is no process at the official level which might allow for an explanation other than the Hutu perpetration of violence against Tutsi victims. There is no room for an explanation of the political dimension to the genocide or its parameters. The division between Hutu and Tutsi is now extreme and the population is now more polarised than ever before. Although this can be expected in the wake of a genocide—and indeed it can be questioned whether there can be deep reconciliation at all in the wake of such crime— the approach taken by the Rwandan government certainly does not encourage or stimulate societal reconstruction.

The explanation which is reflected in the path taken by the Rwandan government is one in which "ethnic hatred" fuelled attacks against Tutsis in Rwanda, that individual Hutus took it upon themselves to kill their neighbours. It denies the level of orchestration by the elites which saw the training of the Interhamwe for an estimated 18 months before the killings began, the initial killing of moderate Hutu and Tutsi leaders who would have opposed the genocidal plan, and the role played by the Interhamwe and supportive officials at the commune and cell level. Clearly many individual Hutus did take it upon themselves to "settle old scores" and join the violence. But many did not. There are known instances of Hutu who hid Tutsis. Situating responsibility only at the individual level does not account for the genocide. Genocide does not just happen, it is not the "inevitable" result of long-standing divisions. It is planned and systematic, and it relies on the exaggeration of division and the coercion of segments of populations in order to fulfil the vision of a political elite. The revelation of this is a crucial part of the "truth-telling" function of legal process.

While official rhetoric supporting societal reconciliation can be heard in Rwanda, there are few officially supported or endorsed attempts on the ground to achieve this reconciliation. On the other hand, the greatest emphasis has been on fostering division through law, the use of law in the form of the national trials against *génocidaires* as an essentially political tool. The interest of the government is not in justice in a broad sense, but in justice as retribution and a means of consolidating power. Criminal law is being used as a tool for "containment", for sealing the society in its differences: Hutu and Tutsi, killer and victim. Rather than law being a window to the future, it stops at addressing the past. The vast numbers of alleged *génocidaires* in jails have played an important role for the government in fostering rule by fear. The threat of being accused of involvement in the genocide is real for all Hutus. The connections—and thus any solidarity— between the new urban elite and their rural Tutsi brethren (who were the victims of the 1994 killings) are said to be slight.[33] As Gérard Prunier

---

[33] Prunier stresses that rather than delineating between Hutus and Tutsis, the more

writes, although Tutsi talk about "national reconciliation", in practice they act as if all Hutus were *génocidaires* and bear a collective guilt.[34]

In this political context, the statement in the preamble to the Organic Law No. 08/96 of 30 August 1996 which established the trial process, that "...in order to achieve reconciliation and justice in Rwanda, it is essential that the culture of impunity be eradicated forever", can be viewed as mere decoration. The decision by the government to resurrect customary law and formally establish *"gacaca"* tribunals to try sections of the accused, can in this light be viewed as a strategy to move quickly through the estimated 122,000 persons still in Rwanda's jails on genocide charges, rather than a better or fairer form of adjudication.

Negotiated transitions

Negotiated transition presents some different issues to the non-negotiated transition. The securing of a broad base of acceptance of the new state of affairs can mean a path bordering on amnesia is taken, or it can form the basis for an inclusionary institutional approach. South Africa is an example of the latter. The post-Communist transition in East-central Europe lies somewhere in between.

The South African Truth and Reconciliation Commission has been a nationwide public process, or at least one which consciously attempted to be that. The TRC defined apartheid as state crime. It identified the individual and the institutional actors, and was designed with these parameters in mind. The combination of individual human rights violations hearings and institutional hearings was a recognition that to look at one or the other in isolation was neither to gain the full story, nor to apportion responsibility accurately. The combination worked in that not only could individual stories now be located within institutional perspectives, but also

important division in Rwanda has always been between moderates and extremists, both Hutu and Tutsi. This is clear in post-1994 Rwanda. Although in the wake of the genocide, a more moderate approach was discussed by members of government, with the rise of the extremists in the government, this changed to a more punitive approach. In August 1995, three senior Hutu members of the government were sacked: the Prime Minister Faustin Twagiramungu (the designated Prime Minister of the Arusha Accords, sworn in in the wake of the genocide), the Minster of the Interior, Seth Sendashonga, and the Minster of Justice, Alphonse-Marie Nkkubito. The subsequent Minister of the Interior, Colonel Alexis Kanyarengwe, described by Prunier as a former Hutu power devotee and willing tool of the RPF's Tutsi power structure during the war years (he joined in 1990 after ten years in exile, the consequence of a failed *coup d'état* against his former close associate, General Habyarimina), was forced to resign in March 1997. Prunier notes that his removal is a symbol of the total elimination of the Hutu community as a political partner in the so-called "coalition government": G Prunier, "'Rwanda: The Social, Political and Economic Situation in June 1997", *Writenet* Issue Paper, July 1997, p. 8.

[34] *Ibid.*, p. 5.

that the parameters of the crime as a political crime could be recognised and analysed as such.

Mahmood Mamdani commented that "the power of the [Truth and Reconciliation] Commission is really to define the terms, to set the terms of a social debate",[35] and in this sense is quite different from the International Tribunals for former Yugoslavia and Rwanda. No matter how much South Africans may try to ignore it or argue vehemently against it, the TRC has become a reference point around which the past and the future can be discussed and debated. It was created as a public forum,[36] a structure within which "ordinary people" can scrutinise and face up to their place, their role and the harm they either experienced, committed, or observed, within the apartheid regime. Many South Africans may have needed to have nothing to do with the TRC—they may be neither victim nor perpetrator—yet the TRC may change the reference points of their lives in a way in which the change of government did not. Governmental change can be explained as a political exercise, put down to politics and regime change. The TRC, however, forced many people, mainly white South Africans, to engage with the reality of apartheid in a way in which they had never previously been forced to do. It forced many South Africans to confront their place in this system. Its very presence provides a tangible set of reference points to which people were and are forced to respond.

Thus the TRC process became something much more than a legal process. As the journalist Antjie Krog wrote, in respect to the process of amnesty within the TRC, it has become the only forum where South Africans can say: "We may not have committed a human rights abuse, but we want to say that what we did—or didn't do—was wrong and that we're sorry". She relates a story of six black youths walking into the TRC's offices in Cape Town, shortly before midnight on Saturday, 10 May 1997, the final deadline for amnesty applications. They filled out the forms and took the oath. Their application read: "Amnesty for Apathy".[37] In all this, not only did the TRC provide the space within which a "legal" accounting of the past could take place, it also stimulated processes outside of this framework. The success of the TRC is that in its being a public, inclusive, and holistic process, it can be said to be an enduring process. This is

---

[35] M Mamdani, *Truth and Reconciliation Commission Public Discussion: "Transforming Society Through Reconciliation: Myth or Reality?"*, Cape Town, 12 March 1998, p. 24, TRC website www.truth.org.za. He has argued, however, that in not facing up to the "banal reality" of apartheid—the reality of Pass Laws, forced removals, Bantu education, the reality of racialised poverty alongside racialised wealth—the TRC has missed this opportunity. A Commission that does face up to its truth, notes Mamdani, would be a Commission that would put social, not criminal justice, at its forefront: Mamdani, p. 27.

[36] Note the inclusion of an elective directed apology within the amnesty hearings. In addition, public fora which addressed the topic of reconciliation were established by the TRC.

[37] A Krog, *Country of My Skull* (South Africa, Random House, 1998), pp. 121–2.

something that processes of lustration in the post-communist countries, or even individual war crimes trials, cannot claim.

The lustration procedures and the opening of secret service files are processes which function at an individual level. Lustration procedures operate as a dialogue between the State and the individual. Although the process has stimulated some societal discussion,[38] it does not consciously involve a broader section of the population, it does not seek to address those who may have been the most responsible for abuses committed,[39] nor does it address the crimes committed in a holistic manner. Similarly, the access given to secret service files (for example, in the former East Germany), is also individually-oriented. It is an individual, not a national process. The recognition and official inclusion of the institutional parameters of State crimes should not, of course, avoid individual responsibility. What it can do, however, is avoid the cementing of identities into killer and victim, and encourage the acknowledgement of a wider range of responsibilities across the whole of the political community.

LAW AND RECONCILIATION

Reconciliation as multi-dimensional

Reconciliation has been defined by one commentator as meaning at its core the restoration of relationships, the rebuilding of trust, and the overcoming of animosity.[40] It can occur at the national, the communal and the personal levels. It can take the form of a reckoning of two communities, of two nations, or a bringing together of two persons. In all cases it is a multi-layered process, marked by certain acts. Although the term "healing" is often used in discussions of reconciliation, healing is something different from reconciliation. The paths of healing and reconciliation have the same beginning—acknowledgement of harm and the establishment of what happened—but the path of healing, for individuals, communities and nations, is a different but connected one. Reconciliation has a public dimension to it that healing does not necessarily have.

[38] See J Siklova, "Lustration or the Czech Way of Screening", (1996) 5:1 *East European Constitutional Review* pp. 57–62.

[39] The focus of the lustration process is narrow, targeting those who are presently in official positions. Those formerly in official public positions, who may now work in the private sector, are immune from any penalisation. This means that many who were the most culpable, the higher political elites, if they avoid the public sphere and go into private business, can also avoid censure for their actions. There are many of the old nomenclature, now operating (and influencing) the private sphere. See A Zybertowicz, *W Uscisku Sluzb Tajnych (In Secret Services' Embrace)* (Warszawa, Antyk, 1993).

[40] P Gobodo-Madikizela (Chairperson), *Truth and Reconciliation Commission Public Discussion: "Transforming Society Through Reconciliation: Myth or Reality?"*, Cape Town, 12 March 1998, p. 1.

National reconciliation and personal reconciliation in the wake of State crime may be different, yet they require as a basis the same dimension of public acknowledgement, public recognition of harm, and public accountability. They require the same reckoning, the same restoration of goods and of rights.

If enduring reconciliation—structural reconciliation—is to be achieved, then this must be framed by institutional change. This can take the form of the establishment or restoration of rights, the creation of new types of institutions, the return of land or belongings, or the establishment of processes of restitution. Such institutional reconstruction provides a necessary public dimension to societal reconstruction.

Reconciliation without a level playing field is not full reconciliation. The stretching out of the hand should be from equal positions of power. In this way we can conceive of Australia as an example of a *stagnating* transition:[41] despite the *Mabo* decision, the nation has not moved far along the road of institutional reconstruction, because of its political failure to acknowledge publicly the dispossession of the Aboriginal people, to acknowledge publicly the kinds of harm perpetrated, to address this on an institutional level, and to provide an official apology. Without this institutional level, it can be questioned how enduring the processes of reconciliation at the civil societal level can be.

And this is the key point: reconciliation requires a structural and institutional dimension (justice, rights, law) for its sustainability. It is not that reconciliation cannot possibly occur without justice—on a personal level it may do—but rather that in its public dimension reconciliation is dependent upon a framework of rights and justice; a framework, ultimately, of institutional change. Institutional support is thus a necessary, but not a sufficient, condition for processes of reconciliation. Processes of forgiveness, mercy, and healing are locally contingent, and they cannot be thought to be determined by legal decision-making or legal processes[42] since that which makes reconciliation enduring is conditional both on the institutional structure and on local factors.

Enduring reconciliation may not occur in the first instance, even with the structural institutional dimension contributed to by legal process. The temporal dimensions of reconciliation are different to those of other processes such as accountability. It may not occur in the first generation, nor even in the second generation—it may never fully occur. All law can do is attempt to stimulate this process. What the state can do is, to push for

---

[41] I am grateful to Valerie Kerruish for this point.

[42] For example, the centrality of religion, in particular Christianity, in South Africa, meant that the design of the TRC with its emphasis on confession and confrontation, as well as the language used (healing and forgiveness were central terms) was both in the main acceptable and effective in opening up channels of communication between South Africans. The design and language of the TRC may not have the same impact elsewhere.

structural harmony—not for love, but for tolerance and harmony, ways of "living together". This can be done through a policy of amnesia, but this is clearly a risk (as might be demonstrated by Tito's policy of suppression of ethnic and religious identities in the former Yugoslavia which was also a suppression of the particular roles played by these groups during the Second World War). It is far better to push for this through a policy of transparency and accountability, and to move away from any kind of enduring stigmatisation. If groups are to continue living together it is an important question for new governments to ask how divides will be healed, and thus, how reconciliation may come about. If, on the other hand, they wish to use these divides to their own political advantage (as can be seen in Rwanda and in the former Yugoslavia in part), the question of reconciliation will only be a rhetorical, not a real one.

Law and the debate on reconciliation

One of the most striking features of the role of law in both South Africa and Australia is how it has in so many ways framed the debate on reconciliation. The Australian *Mabo* decision, with its repudiation of the doctrine of *terra nullius* and appeal to the "enduring values of all Australians", created a foundational moment in its institutional recognition of a different historical narrative, opening up a public space for discussion of reconciliation. In South Africa, law is consciously aimed at societal reconciliation, eschewing more traditional Western notions of accountability in favour of a new model. The architects of the Truth and Reconciliation Commission presupposed that reconciliation is a necessary institutional goal.

There is unfortunately no guarantee that the combination of official acknowledgement and statement of facts will even mean acceptance of the perpetration of harm and this "new reality". This can be observed in the Australian case, where the (partial) "statement of the facts" in *Mabo* has not ensured the uniform acceptance of these facts.[43] It has also sparked— or been the cover for—a wave of "not in my backyard" racisms (which included land claims scare-mongering, where land owners were falsely told that all Australian land was subject to native title claims). As Udesthra Naidoo has written in this context:

> "We believed that the truth would dispel the web of lies, myths and stereotypes
> that sustain racial antagonisms. We believed that the truth would lead to recon-
> ciliation, which we understood in fairly vague terms, as an era of racial
> harmony. To an extent, we were right. Arguably, we could point to an
> increased awareness of social injustice, past and present. But it is impossible to

---

[43] Even the impact of the *Stolen Generation Report* can be questioned in light of the statements made in April 2000 by Australian Aboriginal Affairs Minister, Senator Herron, that "there was no such thing as a Stolen Generation".

ignore the existence of a wide array of other responses ranging from indifference and excuses right through to a rise in racism, in light of which our initial optimism was a little ill-founded, if not naive".[44]

In tying the success of reconciliation to legal successes, it can be argued that an unnecessarily overbearing link is drawn. Legal clarity will not necessarily result in the success of reconciliation. If victims' claims are met, this does not mean that reconciliation will ensue. What it will mean is that a firmer base for reconciliation on the societal level will have been established. It will also mean that a type of political reconciliation will have been achieved. The danger in firmly tying reconciliation to legal discourse is that this could hinder the process of societal reconciliation. This is because legal concepts often cannot accommodate—indeed cannot even recognise—reconciliation's demands. Current Australian property law, for example, which deals with issues of Aboriginal native title according to an understanding of Western land ownership, is based on a fundamental misunderstanding of what it is that the land means to indigenous people, being based as it is on a non-indigenous philosophy that land can be bought and sold, given and taken.[45] As such, there are severe disjunctures between the law dealing with these issues and any hopes of deep reconciliation, if reconciliation is to be based on understanding, not just on attempts at settling accounts, important as this is.

Rather than law opening up discussion, law has in many ways confined the discussion. For law certainty is the holy grail, whereas certainty is not all that reconciliation need be about. Reconciliation is a process: a process which is uncertain, located in a no-man's-land in which a new relationship is attempted to be forged in a gulf between different cultures and understandings, and often after years of conflict or hatred. Yet, as I have suggested, enduring reconciliation is conditional upon official institutional—legal—acknowledgment of harm perpetrated. Without the authority of law and political-legal acts which frame and kick-start these processes, any reconciliation has less chance of being an enduring one. Yet the substance of reconciliation, that which *becomes* reconciliation, that fuels the process and permeates the institutional frame, cannot be spoken of legally or take the form of legal discourse. Rather, it must take a different track, grounded in the realities of peoples' lives and fears and hopes. It is an uncertain path, and one which law can only support from a distance.

---

[44] U Naidoo, "The Truth Hurts: Psychoanalytic Speculations on Racism", (1998) 25 *Melbourne Journal of Politics* p. 133.

[45] See J Clarke, "Racial non-discrimination standards and proposed amendments to the Native Title Act", Australian Institute of Aboriginal and Torres Strait Islanders Studies Issues Paper 16/1997, pp. 4–5, J Clarke, "The Native Title Amendment Bill 1997: a different order of uncertainty?", Centre for Aboriginal Economic Policy Research (ANU) Discussion Paper 144/1997, pp. 23, 26.

All law can do is to stimulate conditions for reconciliation. It can do this through providing the building blocks, in the form of authoritative acknowledgement of the past, and, in partnership with the political process, by ensuring the optimum institutional framework for reconciliation. Political reconciliation will only occur once certain structural and institutional changes have been made. Yet even if a victim community is "restored" politically, this does not mean that a deep level of harmony will have been reached within that society. That is dependent on further processes which are outside the law.

CONCLUSION

In the wake of genocide and state crime, an enduring reconciliation cannot be achieved without just and accountable mechanisms, without the political will for this to happen, and without a strong institutional framework, including the fundamental restoration and respect of rights. Foregoing judgement will not necessarily achieve reconciliation. Mechanisms of accountability are essential; how they are designed, whether the political will exists to support an integrative approach, and whether local realities will support the opening of such channels, all impact on the potential stimulation of processes of reconciliation. The belief that reconciliation somehow requires a "lesser" use of law, or even the absence of law, must be questioned. This chapter has suggested that building into the legal process the investigation of certain crimes *as* State crimes allows communities and societies to develop their own formative structures and spaces for reconstruction. These will be developed and acted upon outside of law, but can, potentially, be fuelled by law and legal political acts which themselves will come to be seen as foundational moments.

This chapter has attempted to show that the role which legal proceedings play does differ, according to the types of crime addressed, and according to the circumstances and the form of the legal proceedings. A State-initiated spirit of reconciliation, reflected in legal institutional design, has the potential to create a climate where such acts of truth, justice and reconstruction can occur, outside of law. Equally a State-initiated pursuit and authoritative articulation of truth may lay the foundations for reconstruction, justice and then reconciliation. These dynamics can be stimulated outside of law, however they must be supported by the law in its establishment of what happened, its acknowledgement of harm, and its establishment of structures to uphold justice and to promote restitution for victim communities.

Even when these conditions are met, legal process cannot guarantee reconciliation. For example, the TRC by itself cannot be *the* forum for reconciliation and reconstruction. It can provide an initial structure but it cannot be the sustaining structure. It may provide certain essentials: the knowledge of what apartheid meant, the "facts" of what was done, an institutional push for reconciliation, the basis for further reconstruction, a means of restitution. Yet it has a certain life-span and culminates in a Final Report. The most crucial role law must play is in establishing these possibilities: institutional and societal reconstruction and reconciliation. What is significant then is for law to constitute spaces for reconstruction and reconciliation that are just and accountable, rather than to pursue these objectives as legal objectives. In so doing, law as formal and state-authorised has the potential to stimulate and to frame the normative sphere, and create conditions through which societies may find ways of living together.

Part III

Memory and the Ethics of Reconciliation

9

Justice or Reconciliation?
The Politicisation of the Holocaust
in the Kastner Trial

LEORA BILSKY

It was not the trials of Nazi perpetrators such as Adolf Eichmann that first brought the Holocaust to the attention of Israeli courts but rather trials involving their Jewish victims. In the 1950s the Israeli Law of Punishment of the Nazis and their Collaborators led to a number of trials in which judges were obliged to confront the actions of the Jewish leaders and functionaries during the Holocaust.[1] These trials did not receive much public attention and were mainly discussed in the communities of survivors involved in them. One trial, however, stands out as the exception: Criminal case 124/53, The State of Israel against Malchiel Gruenvald, better known as "the Kastner trial" which took place in the district court in Jerusalem during the years 1954–55. This was the first Holocaust trial that succeeded in making itself relevant to the Israeli public at large. How did this change come about? Was there something that distinguished the facts of this case from the many forgotten trials conducted at that time under the Law of Punishment of the Nazis and their Collaborators? No doubt, the Kastner trial differed in important respects from other "Holocaust trials": not only was it the first (and only) trial that dealt with the actions of a Jewish leader as opposed to those of low-ranking Jewish functionaries (Kapos and policemen), but the central issue it raised—the negotiations conducted between Kastner and Eichmann about the "blood for trucks" bargain—had the power to capture the imagination of ordinary people. Moreover, the fact that this case was brought to court as a criminal libel trial concerning the free speech of an Israeli citizen endowed it with far more immediate interest

---

[1] Law of Punishment for Nazis and their Collaborators, 5710-5950, 4 L.S.I. 154; H Yablonka, "The Law of Punishment for Nazis and their Collaborators: History, Implementation and Point of View", (1996) 82 *Kathedra* (Hebrew); T Segev, *The Seventh Million: The Israelis and the Holocaust* (Haim Watzman trans.), New York, Hill and Wang, 1993), pp. 260–2, Y Weitz, "The Law for Punishment of the Nazis and their Collaborators as Image and Reflection of Public Opinion", (1996) 82 *Kathedra* (Hebrew) 153.

for the Israeli public than the trials judged under the retroactive and extra-territorial Law of Punishment of Nazis and their Collaborators. These differences, I argue, were not sufficient to explain the fierce political debate about Israeli collective identity and memory that the Kastner trial engendered. Rather, it was the brilliant defence lawyer associated with the right-wing Revisionist Party who was largely responsible for its transformation from a trial about past events in a distant land into a full-blown political trial, perceived by the Israeli public to touch upon the most urgent issues of the day. This chapter is devoted to exploring the transformation that took place during the trial and the role of the defence lawyer in effectuating it.

The Kastner trial began as a libel trial against an old Hungarian Jew, Malchiel Gruenvald, who was accused of defaming the Zionist leader of Hungarian Jewry, Rudolph (Israel) Kastner, by alleging that he had collaborated with the Nazis.[2] Kastner had lived in Budapest during the Second World War and organised, together with other Zionist activists (among them Yoel and Hanzi Brandt), a committee for the rescue of Jewish refugees who were fleeing to Hungary in an attempt to escape the Nazi terror in neighbouring countries. After the 1944 German take-over of Hungary, Kastner had served as chief negotiator with Adolf Eichmann, the top Nazi official responsible for the deportation of Jews to German concentration camps, and with other Nazi officials on behalf of Hungary's Jewish community. The "blood for goods" deal sought by Kastner and seriously considered by the Nazis was intended to save the lives of nearly one million Jews in exchange for ten thousand trucks to be delivered to the German Army. This ambitious goal was not achieved and approximately 400,000 Hungarian Jews were eventually sent to their deaths in Auschwitz. However, Kastner did succeed in saving a group of 1,685 Jews who were shuttled to safety in Switzerland. This transport included a disproportionate number of Kastner's friends and relatives.

After the war, Kastner's involvement in this capacity was questioned; at the 1946 Zionist Congress he was accused by a Hungarian activist of being a cynical opportunist who had selfishly sacrificed Hungarian Jewry in return for his personal safety. Kastner responded with a libel suit against the accuser, submitted to the Congress's Honor Court. He also wrote a long report accounting for all his war-time activities in Hungary. However, the panel decided that it did not have enough evidence to reach a conclusive decision and recommended that the matter be investigated in depth in the future.[3] Thereafter, Kastner moved to Israel and became active in the

[2] For detailed descriptions of the Kastner affair see T Segev, above n.1, pp. 255–320; Y Weitz, *Ha-Ish she-Nirtsah Paamayim (The Man Who Was Murdered Twice)* (Jerusalem, Keter, 1995); Y Bauer, *Jews for Sale? Jewish Negotiations, 1933–1945* (New Haven, Yale University Press, 1994), pp.145–71. For a discussion of the decisions in the trial and appellate courts see Lahav P: *Judgment in Jerusalem: Chief Justice Simon Agranat and the Zionist Century* (Berkeley, University of Califonia Press, 1997), pp. 123–5, 132–3, 142–4.
[3] Weitz, above n. 1, pp. 60–1.

ruling Labor Party, Mapai; by 1952 he served as spokesman for the Ministry of Trade and Industry. Kastner was also on the Mapai candidate list for the first and second Knessets (Israeli Parliament). Though he did not get elected, there was a good chance he would be successful in the third elections to be held in 1955.

It was at this time that Malchiel Gruenvald embarked on a campaign against Kastner. A devoted member of Ha-Mizrahi (the religious wing of the Zionist movement) and a refugee who had lost most of his family in Hungary, Gruenvald had a political as well as a personal agenda. In addition to seeking to expose Kastner's crimes, Gruenvald hoped to denounce Mapai, demand Kastner's removal, and facilitate the appointment of a commission of inquiry to investigate the events that had led to the decimation of Hungary's Jews. The target of his criticism was the negotiations that Kastner had conducted with Adolf Eichmann.[4] Gruenvald asserted that these negotiations had facilitated the destruction of Hungarian Jewry while benefiting Kastner personally. In a pamphlet he sent to Ha-Mizrahi members in the summer of 1952 Gruenvald phrased his charge that Kastner had collaborated with the Nazis in vivid and offensive terms:

> "The smell of a corpse scratches my nostrils! This will be a most excellent funeral! Dr. Rudolf Kastner should be eliminated! For three years I have been awaiting this moment to bring to trial and pour the contempt of the law upon this careerist, who enjoys Hitler's acts of robbery and murder. On the basis of his criminal tricks and because of his collaboration with the Nazis . . . I see him as a vicarious murderer of my dear brothers."[5]

According to Gruenvald's allegations, Kastner had become friendly with the Nazis through their negotiations and as a result had been allowed to save his relatives and a small number of Jewish dignitaries. In return, Kastner had let the Nazis use him by not informing Hungarian Jews of the real destination of the deportation trains. Gruenvald also alleged that Kastner, in collusion with some Nazis, had stolen Jewish money and then helped save the life of Kurt Becher (one of the Nazi officers with whom Kastner negotiated) with favourable testimony at the Nuremberg war crimes trials. Warned by the Attorney General that he either sue Gruenvald for libel or resign from his government post, Kastner sued, and since he was a senior government official he was represented at the trial by the Attorney General, Haim Cohen, himself. In the course of the trial, however, it was Kastner, not Gruenvald, who found himself on the defensive.

---

[4] For a detailed examination of the negotiations see Y Bauer, above n.2, pp. 145–71.

[5] Translated by P Lahav, above n. 2, p. 123. The Hebrew quotation in S Rosenfeld, *Tik Plili 124: Mishpat Gruenvald-Kastner (Criminal Trial 124–The Gruenvald-Kastner Trial)* (Tel Aviv, Karni, 1955), pp. 16–17. The full version is quoted and translated into English by Segev, above n. 1, pp. 257–8.

Shmuel Tamir, the defence attorney, answered the accusation against his client with the response: "He spoke the truth". Tamir did not deny that Gruenvald had written the offending pamphlet. Quite the contrary—he set out to prove that everything in it was true. Tamir claimed that had the Jews been informed of the Nazi extermination plan, many of them could perhaps have escaped to Romania, revolted against the Germans, or sent calls for help to the outside world, all of which could have significantly slowed down the Nazi killing process.

Tamir's main aim was to turn the trial into a political trial, a means for delegitimating the ruling Mapai party. But here he confronted formidable obstacles. In the 1950s the Israeli public regarded the Holocaust as belonging to "another planet", and saw the Holocaust survivors who had immigrated to Israel as "Others" to the Israeli collective. This attitude was supported by the prevailing Zionist ideology known as "the Negation of the Diaspora", according to which the state of Israel epitomised a rupture with the two thousands years of Jewish life in the Diaspora. It envisioned a "New Jew" who would develop in the land of Israel with characteristics diametrically opposed to those of the Diaspora Jew. The New Jew was to be connected to the land, leading a productive life and relying on self-help in economic and security matters, as symbolised by the figures of the *halutz* (the pioneer farmer and builder) and the *shomer* (defender and warrior). This ideological background can explain why the Holocaust trials of the 1950s had until then been perceived by the Israeli public as internal matters involving the communities of survivors alone. Thus, Tamir had to find a way to make a trial that dealt with events that had occurred in that "other planet" of occupied Europe relevant to the political controversies of the day.

The Kastner affair could have signalled a first questioning of the Zionist ideology that opposed the proud "New Jew" of the land of Israel to the submissive Jews of the Diaspora. After all, Kastner was a *Zionist* leader who had chosen negotiations and co-operation with the Nazis rather than military resistance. This moment of recognition, when the simplified stereotype of myth confronted the complexities of concrete historical realities, had an explosive potential. It could have led to a searching critique of this aspect of Zionist ideology, and in particular, of its disparaging treatment of Holocaust survivors who had not belonged to the resistance. Tamir, however, who had no intention of undermining an ideology he himself upheld, was quick to notice the political potential of the Kastner trial and chose to take it in another direction that could be used to sully the Zionist credentials of his political opponents. Thus, instead of examining Zionist ideology in light of the historical reality of occupied Europe, he chose to distort that reality to make it fit the ideological dictum, thus strengthening the blindness that this ideology produced. In other words, Tamir sought to show that it was not the ideology that was at fault but the leaders (Kastner and, by association, Mapai) who had failed to live up to it. In order to sustain this argument Tamir skillfully exploited the legal process, building his case on three central strategies which involved (a) adapting historical reality to the binary structure of Zionist ideology; (b) re-enacting past trauma in the courtroom; and (c) manipulating the legal discourse of "truth".

A SOCIO-LEGAL BINARY STRUCTURE

The legal process of Israeli law is adversarial. The struggle between the two sides—the prosecution and the defence—generates a drama, which is intensified in criminal proceedings that continue from day to day and take place within a relatively short period of time. The binary structure of the trial, which creates the impression that there are only two possibilities—acquittal or conviction—was perfectly suited to the story Tamir wished to promote, according to which people were faced with two mutually exclusive choices—heroic resistance as opposed to collaboration and treason. The formal positions of prosecution and defence in a criminal trial thus came to symbolise two ideological positions: co-operation and defiance. Kastner's actions were associated with the cowardly path of collaboration while Tamir's political stance was associated with the heroic path of resistance. The entire intermediate range of actions between these two poles, such as the different ways in which the underground movement co-operated with the official *Judenrat*, was disregarded. The binary framework thus excluded serious consideration of the issues actually faced by Kastner and other Jewish leaders who had to take decisions on the basis of weighing probabilities without the benefit of hindsight, the immense difficulties of saving the victims, the impending end of the war as a factor that was considered in the negotiations, etc. Moreover, this binary structure (both ideological and legal) that was imposed on the facts obscured the tragic nature of the decisions taken by people who were forced to make the cruel choice of sacrificing the few in the hope of saving the many.

Tamir presented his arguments within the framework of the Zionist narrative that exalted the New Jew as the opposite of everything represented by the Jew in the Diaspora. According to Tamir, Kastner's compliance with the authorities was typical Diaspora behaviour, which had led to full collaboration with the Nazis and to the annihilation of the Jewish people of Hungary. The Zionist alternative to "Kastnerism", however, could not come from Tamir's client, Malchiel Gruenvald, himself a typical Diaspora Jew who was ultimately a marginal character in the legal drama.[6] Rather, it was Defence Attorney Tamir himself who was offered as a model

---

[6] Judge Halevi even had difficulties remembering Gruenvald's name. See Segev, above n. 1, p. 255.

of the proud *Sabra* (native-born Israeli Jew). The contrast between the "new" and "old" Jew was especially evident in the cross-examination of Kastner. Tamir's eloquent rhetoric and perfect fluency in Hebrew were in stark contrast to the broken Hebrew of Kastner's testimony, which was filled with "foreign" expressions.[7] Moreover, by managing to transform his position in the trial from that of a formal defence lawyer into that of a *de facto* prosecutor, Tamir re-enacted the national myth of heroism—the weak and few overcoming the strong and many by turning a defence into a victorious offensive.

The Zionist narrative, which Tamir so skillfully put to his use in the trial, was well known to the Israeli audience and made it receptive to his critique. Although Tamir's criticism failed to reveal the sordid secrets and sensational facts that he promised, he succeeded in transforming his defence of Gruenvald into a political attack by extending the patterns of behaviour he had identified in Nazi-occupied Hungary to the situation in pre-state Palestine, implying that the leadership of the Yishuv (the Jewish population in Mandatory Palestine) during the war had played the role not of the "heroic Zionist" but, like Kastner, of collaborators with the foreign ruler.

During the years of the Holocaust, one of the central divisions among the different Jewish political groups in Palestine had involved the relationship with the British authorities. Mapai, the leading party, had chosen co-operation with the British in their war efforts against the Nazis, while the Revisionists had believed that the military struggle for liberation from the British in Palestine should continue. At first glance, the Kastner trial seemed irrelevant to this controversy since it dealt with the actions of Jewish leaders in Nazi-occupied Hungary. However, in his effort to discredit the Mapai party, Tamir used Kastner's political affiliation with Mapai leaders to imply an underlying resemblance in their political approach. Both, he argued, had preferred negotiations and co-operation to military resistance. In Europe this choice had proved to be catastrophic since it had facilitated the Nazi annihilation of European Jewry. The trial, in Tamir's vision, should serve to demonstrate this "lesson" to the Israeli public, a warning against the pragmatic path of negotiations. This, he argued, was the essential meaning of the Zionist message of the "negation of the Diaspora", since Jews in the Diaspora throughout the ages had relied on compliance and co-operation with the authorities for their survival. The Israelis, as the New Jews, should abandon this path and criticise the Mapai leadership for demonstrating a "Diaspora mentality". In short, the trial should serve to legitimate the Revisionist approach as the only "authentic" Zionism capable of guarding against the recurrence of similar catastrophes to the Jewish people in the future. It was here for the first time that the political path of "negotiations" acquired the defeatist

---

[7] Weitz, above n. 2, p. 126.

connotation that was to be evoked in future political debates concerning the legitimacy of the negotiations of Israeli leaders with Arab and Palestinian leaders.

By removing the Mapai leaders from the category of "heroic Zionists" Tamir rendered this slot vacant. In Tamir's version, the right-wing underground movements (to which Tamir himself had belonged) which had urged that all contacts with the British cease, were the only ones fit to bear that title. He completed his subversive narrative by representing the Jewish population in occupied Europe not as passive victims but as heroes ready for battle who had been misled by incompetent leaders and had therefore gone "like lambs to the slaughter". Tamir's revisionist history met little resistance, since the Israeli public did not have to make a major conceptual change, as would be required by a truly critical approach to the prevailing ideology, but merely had to switch the positions of the participants in a narrative with clearly defined roles. Moreover, it helped ordinary people deal with their own guilt feelings for not having done enough during the war to save their Jewish brethren, since the failure could now be attributed to an incompetent and deceitful leadership.

Tamir's portrayal of the events was deliberately non-linear and non-chronological. Instead he opted for analogical story-telling, jumping constantly in space (Israel/Hungary) and in time (war-time/trial time) in order to make comparisons between Kastner's leadership in Hungary and Mapai's leadership in Palestine.[8] This analogical story-telling helped create a drama in black and white, since historical time with its elements of contingency, uncertainty and ambiguity was expelled from the courtroom. Moreover, this method transformed the audience into capable participants in the legal drama, because each one was invited to fill in the gaps in the story of Kastner by making analogies to what had happened in Mandatory Palestine and on the basis of his or her knowledge about the present. Since the actions of the leaders on both sides were depicted as determined by internal tendencies ("Diaspora mentality") rather than external exigencies, knowledge of historical details was not required. Gone also were the important differences between the situations in Hungary and in Palestine during the war, and the actions of leaders under colonial rule and in a sovereign state. In this narrative there was no longer a difference between

---

[8] Among the analogies, the analogy between Kastner's cover-up of the "Auschwitz secret" and the fact that the news about the Holocaust were kept quiet in Israel; between Kastner's collaboration with the Nazi's and the Mapai party leadership's collaboration with the British; between Kastner's responsibility for the failure of the paratroopers' operation in Hungary and Mapai's role in the failure of Yoel Brand's mission. A closer look at these analogies, however, demonstrate their implausibility. Tamir was making a contradictory argument: on the one hand, he condemned Kastner for collaboration saying that this road was futile from its inception, on the other hand, he blamed the leaders of Mapai for not co-operating with Kastner (by failing to attend to his messenger Yoel Brand) and attributed the responsibility for the failure of the negotiations with the Nazis onto them.

the past and the present. Unlike ordinary trials that are directed to determine the truth about past events, the Kastner trial was future-oriented, intended to encourage the public to draw lessons from the affair in order to choose between different courses of action in the future.

THE RE-ENACTMENT OF A PAST TRAUMA IN THE COURTROOM

"The prominent" versus "the masses"

Tamir's narrative offered an alternative framework in which to judge the actions of the Yishuv's leadership during the war. The trial thus went beyond a representation of past events to create connections and symbols that did not inhere in the events themselves but were the product of an analogical story-telling in the courtroom. However, in order to render historical events part of a living collective memory, it was not sufficient merely to switch the roles of the participants in the Zionist narrative. It was essential to revive the past and recreate the trauma in the courtroom. For this purpose Tamir relied on testimonial witnessing. Tamir's early recognition of the value of survivors' testimonies as a privileged site for memory preceded the proliferation of current studies on the issue of history and memory. Indeed, testimony has recently become a prevalent and important genre of non-fiction, and witnessing—typically, witnessing based on memory—has emerged as a widely used mode of access to the past and its traumatic occurrences. Recent studies reveal that testimonial witnessing transforms the audience itself into a secondary witness, but that its reception depends on the extent to which the audience is capable of real empathic listening.[9] However, as we shall see, Tamir was interested in reviving the trauma through the testimonies of eye-witnesses not in order to deepen historical understanding of the full complexity of the events but in order to reinforce his own political message,and he did not therefore bother to create the proper framework for real listening.[10]

---

[9] D LaCapra, *History and Memory after Auschwitz* (Ithaca and London, Cornell University Press, 1998).

[10] Psychoanalyst Dori Laub explains that "bearing witness to a trauma is, in fact, a process that includes the listener". See S Felman and D Laub, *Testimony—Crises of Witnesses in Literature, Psychoanalysis and History* (New York and London, 1992), p. 70. Therefore, to recover from a trauma it is not enough to tell the story. One's story has to be received by an empathic audience. However, people are often reluctant to listen to stories of traumatic experiences because the story "forces us to acknowledge that we [the listeners] are not in control of our own". See S J Brison, "Outliving Oneself: Trauma, Memory, and Personal Identity", in D Tietjens Meyers (ed), *Feminists Rethink the Self* (Westview Press, 1997), p. 26. On a societal level, Israeli society found it difficult to face a collective experience of such helplessness and horror and preferred to hear about the heroic moments of the ghetto fighters and Jewish partisans. In order to overcome the societal pressures on the survivors not to tell their stories, more than individual occasions of listening were needed.

Tamir used the structure of the testimonies in the trial in order to recreate the painful moment of "selection" between "the prominent Jews" who were rescued and the "Jewish masses" who were sent to their deaths. This tactic was made possible as the result of an unwise decision by the prosecution to call Kastner as its first witness in order to allow him to present his version of the events. Kastner's tendency to exaggerate, to be somewhat vague and to sometimes take more credit than he deserved may have worked to his advantage in his negotiations with the Nazis when he had had nothing substantial to offer, but was exploited by Tamir to Kastner's detriment in the trial.[11] Through his aggressive cross-examination of Kastner, Tamir exposed many weak points in his testimony. The prosecution, therefore, had to call a large number of "political" witnesses who had worked with Kastner to substantiate and complete his testimony. The witnesses for the prosecution included people like Menachem Bader, Ehud Avriel, Yoel Palgi and others who were prominent political figures and who had played key roles in rescue operations in Europe.[12] Some, like David Berman, had been *Judenrat* members and some held public positions in the young state of Israel.[13] By extending the scope of the trial and causing it to become more political, Tamir set a trap for the prosecution. Instead of countering the prosecution's well-known political witnesses with other well-known political figures—a move that in any case was not possible for Tamir because of his marginal position in Israeli politics—he decided to call a number of mostly unknown Holocaust survivors whose voices had not yet been heard by the Israeli public.[14] These people, from various walks of life and affiliated with a broad range of political parties, formed a vivid contrast with the witnesses for the prosecution, most of whom belonged to the Israeli socio-economic elite and were affiliated with Mapai. Tamir emphasised the fact that his witnesses

---

The solution of using the trial as a controlled environment in which survivors' testimony could gain such empathic listening was not attempted in the Kastner trial but had to wait for the Eichmann trial of the 1960s.

[11] Weitz, above n. 2, p. 353.

[12] Menachem Bader was a member of the left-wing Mapai party and a member of Knesset; Ehud Avriel was the Israeli delegate in Budapest and the director of the Prime Minister's office and the Finance Ministry.

[13] Witnesses like Prof. Benjamin Aktzin, dean of the law school at the Hebrew University, and Shmuel Benzur from the Foreign Ministry, were not connected directly to the affair and were summoned by the prosecution as part of its policy to call important people who would make a better impression on the court because of their public credentials. Weitz, above n. 2, p. 132.

[14] Among the survivors were Irena Hirsch, Yosef Kats, David Rozner, Paul Gross, Friedrich Mund, Eliezer Rozental. Weitz notes that the idea of bringing these witnesses, all survivors from Kastner's home town Kluz, all simple, hard-working people who had lost many of their relatives in the Holocaust, was a wise decision. "Their words sounded reliable and authentic, and the story they told was engaging" *ibid.*, p. 195. The contrast was also between the "simple people" and the "political elite".

were not affiliated with any particular political party, arguing that it proved that "the spontaneous truth" was on his side. Their true testimonies were being repressed by the authorities who had initiated the libel trial in order to keep them from the public gaze. Thus, the contrast between the prosecution's list of prominent political figures and the unknown witnesses of Tamir had the powerful effect of recreating the traumatic moment of "selection" within the courtroom. The result was a complex tale of a dual act of selection—the original selection of the few privileged Jews who had boarded Kastner's train, re-enacted by this second selection of "privileged witnesses" by the prosecution who had been summoned to defend Kastner.[15]

In order better to understand Tamir's procedural tactic we should consider the legal method of proving the truth through first-hand testimony and direct observation.[16] The law privileges the human voice as the basis for proving the truth. For this reason establishing the trustworthiness of the witness becomes an issue of critical importance in the trial. As Lawrence Douglas observes, "in this jurisprudential model, the witness identifies himself to the court before he tells the court what he has seen. His identity, once defined and secured, is considered anterior to, and enabling of, the act of bearing responsible witness".[17] Tamir was doubly burdened in this respect. The prevalent Zionist ideology of the day rendered the "ghetto fighters" and "resistance members" as the only trustworthy witnesses of the period.[18] Ordinary survivors, on the other hand, were deemed suspect. Their very survival was taken by Israelis to be a sign of their moral failure, an attitude that has been succinctly captured by Primo Levi: "the worst survived, that is the fittest: the best of all died".[19] These survivors were transformed into "victims" in the extreme sense of the word described by Lyotard, indicating those who cannot even express their victimisation because their words are considered unreliable.[20] The

---

[15] For a discussion of a similar educational technique of creating double-layered experience of the past as a device of memory in museum tours see T Katriel, "Remaking Place: Cultural Production in an Israeli Pioneer Museum", (1993) 5:2 *History and Memory*, 104–35.

[16] Strong (ed.), *McCormick on Evidence* (The West Group, 1992), pp. 37–40.

[17] L Douglas, "Wartime Lies: Securing the Holocaust in Law and Literature", in 7 *Yale Journal of Law and Humanities* 367–95, at 389.

[18] Throughout the 1950s the only historical accounts of the Holocaust in Israel were written by people associated with the Jewish resistance.

[19] P Levi, *The Drowned and the Saved* (W.Weaver trans.) (New York, Vintage Books, 1982), p. 9.

[20] "This is what a wrong would be: a damage accompanied by the loss of the means to prove the damage. This is the case if the victim is deprived of life, or of all her liberties, or of the freedom to make his or her ideas or opinions public, or simply of the right to testify to the damage, or even more simply if the testifying phrase itself is deprived of authority. In all these cases, to the privation constituted by the damage there is the added impossibility of bringing it to the knowledge of others, and in particular the knowledge of a tribunal": see

prosecution used this "economy" of uneven credibility and packed its list of witnesses with "heroes" and "political leaders". Tamir, because of his marginal political position, was left to rely on the testimonies of those considered to be the least reliable in the young Israeli society—the Auschwitz survivors. However, by using the symbolic structure of witnesses in the trial as a re-enactment of the past trauma of selection, Tamir was able to turn a disadvantage into an advantage. In his defence the very "respectability" of the prosecution's witnesses was presented as a sign of their unreliability, since they were the ones deemed most interested in "covering-up" the selection of themselves and their friends to be rescued by Kastner's train. In other words, the same logic that undermined the reliability of Holocaust survivors (the mere fact of their survival) was now used to discredit a specific group of survivors—the leaders—simply by virtue of their having belonged to the *Judenrat* or their present affiliation with the Mapai establishment. With this performative hyperbole Tamir transformed the "ordinary survivors" into reliable witnesses who were perceived by the public as doubly wronged, once by their Nazi persecutor, and again by the Israeli prosecution.

Giving Voice

The defence repeatedly declared its intention to allow the survivors, who had never before been given the chance to tell their stories in public, to report "the whole truth". However, a scrutiny of the actual testimonies reveals a different view of what went on in the trial. Legal rules of procedure limit the testimonies of witnesses in court, mainly by subjecting them to the form of questions and answers that are controlled by the attorneys. Tamir's questions did not allow for hesitation or confusion in his witnesses' testimonies. Their words were meant to be heard only insofar as they supported the Zionist "lesson" in favour of military resistance advanced by Tamir. Consequently, the question repeatedly presented by Tamir to the survivors was "What would you have done if you had known about the secret of Auschwitz?" The answer was inevitably that they would not have boarded the trains. Tamir's question took advantage of the understandable anger felt by the passengers of the death transports who had not been fortunate enough to be rescued by Kastner's train. His questions were aimed to elicit a simple answer, an answer that would place all the blame squarely on the leaders who had known about the atrocities but had not warned their communities about them. Any other answers, which suggested that the leaders' decision to co-operate with the Nazi authorities had been complex, influenced by the Nazis' own deceptions and by extremely uncertain circumstances, were presented by Tamir as efforts to

J-F Lyotard, *The Differend* G Van dAbbeele (trans), (Minneapolis, University of Minnesota Press, 1988), p. 5.

conceal the truth. He ignored the crucial issue of whether "knowing" about Auschwitz at that time could have been the same as comprehending its meaning. Thus, Tamir created the impression of breaking the silence about the Holocaust without actually giving the public a chance to listen to the accounts of Holocaust survivors in all their complexity and ambiguity.

The difficulty of listening to testimonies of Holocaust survivors within an ideological framework and within the constraints of legal questioning is particularly evident in Tamir's cross-examination of Hillel Danzig. Danzig had been affiliated with the Jewish Council in Kastner's home town, Kluz. Notwithstanding Danzig's efforts to explain the difficulty of judging past events in today's courtroom, his words were dismissed as perjurious and unreliable:

> "*Question:* . . .If you had known that the train was going to Auschwitz, how would you have acted in relation to your family and yourself?
>
> *Answer:* I don't know...I can think about it today and give you an answer, but it has nothing to do with the situation then, with what I would have done under those circumstances.
>
> *Question:* Why doesn't it have anything to do with it?
>
> *Answer:* Because we are sitting here today in completely different circumstances. What one asks and answers here in the state of Israel, after ten years, is not at all related to the situation then.
>
> *Question:* Can you remember the situation then?
>
> *Answer:* I remember. But I can't tell you what I would have done given the way things are now. Since all the Jews boarded those trains, I guess that my family and I would probably have gotten on the train too, if there were no other possibility".[21]

In his study of the testimonies of Holocaust survivors, Lawrence Langer discovered a split between past and present experiences, which prevented the survivors from presenting a coherent chronological account.[22] The rules pertaining to legal evidence are based on the assumption that there is chronological continuity between the past and the present, and any discrepancy is interpreted as a sign of lying or evading the truth. The law is accustomed to dealing with a witness who either does or does not remember, but lacks tools that are sensitive enough to deal with a witness who remembers all too well but is incapable of reproducing the past in the present. Thus, in Kastner's trial, the silencing of the survivors took on a new dimension—even when they came to testify in public, their testimonies were not really heard.

[21] Recited in the court's decision, C.C. 124/53 Attorney General vs. Greunvald P.M. 44 at pp. 85–8.

[22] L Langer, *Holocaust Testimonies: the Ruins of Memory* (New Haven and London, 1991).

Several years later, in the Eichmann trial, the Attorney General Gideon Hausner faced a similar problem. In order to facilitate meaningful listening to survivors' testimonies he decided to relax some of the rules of procedure, in particular, the format of questions and answers.[23] Each personal narrative found its place in Hausner's comprehensive narrative about the history of Nazism that portrayed the different stages of the destruction chronologically and geographically, addressing the fate of Jews in the different European centres.[24] In Eichmann's trial, the geo-historical narrative of the Holocaust was thus built upon a long procession of over ninety survivors' testimonies whose stories were heard as personal and representative at the same time. Indeed, Hannah Arendt who came to report the trial described these testimonies as resembling a "town meeting" more than legal proceedings.[25] Arendt, however, failed to notice the barriers of silence that had to be overcome to facilitate the telling of a traumatic experience. Hausner tried to do this by providing a new framework for listening to the survivors. Arendt also criticised the prosecution's decision in Eichmann's trial for its failure to meet the basic legal requirement of concentrating its case upon the actions of the perpetrator and not upon the suffering of the victims-witnesses.[26] But this narrow legalistic view fails to address the problem of bearing witness to a traumatic event, and using the courtroom as means of overcoming silence.[27]

Hausner's procedural decisions in Eichmann's trial may have been influenced by the earlier Kastner trial in which the traumatic moment was re-enacted without resolution. Tamir's unwillingness to create an adequate

---

[23] For this purpose he relied on the permission given in art. 15 of the Law for Punishment of Nazis and their Collaborators (1953) under which Eichmann was tried, which stipulates that the court "may deviate from the rules of evidence" provided it "places on record the reasons which prompted" such deviations.

[24] For elaboration of the need to create such a framework for listening in overcoming a traumatic experience see Brison, above n. 10, pp. 12–39.

[25] H Arendt, *Eichmann in Jerusalem* (Harmondsworth, Penguin Books, 1963, reprint 1994).

[26] *Ibid.*, p. 5.

[27] I do not mean to conflate the therapeutic and juridical settings of testimony. For obvious reasons juridical testimony cannot replace therapy. However, when the barriers of silence are not only individual but also collective, trials can have a therapeutic function by reconciling the personal traumatic story with the larger framework of collective memory. In such instances the ordinary direction of telling from the private to the public sphere is reversed. (For a sociological account of the movement of stories from the private to the public see, W Felstiner, R Abel and A Sarat, "The Emergence and Transformation of Disputes: Naming, Blaming, Claiming", in (1980) 15 *Law and Society Review*, 631–87. This function of a trial as a facilitator of testimony can be seen in the Eichmann trial and also in the Truth and Reconciliation Commission in South Africa. For the Eichmann trial and psychotherapy see Judith Stern "The Eichmann Trial and its Influence on Psychiatry and Psychology" (2000) 1(2) *Theoretical Inquiries in Law* 393–428 for testimonies of survivors in South Africa see M Minow, *Between Vengeance and Forgiveness* (Boston, Beacon Press, 1998), pp. 61–74.

framework for listening to the survivors reduced their testimonies to a pathological repetition of the original trauma. The survivors were deprived of a sense of control and empowerment in relating their story, especially as they were brought in as defence witnesses and expected to limit their narrative to pointing an accusatory finger at Kastner. In the Eichmann trial, by contrast, survivors were brought in as witnesses for the prosecution, a structural change that allowed them to direct their accusations where they really belonged—at the Nazi perpetrators.[28] With no legal resolution to the painful past (the acquittal of Gruenvald was not accompanied by the conviction of Kastner), the emotions aroused by the Kastner trial exploded in the murder of Kastner—the first political assassination to occur in the state of Israel.

THE MANIPULATION OF THE LEGAL DISCOURSE OF "TRUTH"

Cross-examining national myths

Two testimonies were particularly important in rendering Tamir a social iconoclast who shattered national myths. One of the main heroic myths in Israeli memory of the Second World War was that of young Israeli paratroopers, who were sent by the British to war-torn Europe on a mission of espionage, and who also undertook to help the Jews organise resistance to the Nazi occupiers.[29] Tamir challenged the accuracy of this myth in the trial, but without undermining the basic Zionist narrative. He did not try to challenge the standard of heroism against which the actions of *Judenrat* members were judged. Nor was he willing to discuss the limitations of heroism as a rescue device by showing how the paratroopers' actions had proved futile in the reality of the Holocaust since they had become a burden on the local Jewish leaders and endangered their rescue attempts. Instead, Tamir sought to discredit one of those paratroopers, Yoel Palgi, who was a witness for the prosecution, and through him the Mapai party with which he was affiliated.

National myths, woven on the basis of actual events but replete with historical inaccuracies, are not likely to withstand cross-examination in court. Yoel Palgi, the only paratrooper who had survived that mission and

---

[28] For further discussion of the novelty in Hausner's approach to testimonial witnessing see L Bilsky, "The Competition of Storytellers in Eichmann's Trial" in Steven Aschhelm (ed.), *Arendt in Jerusalem* (Univeristy of California Press, forthcoming).

[29] Three of the paratroopers were directed to Hungary. Senesh Palgi and Goldstein intended to arrive in Hungary before the Nazi invasion in order to organise rescue and were given Kastner's address as their connection person. However, they were late, Senesh was caught crossing the border while Palgi and Goldstein's arrival was known to the Nazis who threatened to cancel the rescue train if they were not handed over. After discussing the matter with Kastner and his partners, Palgi and Goldstein gave themselves up to the Nazi authorities.

managed to return, was known for his autobiographical book *And Behold a Great Wind Came,* which described the mission and its failure but glorified the courage of the Israeli paratroopers, particularly that of Hanna Senesh who was executed by the Hungarians.[30] Tamir cross-examined Palgi on his book, aiming to re-tell it as a story about Kastner's treason and Palgi's cover-up. For this purpose he wanted to establish that Kastner was told by Palgi about the military espionage mission of the paratroopers, that Kastner delivered one of the paratroopers, Peretz Goldstein, to the Nazi authorities, and that Palgi deliberately concealed these facts in his book. This line of inquiry can be seen in Palgi's cross-examination:

> *Tamir:* . . . I tell you that you did not disclose your military mission to Kastner.
>
> *Palgi:* If you say so, you are lying.
>
> *Tamir:* But on page 116 to your book you write: 'to sum up, for the moment we should not disclose our military mission'.
>
> *Palgi:* The book lies intentionally about this point . . . *I wrote a novel and not a history book,* there are two points in the book that I intentionally blurred and changed.
>
> *Judge Halevi:* Why did you find it necessary to change the truth about Kastner and the transmitter?
>
> *Palgi:* Maybe it is a bad habit of a liar—when he does not want to tell the truth he exaggerates. I did not know what would be the implications of my writings. There were numerous trials in Europe against people who delivered Allied soldiers and were later executed. Dr. Kastner, technically, delivered Goldstein to the enemy. This is why I did not write the true version about the arrest of Goldstein. Not only in order to save Goldstein, if he remained alive, but also to protect Kastner and the whole affair. And as to the transmitter, I added that Kastner did not know about it as an emotional reaction to the lie. I wanted to emphasize that Kasnter had nothing to do with it".[31]

Tamir restricted his criticism of the paratroopers' affair to question Palgi's willingness to co-operate with Kastner and to hand himself in to the Nazis. Tamir refrained from investigating whether the heroism of the paratroopers could realistically offer an alternative to Kastner's rescue efforts, and was unwilling to admit the possible "price" of such heroism, the undermining of the rescue attempts of Kastner's committee. Instead, he exploited the structure of the criminal process to offer a simple solution to the discrepancy between the myth of heroism as related in the book and the reality of collaboration with the Nazis. Tamir presented Kastner as an all-knowing figure whose actions had sabotaged the paratroopers' mission from the very beginning. This dichotomous view of heroism and treason was strengthened with the testimony of Katherine Senesh, Hanna Senesh's

---

[30] Y Palgi, *And Behold, a Great Wind Came* (Tel Aviv, 1946, reprint 1977) (Hebrew).

[31] Rosenfeld , above n.5, pp. 130–1 (emphasis added L.B.).

mother, who was brought in as a witness for the defence. Senesh presented a pure version of heroism, in the eyes of a mother who had unsuccessfully tried to meet Kastner in order to deliver a package to her imprisoned daughter. Since the dead cannot be called to testify and there is no need to fear their response, Tamir could strip Palgi of his heroic aura and reconstruct the myth of heroism around Hanna Senesh, "the paratrooper who did not return". Interestingly, in this trial, the reconstructed myth of heroism revolved around two women, Katherine Senesh, the mother, a symbol of sacrifice, and Hanna Senesh, the daughter, an Israeli Jeanne d'Arc.[32] Again, the binary ideological framework was supported by a re-enactment in the courtroom of the tragic conflict of Senesh (the mother) versus Kastner, heroism versus treason.

The defence: "I told the truth"

It is ironic that the first political trial in Israel concerning events during the Holocaust took place in the framework of a libel trial, the very framework that became typical for what came to be known as "Holocaust denial trials" in the 1980s and 1990s.[33] The prosecution in such cases has to prove that the denials of the Holocaust are "false" and the courts often find themselves functioning as tribunals burdened with determining the truth of the Holocaust according to legal conventions of proof and evidence. In the Kastner trial, however, this structure was reversed since it was the attorney for the defence, and not the prosecution, who claimed that the state authorities were involved in an attempt to silence the truth about the Holocaust. Tamir drew an analogy between Kastner's alleged efforts in Budapest to conceal the truth about the destination of the trains to Auschwitz and what he saw as the concealment of the information about the Holocaust by the Mapai leadership in Palestine. Tamir thus presented the trial against Gruenvald as an attempt to censor the truth about the Jewish leadership's part in the failure to stop the catastrophe.

[32] The newspapers called Katherine Sensesh "a Hebrew mother" (erasing her "Diaspora" origins). By contrasting Kastner to Senesh, Tamir succeeded in creating an implied gender opposition between "the heart" (Senesh) and "the brain" (Kastner).

[33] See for example the trial of Ernst Zundel, a German-born Canadian citizen who had arranged for the publication of *Did Six Million Really Die?* a pamphlet that alleged that the Holocaust was a Zionist hoax (*Regina v. Zundel*, 58 O.R. (2d) 129). Many of the court documents associated with the suit are reproduced in B Kulaszka (ed.), *Did Six Million Really Die? Report of the Evidence in the Canadian "False News" Trial of Ernst Zundel— 1988* (Toronto, 1992). For legal articles on the topic of "Holocaust Denial Trials" see Douglas, above n. 17; E Stein, "History against Speech: The New German Law Against 'Auschwitz' and Other Lies", in (1986) 85 *Michigan Law Review* 277–324. For historical assessments of the phenomenon of Holocaust denial see, P Vidal-Naquet, *Assassins of Memory: Essays on the Denial of the Holocaust* (foreword and translation by Jeffrey Mehlman) (New York, Columbia University Press, 1992) and G Seidel G, *The Holocaust Denial: Antisemitism, Racism and the New Right* (Leeds, Beyond the Pale Collective, 1986).

The law usually tries to make a clear distinction between historical truth and legal truth, leaving the former to historians. Tamir could, of course, have based his defence on a lack of intention (*mens rea*) on the part of Gruenvald who had written the pamphlet allegedly slandering Kastner. Although it could have helped his client, this option would not have given Tamir the chance to present the "truth" as being on his side and to use it as a political leverage. By adopting the "I told the truth" line of defence, Tamir forced the court to employ legal means to clarify complex and difficult historical issues. Tamir promised to present "the naked truth" in the trial. However, the truth in a trial is always the result of complex procedural rules, which involve additional considerations such as the finality of the legal proceedings, due process, predictability, etc. In addition, Tamir exploited the procedural advantage afforded him as the attorney for the defence to make serious charges against Kastner and the Zionist leadership but supported his version without fully substantiating it (for example, the defence was exempt from proving its version beyond reasonable doubt, and did not have to present its charges at the beginning of the trial in order to allow for appropriate preparation of the prosecution). In contrast, because his official status in the trial was that of a witness for the prosecution, Kastner, who was the *de facto* defendant, did not enjoy any of the procedural rights and protections that the adversarial system grants criminal defendants. Although these procedural rules shaped the "truth" that was presented at the trial and tilted it in favour of Tamir's version, they were not apparent to the public which was only concerned with the question of which version would receive the court's stamp of approval. Thus, the public was all too responsive to the "verdict" that acquitted Tamir's client (and thereby condemned Kastner) without realising the circumscribed character of the narrative frame of the trial. The complex reality in which Kastner had acted was neatly trimmed to serve the purposes of a mythical story of heroism, appropriated by one side of the Israeli political spectrum.

Conspiracy theory

The only persons who could present a whole story without interruptions and outside the constraints of the question-answer framework were the attorneys in their closing arguments, and the judge in his decision. In its closing arguments, the prosecution attempted to limit the wide range of facts presented in the trial in order to re-focus attention on Gruenvald's actions. Accordingly, it presented a legal analysis of the various sections of the law of libel. By contrast, the defence chose to concentrate on the factual aspects of the trial in order to re-assemble them into a coherent story. In opting for suspenseful narrative rather than dry law, Tamir managed to capture the public's imagination. Tamir's narrative left nothing to chance and all the elements in the narrative were linked together in order to posit a conspiracy theory according to which the leadership in Budapest had allegedly worked together with Yishuv leaders in Palestine in order to mislead the masses. Tamir's version was consistent with popular conceptions of crime as represented in literature—every single fact in the story serves to move the story forward. However, as noted by Alan Dershowitz, a law professor and well-known American criminal lawyer, real life is not a dramatic narrative and is full of irrelevant details and coincidences. In real life, a person who coughs a little in the evening isn't necessarily about to die, and a gun revealed in Act I does not necessarily go off in Act III.[34]

The plausibility of the conspiracy story was enhanced by the structure of a criminal trial that focuses the charges against a specific individual. Although the charges were *de jure* against Gruenvald, Tamir succeeded in turning Kastner into the *de facto* defendant. The individualistic nature of a criminal trial allowed Attorney Tamir to disregard the broader background of the Holocaust, which could have served to situate Kastner's actions in their appropriate historical context, and to present the public with a simplified version of the grave ethical dilemmas posed by the Nazi regime. Tamir re-directed the blame onto the victims' leader by accusing Kastner of having conspired with the Nazi leaders to save his relatives and thus having facilitated the destruction of the Jews of Hungary.[35] Since the charge was against one particular person, the Israeli public at large was absolved from the need for self-examination, and since the trial channelled all the blame onto Kastner (and the Mapai leadership) it offered an easy solution to the mounting feelings of guilt of the Israeli public for not having done enough to rescue Jews during the Holocaust—convict Kastner and thus avoid confronting the past. And as the formal charges were against Gruenvald, his acquittal by the judge was read as if it were a conviction against Kastner, thus serving as the justificatory basis for his subsequent assassination. Instead of facilitating a critical public debate, the trial cut short such a debate before it had even begun. It provided a simple answer to the troublesome question "Like lambs to the slaughter?"—an answer repeated by witness after witness like a Greek chorus: "because our leaders betrayed us!"

[34] A Dershowitz, "Life Is Not a Dramatic Narrative", in P Brooks and P Gewirtz (eds), *Law's Stories* (New Haven and London, Yale University Press, 1996), pp. 99–105.

[35] The Israeli journalist Alex Barzel criticised this move at the time of the trial: "this was a typical Jewish response of self-hate. The direction of the blame for the Holocaust to the near and most venerable—the other Jew". Cited in Weitz, above n. 2, p. 265.

CONCLUSION: BETWEEN MEMORY AND HISTORY

Alain Finkielkraut opens his reflective book on the Klaus Barbie trial with an observation about the way in which a criminal trial can transform history into a living reality:

> "We were able to see an already historical past transmuted into a judiciary present. For two months at the Palais de Justice in Lyon, within the framework of a criminal debate, protagonists from an era believed bygone reclaimed their story from the historians. By focusing our attention on the sentence and no longer simply on knowledge or on commemoration, this judiciary ceremony filled in the abyss that had separated us from the era of Barbie and his victims. The very fact that we waited along with them for the verdict made us their contemporaries. What had happened more than forty years ago was receiving today, before our eyes, its epilogue".[36]

These observations apply with similar force to the Kastner trial. Moreover, it seems that Barbie's defence lawyer Jacques Verges employed many of the disruptive techniques that were used by Shmuel Tamir in order to prevent the state authorities from using a criminal trial to dictate the script of collective memory. Notwithstanding the difference in the context of the two trials, both defence lawyers chose to undermine the official story of "heroism" by exposing the scale and scope of the phenomenon of collaboration that it covers up. Thus, in both trials "heroism" and "collaboration" were presented as two mutually exclusive courses of action between which the judges (and the public at large) had to choose. In both, past and present were conflated in the interest of an ideological re-telling of history.

However, there is an important difference between the Barbie and Kastner trials. Barbie's trial took place forty years after the event and hence the lawyers were faced with the formidable task of unfreezing history and turning it into a living memory. In Kastner's trial, Tamir had to deal with the opposite problem since it took place only ten years after the end of the war when survivors were still struggling with their personal losses and traumas, and when the Israeli public at large had yet to process the collective trauma of losing a third of the Jewish people. The historical perspective that is gained from the passage of time and historical research was still lacking. The narrators of history at this time were "story-tellers" in the traditional sense of relating their personal experiences as underground fighters and Jewish partisans. This was a history told exclusively by representatives of what was then considered the "heroic" side of the Holocaust, and their stories deflected attention from the much wider phenomenon of mass victimisation. Their stories were seen as supplying the moral standard against which to judge the Jewish leaders' co-operation

---

[36] A Finkielkraut, *Remembering in Vain* (R Lapidus (trans.), introduction by AY Kaplan New York, Columbia University Press, 1992), p. 2.

with the Nazis. These stories were also used to consolidate the collective identity of Israelis as the New Jews in the tradition of the heroic and fearless underground fighters of the Warsaw and Vilna ghettoes.

Within this ideological framework Tamir sought to exploit the forum of a criminal trial to direct political criticism against the ruling party, Mapai. Delegitimation of Mapai required telling the story of the collaboration of *Judenrat* members and drawing an analogy between their collaboration and Mapai's actions in Palestine. As we have seen, Kastner provided Tamir with the perfect opportunity to redirect the criticism of the behaviour of the mass of Jews during the Holocaust to the political leadership of Israel since Kastner, the Jewish leader who had allegedly betrayed his community to the Nazis, was also the spokesman for the Ministry of Trade and a Mapai candidate for the Knesset. But Tamir needed to sustain the Zionist myth of heroism in order to legitimise his own political stance, which glorified military resistance and opposed negotiations with the enemy, in the past the Nazis or the British, in the present the Arabs. Moreover, in order to gain popularity with the Israeli public at large, Tamir had to offer a resolution to the painful reality exposed during the trial of the Jewish mass victimisation and their leaders' collaboration.

In light of this tension in Tamir's political stance, the law can be seen as a forum that enables the political lawyer to present his criticism as exhaustive (telling the story that was not told, giving voice to the victims, cross-examining myth, establishing the truth) while at the same time reinforcing the frameworks of collective myths. Thus, instead of being used as an opportunity truly to question the rescue possibilities that military heroism offered under Nazi rule, and comparing it to the co-operation options, the trial provides the political lawyer with a scapegoat. Kastner, the *de facto* defendant, was demonised as an "Other" to the Israeli collective (of New Jews) and his party Mapai as the one that had betrayed the people and the authentic Zionist path. The binary framework of a criminal trial enabled Tamir to offer an easy solution to the moral dilemma—all that was needed was to convict Kastner and to replace the ruling party in the coming elections. The short-term consequences of this criticism are well known in Israel: Tamir won his case in the district court (a decision that was later reversed by the Supreme Court), Kastner was assassinated by people affiliated with the radical right, Mapai, though not defeated, lost a substantial portion of its votes in the elections. However, the long-term consequences of the Kastner trial have rarely been explored. I had already suggested that the traumatic re-enactment of the past in the Kastner trial can explain many of the legal strategies adopted by Attorney General Gideon Hausner in the Eichmann trial, such as the focus of the trial on victims' testimonies, the relaxation of the rules of evidence, and, most importantly, the deliberate attempt to exclude the Kastner affair and the story of the *Judenrat* from the Eichmann trial.

Hannah Arendt, who came to report the Eichmann trial for the *New Yorker* and who knew very little about the Kastner affair, could only discern the pathological symptoms without understanding their roots. She was quick to condemn and harsh in her criticism of Hausner. In a reflective essay written several years after the controversy that her book *Eichmann in Jerusalem* ignited, Arendt returned to the silencing of the Kastner and *Judenrat* affairs that she had detected in the Eichmann trial and explained the danger she attributed to their suppression:

> "The facts I have in mind are publicly known, and yet the same public that knows them can successfully, and often spontaneously, taboo their public discussion and treat them as though they were what they are not—namely, secrets. That their assertion then should prove as dangerous as, for instance, preaching atheism or some other heresy proved in former times seems a curious phenomenon . . . Since such factual truths concern issues of immediate political relevance, there is more at stake here than the perhaps inevitable tension between two ways of life within the framework of a common and commonly recognized reality. *What is at stake here is this common and factual reality itself, and this is indeed a political problem of the first order*".[37]

In Arendt's view the public reaction to the Kastner affair, the refusal to confront the painful issues it had raised and their treatment as taboo, as was manifested in the trial of Eichmann, was dangerous to a democratic regime. This constituted more than a "free speech" problem of suppressing one side of the debate. What was at stake was the narrowing of the very framework of reality that could become the subject of public debate and contestation. Unlike opinions, Arendt contended, "facts" of this kind are the most fragile and therefore most in need of our protection since they depend on collective recognition and exist only to the extent that they are spoken about in public.[38] Of course, once admitted, a whole range of interpretations is possible, a process that cannot even begin when a subject is treated as taboo. It may be an irony of history that Tamir, a lawyer who took upon himself to defend freedom of speech against its suppression by the mechanism of criminal law, ended up producing a collective memory (or rather collective amnesia) whose threat to the possibility of free speech discussions in Israel was much more fundamental and long-standing. The traumatic experience of the trial and its aftermath strengthened a tendency in Israeli society to see criticism as unavoidably leading to political violence and, therefore, to prefer the silencing of painful issues to their serious discussion In this way, the Kastner trial postponed the frank and free discussion of a traumatic past for many decades, it perpetuated myths and closed an entire chapter of history to serious deliberation.

---

[37] H Arendt, "Truth and Politics", in *Between Past and Future* (Harmondsworth, Penguin Books, 1968), pp. 236–7 (emphasis added).
[38] *Ibid.*, p. 238.

10

Rubbing Off and Rubbing On: The Grammar of Reconciliation

BERT VAN ROERMUND

INTRODUCTION: RECONCILIATION AS A POLITICAL PROCESS

Reconciliation is a different process in different contexts. When we speak of reconciling contradictory statements made by a politician at different occasions, or of reconciling seemingly unbridgeable positions in negotiations about wages, or even of reconciliation between former friends who became alienated by a serious opposition of views, these are different contexts. But, as a set of different contexts, they all differ characteristically from another set. The examples I gave were about reconciliation given a relation of *opposition* (of statements, of positions, of views). The other set, the one I want to talk about, is to be characterised as a set of situations in which reconciliation is called for, given a relation of *oppression*. The definition of oppressive power is slightly, but all-importantly different from Weber's well-known definition of power. Power, Weber says, is the chance of pursuing one's will notwithstanding resistance, on whatever basis this chance may rest. Oppression, I propose, is the chance of pursuing one's will to destroy such resistance, whatever form it may take. It is the exercise of power squared.

The latter set is again a set of differing situations, of which I will present only two characteristic examples. The first is that of violent criminal offence. In such a case the State is called upon to punish the offender as if the only wrong he had done was to offend the public order (the monopoly of the sword). Modern approaches in criminal law, however, advocate renewed attentiveness to the position of the victim and to the importance of a process of healing between the offender and the victim. Sometimes this process is referred to as "reconciliation". These situations can be called "social". They do not have direct roots in, or bearing on, what I would call the *political* dimension of a society. It is this political dimension which gives rise to a second characteristic example of oppressive relationships. For the purposes of this chapter I will define politics as the sum-total of those acts which aim at (a final account of) the self-organisation of a social group. It therefore requires the identification of this group as a bounded polity: a whole that is contained and united within certain borders. Thus, political oppression characteristically differs from criminal oppression by virtue of the claim it makes: to further the *whole* of such a polity by oppressing *part* of it. In politics, oppression is accompanied invariably by the claim that it occurs *on behalf of* the public order or the general interest. Quite distinct from even large-scale criminal oppression (the Mafia, for instance), political oppression operates at the level of representation. It relies on ideology to legitimise its action. It addresses itself to the oppressed as subjects of law, only to deny them their very status as legal subjects. Political oppression, therefore, is cynical on the part of the perpetrators and humiliating for their victims. Reconciliation needs to address all these aspects. It will have to come to terms not only with the violence of the past, but also with its alleged justification, that is, with the ideological function, with cynicism and humiliation.

Of course, it may happen that crime comes to exhibit a pattern that is related to the political dimension, for instance in the case that, as a matter of regular fact, victims and offenders belong to a certain race, a certain gender, a certain religion, or a certain national minority. But the type of situation I want to focus on is direct political oppression, or rather: on what can happen after such oppression is overthrown and a beginning of freedom is established. Is there, from the perspective of the previously oppressed who are now in power, a reasonable way of establishing a society in which there is a place for the former oppressors? Is there a principle of reasonableness guiding such a transition, which is a transition not from "warre" to law (as contract theories invariably seem to propose), but from oppression to law?[1] These are the kind of questions reconciliation raises from a philosophical point of view.

To lend the analysis some empirical support and context, I will focus on the truth and reconciliation process in South Africa. This process, I submit, will not come to an end in the near future. Much will depend on the follow-up given to the findings of the Truth and Reconciliation Commission (TRC) that initiated the first stage of the process. Within the framework of this chapter it is impossible, and probably unnecessary, to describe the status, the structure, the results and the reports of bishop Desmond Tutu's Commission. The references contain sufficient entries providing such information. Here, I will concentrate on some of the philosophical issues involved in the process.

---

[1] See below.

COVERING AND UNCOVERING: THE AMBIVALENCE OF TRUTH

It is not unlikely that the etymological roots of the Semitic *kpr* or *kfr* reflect the uncanny relationship between truth and reconciliation. Surely they have to do with "rubbing", but they constantly oscillate between "rubbing [something] off" and "rubbing [something] on [a surface]", that is, between "uncovering" and "covering", or between "purging" and "applying", "cleaning" and "treating". Remarkably enough, there is linguistic evidence that the two semantic streams sometimes conflate. There are contexts "where the step between 'rubbing off' and 'rubbing on' is so short that one cannot distinguish between cleaning and treatment".[2] Characteristically, these contexts are "medical" or "magical" ones. For instance, when we use a disinfectant there is a cleaning sense in covering and a covering sense in cleaning.[3] By analogy, this can be extended to healing in other contexts, for instance psychological traumas or socio-political relationships. It might, more particularly, be symbolic of the ambivalence of the role of truth in a process of reconciliation.

Truth and reconciliation do not go together very well. Reconciliation both requires and forestalls the revelation of truth. On the one hand, it forestalls truth in as far as a process of reconciliation seems incompatible with a persistent pursuit of what things have happened, how they have happened, who was to blame for it and who had an excuse. If reconciliation would be the concluding ceremony of a *Historikerstreit*, it would never occur.[4] On the other hand, it requires truth because acknowledging the oppressive facts of the past seems a precondition of reconciliation. Isn't it this preconditional role of truth that is succinctly expressed in the TRC's *Interim Report* of June 1996, by a quote from Babalwa Mhlawuli, the daughter of one of the Cradock Four: "We want to forgive, but whom should we forgive?"[5] The revelation of the "who" implies the disclosure of

---

[2] *Encyclopedia Judaica* (Jerusalem, New York, 1971), vol. 10, c. 1039. *Theologisches Wörterbuch zum Alten Testament (1984)* Bd. IV, c. 303 is pertinent in pointing out that the Arabic *kafara* (to cover) must be distinguished from the Old Testament *kippoer* (to clean). See also H Gese: *Zur biblischen Theologie. Alttestamenliche Vorträg* (Tübingen, Mohr, 1983), with a chapter on *Die Sühne.*

[3] In this respect, the title of G Simpson and P van Zyl, "La commission pour la vérité et la réconciliation sera-t-elle 'le meilleur désinfectant'?", (1995) 50 *Les temps modernes* 394–407, (asking if the TRC will prove to be the best "disinfectant") is a felicitous one.

[4] Which is not to say that a *Historikerstreit* in a certain sense of the term, that is a sincere debate on the ideological manipulation of history, could not be part and parcel of a process of reconciliation.

[5] Bishop Tutu's "Introduction" to the *Interim Report* 1996, as well as the relevant passages in vol. III, ch. 2 of the *Final Report* 1998 render Babalwa's surname as "Mhlauli", while the report of the East London hearings give "Mhlawuli". The name can be spelled in different ways. Babalwa Mhlauli's phrase is also mentioned, though in a slightly inaccurate version, in A Norval, "Memory, Identity and the (Im)possibility of Reconciliation: The

names, agents and acts. In the eyes of the survivors of oppression, obliterating the past is tantamount to killing the victims twice. For them,
revealing the truth is a form of burying the victims in dignity and, thus,
burying the past. *Burying* the past, rather than forgetting or obliterating it.
Burying is, for sure, a way of covering. But it is a way of covering that
uncovers the meaning of what has happened and that one *wants* to
remember or *wants* to forget. Burying, in whatever form, is part and parcel
of a politics of remembrance,[6] i.e. of amnesty by anamnesis rather than
amnesia. Paradoxically, only a concealing memorial of suffering will reveal

Work of the Truth and Reconciliation Commission in South Africa", (1998) 5,
Constellations 250–65, at 258.
    In order not to misuse the phrase for just one more academic enterprise, it is apt to
recall here what the case of the Cradock Four was about. From the TRC final report, III, 2:
    "294 The cases of the 'Cradock Four' and the related 'Motherwell bombing' illustrate
the use of sophisticated covert operations by the security forces in the assassination of both
political opponents and dissidents within their own ranks.
    295 The UDF activists known as the 'Cradock Four' were Mr Matthew Goniwe
[EC0080/ 96NWC], Mr Sparrow Mkonto [EC0029/96NWC] and Mr Fort Calata [EC0028/
96NWC], and Oudtshoorn activist Mr Sicelo Mhlauli [EC0079/96NWC]. They were
abducted and assassinated outside Port Elizabeth on 27 June 1985. Testimony was given to
the first East London hearing of the Commission in April 1996 by their wives, Ms Nomonde
Calata, Ms Nyameka Goniwe, Ms Sindiswa Mkhonto and Ms Nombuyiselo Mhlauli, and
by Mhlauli's daughter, Ms Babalwa Mhlauli. Before their deaths the 'Cradock Four' had all
been frequently detained, tortured, threatened and harassed by the security police.
    296 On 27 June, they drove to Port Elizabeth to attend a UDF briefing. They did not
return home to Cradock, and their burnt and mutilated bodies were found near Bluewater
Bay outside Port Elizabeth about a week later. An inquest in 1987 found that they had been
killed by unknown persons. The inquest was reopened in 1993 and, after the disclosure of
the top secret military signal calling for the 'permanent removal from society' of Goniwe, it
was found that the security forces were responsible for their deaths, although no individual
was named as responsible. The families subsequently filed a claim for damages against the
SADF and the SAP and this was finally settled.
    297 The families requested further investigation to ascertain who was responsible. Ms
Mkhonto requested that the perpetrators be brought to court so that justice could be done.
Ms Mkhonto, Ms Mhlauli and Ms Calata also requested assistance with the education of
their children. Ms Mhlauli requested the return of her husband's hand, which is believed to
have been kept in a jar by the security police at Louis le Grange Square in Port Elizabeth. Mr
Madoda Jacobs [EC0025/96NWC], the former head boy of Lingelihle High School, told the
Commission that while he was in detention in Port Elizabeth in 1985, security police had
shown him a hand in a bottle and told him it was Mlhauli's.
    298 In January 1997, the Commission received amnesty applications from members of
the Port Elizabeth security police for the killing of the 'Cradock Four'. Those who applied
for amnesty were Mr Eric Alexander Taylor [AM3917/96], Mr Hermanus Du Plessis
[AM4384/96], Mr Nicolaas Jacobus Janse van Rensburg [AM3919/96], Mr Harold Snyman
[AM3918/96], Mr Gerhardus Johannes Lotz [AM3921/96] and Mr Johan Martin 'Sakkie'
van Zyl [AM5637/97]. It was revealed that the car in which the four were travelling was
intercepted at the Oliphantshoek pass. The four were shot or stabbed, and their bodies
mutilated, before being dumped in the veld near Port Elizabeth".

    [6] A Margalit and G Smith (eds), *Amnestie oder die Politik der Erinnerung in der
Demokratie* (Frankfurt, Suhrkamp, 1997).

the immeasurable dimensions of what happened during the years of the Holocaust, the Gulag, the Apartheid.[7] Revealing the truth is a way of covering it, and covering the truth is a way of revealing it. As I will argue later on, a piece of "official", or at least "provisionally acceptable", historiography is such a public memorial. Without it, the survivors would not be able to intimate the incomprehensibility of the evil that took place; indeed, they would not be able to survive.

And yet, Babalwa Mhlawuli's phrase "We want to forgive, but whom should we forgive?" expresses an even deeper dimension of how the revelation of truth, in whatever form, relates to reconciliation. On closer inspection, the demand of truth is not a precondition for reconciliation at all. Rather, reconciliation is what makes the revelation of truth possible in the first place. Contrary to its procedural appearance, the quest for truth is a mode, not a term of reconciliation. Let us see how this can be understood.

THE UNCONDITIONALITY OF RECONCILIATION

One of our candid intuitions about reconciliation is that reconciliation is the upshot of repentance and forgiving. Reconciliation seems to be only possible *after* the oppressors have acknowledged that they were wrong and the oppressed have found enough reason to forgive. Only then they can reconcile. No doubt there is some truth to this picture: a process of reconciliation would certainly be frustrated if the perpetrators would not recognise what they have done, if they would not show repentance, or if there would be no forgiveness from the part of the victims whatever repentance was shown. But it would be a mistake to conclude from that that reconciliation can only be the final stage of a process that embraces several other consecutive steps. Babalwa Mhlawuli's phrase strongly suggests the contrary: that the decisive step of reconciliation is already taken at the very beginning of this process and that it is a precondition for the other steps to follow. "Wanting to forgive" appears to be a stage that precedes and, indeed, triggers the search for truth. It is an attitude that sets a framework of fact-finding that is very different from the one set, respectively, by the attitude of getting revenge or doing justice. In particular, it invites perpetrators to come and disclose the wrongdoing they were involved in, not by bowing before coercion and inquisition but by, in fact, voluntarily condemning themselves, and thereby regaining dignity as moral human beings. It should be stressed, though, that it is the victims who allow them to do so, by what I would call: deferring their rights in the first place.

---

[7] The paradox is not that unusual: the famous teflon "cloud" under the Grande Arche in Paris is supposed to reveal the Arche's full dimensions by concealing them partly; in poetry, the fascination is often with what remains unsaid in what is said.

This basic attitude or perspective is not necessarily identical with the psychological motivations of victims to forgive or of perpetrators to come forward. The latter may consist of calculations how to be better off. In fact, in opening this perspective of "wanting to forgive", the victims will have been aware that they were creating a major factor in the calculations of perpetrators to pursue their own interests. But this is only evidence to the fact that, from the part of the victim, there is already an intention to defer those justified claims of retribution that could obstruct peace in the future. Again, this is not a matter of psychology; it is not a manifestation of change in sympathies, or of growing understanding of the position of the former oppressors. Also from the victims' part, the psychological motivation to seek reconciliation may be sheer calculation: getting it over with as soon as possible. That in itself, however, does not contradict what is apparently at stake in the intention underlying the institutional process of reconciliation: to want to forgive. If this is a sincere wish of the oppressed with regard to future relationships with their former oppressors, it implies a specific "frame of mind": to defer one's claims to retribution, however justified, if and when they should appear to be in the way of peace. Reconciliation anticipates and, indeed, eradicates the point where doing justice could become obstructive for civil peace. It steers away from the pitfalls of *fiat justitia, pereat mundus*.

Note that this is precisely why quite a lot of people in South Africa found the TRC process fraudulent or peripheral. Even if they were not after revenge, they believed that the crimes of the apartheid period should be (or should have been) prosecuted under regular criminal law according to international standards. Which strategy would have been best is not for legal theory to judge. In the case of South Africa, it is especially noteworthy that the TRC option was the outcome of a political compromise, in which the agents involved had both power to gain and power to lose. It was not an option chosen by those already in power, let alone by a formal administration. As an outsider, one can only respect and try to understand that decision. It is obvious that the alternative, namely procedures of criminal law, would have had to meet with enormous problems as well. For instance, it would have been much more difficult (a) to demarcate the period of time under consideration; (b) to prosecute as crimes both acts of violence committed by the apartheid regime and those committed by revolutionary movements, not to speak of the problems of evidence; (c) to organise extensive hearings all over the country in order to let people tell their stories. Again, legal theory has not to decide whether these disadvantages outweigh the advantages. It can only help to understand what reconciliation means in relation to a legal order. This meaning is, I submit: to defer the right to retribution to the extent that retribution would obstruct peace.

This sounds like a dangerous formula, and one that cries out for explanation. Before explaining what I think to be the only reasonable account of it, let me just try to set aside two possible misunderstandings.

(1) Note, first, that deferring these justified claims is not something like a move in negotiations about peace, motivated by the expectation that it might seduce the other party to strike a deal and make a contract. If that were what reconciliation amounted to, it would come down to yielding to the oppressor after all. It would mean that the latter is still in a position (though perhaps not very potent) to set the conditions for peace. It would imply that the peace envisaged is a sort of compromise. Instead, the formula implies no such thing at all. The peace envisaged is not a compromise, because it is the oppressed who determine what could be obstructive for what they conceive of as a worthy peace in their future society. If they would not be in a position to determine that much, they would not be liberated from oppression to begin with. A worthy peace is a peace that, among other things, contains promises for the future. Therefore, peace in this context is not "another word for nothing left to do". Civil peace, if it is to have a future at all, commits one, first and foremost, to establish a sound basis for a legal order (civil peace) under the rule of law.

(2) Secondly, deferring claims that would obstruct peace from the victims' point of view does not mean giving up *all* claims to remedies. It does not constitute the offer of gratuitous settlement in which, for instance, no re-distribution of property could be demanded. On the contrary, reconciliation is a way of upholding the demand for such re-distribution, as different from retribution. If redistribution as a sustained policy of the former perpetrators does not come about, the process of reconciliation will certainly meet with massive frustration.

VIRTUAL RECIPROCITY

Let us now ask what would be a reasonable account of the offer by the former victims to defer justified claims to retribution? The only candidate I can see is the belief that must have been already in the background when reconciliation was linked to truth-finding, namely that to find truth does not imply to attribute guilt, and vice versa. This brings us back to the question: what is implied by the belief, exhibited in reconciliation, that there is a cleft between truth and guilt?

It is obvious that this cleft is not about the Humean guillotine between "is" and "ought". Rather, it is about the absoluteness of claims. When we speak about the non-identity between truth and guilt, we refer to the twin beliefs that neither can we expect to have found definitive guilt when we have finally established who committed which acts of violence, nor can we expect to have found definitive truth after we have established who is guilty and who not. To put it in a slightly different way: the TRC process aimed at showing that there is more to the attribution of guilt than the truth about the past and that there is more to the truth about the past than the answer to the question of guilt. By finding the truth one has not yet found those who are guilty, and by finding those who are guilty, one has not yet found the truth. There is clear guilt, certainly, but it does not belong to the transcendental realm of evil. There are undeniable facts underpinning the attribution of guilt, true, but they tell neither the whole story nor the pure story of violence and suffering. These phrases formulate two sides of the same coin. I will explain them below as deriving from one fundamental awareness. They should not be read as immediate descriptions of TRC activities. They do not question the fact that in TRC procedures the truth at stake is the truth about those guilty of violent crimes under political oppression and about those who suffered under these crimes. What they point to is a philosophical presupposition behind these procedures: that the guilt found in these procedures cannot be hypostasised as natural property inherent to a certain part of society, or that a historical truth that is in itself indelible, can be transformed into trans-historical ideology for the legitimation of a new state.

Truth is not absolute guilt

Reconciliation can only be initiated in a sincere way by the former victims of oppression if they have regained a significant degree of freedom. The attitude implicit in this initiative is one of recognition: reconciliation amounts to *the victim recognising the humanness of the perpetrator*. This does not mean that the oppressed are suddenly willing to admit that, after all, the oppressors have their good sides. Nor does it suggest that the oppressed have changed their minds and are now able to comprehend the period of oppression as an understandable course of action for reasonable human beings. Nor is it an effort to create a common denominator "human being" for both the oppressed and the oppressors, on which shared interests can be claimed. What is recognised here from the part of the oppressed concerns an almost unspeakable aspect of their relationship to the oppressors; the awareness that there is a virtual reciprocity in what the oppressors did to the oppressed. Of course, this reciprocity is counter-factual.[8] The recognition involved is that of the counterfactual possibility that the victim could have been the perpetrator but for the actual course of history. In theological terms one would perhaps say that reconciliation as an initiative of the victim is only possible if and when (s)he acknowledges

---

[8] By using "virtual" in the sense of "counterfactual" I take issue with Habermas's use of "counterfactual" presuppositions of communication. In his view, these presuppositions invariably seem to be positive "ideals". To that extent they pay tribute to the very form of "idealism" Habermas wants to criticise. I submit that counterfactual presuppositions of "communication" can also be morally negative in the sense of "that which we seem to head to but want to steer away from at all costs".

being a sinner. In a philosophical framework a similar awareness is probably better articulated by saying that what the oppressors did to the oppressed *belongs to the evil humans do to each other, and not to a mythic evil that intrudes on the world of humans from outside. In reconciliation, evil becomes "ordinary" in the profound sense of "among us".*

It cannot be overemphasised that this is an account of a counterfactual state of affairs, not a historical one. It certainly does not say that both the oppressors and their victims are equally guilty of what has happened. Historically speaking it is quite clear, for instance in the case of South Africa, who were (or are) the oppressed and who the oppressors. Under the aegis of apartheid, the latter developed a whole system of law to justify their superiority over the former. The virtuality alluded to only functions as an implicit presupposition of reconciliation. This presupposition is tantamount to the fundamental doubt as to whether it is possible for humans to live under the assumption that absolute evil ("the devil") has daunted them. Reconciliation rejects such metaphysical explanation of political oppression as too easy. It bears testimony to the doubt whether it is possible to comprehend the evil that people in certain circumstances do to each other; whether it is possible to punish wrongdoing that is incomprehensible; whether it is possible to control wrongdoing that cannot be punished in an alternative way without oneself becoming a partner in crime. These are all forms of doubt, which derive from the firm belief that it may turn out to be possible to live with evil, but certainly not with its hypostasised form. In reconciliation is expressed the awareness of victims that they did not take part in wrongdoing as a matter of historical fact; not because they were on the side of the good as a matter of principle, i.e. not because they are "the good people". Having found the truth of a violent past is, in this sense, not tantamount to having found perennial guilt in a trans-historical sense. It never amounts to having found those who not only were guilty, but will be so forever.

Guilt is not absolute truth

Let us look at the other side of the same coin: having found the guilty ones is not tantamount to having reached perennial truth. What do we mean by this? It is generally acknowledged that the work of the TRC may well have a purifying, or cathartic, effect, to the extent that people are encouraged to relate their own version of the violent past. What is not meant, at least in most cases, is that the TRC is a decompressor in a tense political atmosphere. If that would be the only purpose, the TRC operation could have taken the form of quasi-therapeutic sessions, the contents of which could have evaporated as soon as they were over. But the individual or socio-psychological effect is not what these TRC sessions are about. Their primary purpose is what could be called: naming violent evil. This naming is not just a matter-of-fact-like labelling of past occurrences, so that this information can be easily restored, retrieved and researched, for instance in order to draft adequate advice and eradicate the causes of violence in the future. That, too, is what is done, and it is far from unimportant. But the heart of the matter lies somewhere else; it lies with naming the evil that hides in violence.

Above I referred to the "ordinariness" of evil in a sense that rarely surfaces in our experience of evil, to wit that there is a counterfactual reciprocity in wrongdoing acknowledged in reconciliation. But evil is "ordinary" also in a different sense, a sense which *is* at the surface of our experience, even to the point where it is taken for granted. It is therefore necessary to aggravate, so to speak, the evil that has occurred, because when it occurred it had this ordinariness and noiselessness which, in retrospect, can become almost suffocating. Often enough, it is indeed only in retrospect that we realise the full dimensions of what has happened, not only in cases where it occurred at our doorstep, but also in those where we ourselves were the victims. The genocide committed by the Nazi regime cannot be described without taking into account what Hannah Arendt characterised as the "banality of evil". The Yad Vashem Memorial in Jerusalem exemplifies the effort to disrupt this veil of banality by a certain dramatisation of the evil that occurred. It chooses to do so not by the use of definite descriptions of a certain scope and vividness; the reason being that such descriptions would only force the spectators to turn their faces and—which amounts to the very same thing—to push the evil away into a trans-historical realm of bestiality. Rather, the dramatisation takes place mainly by a much more effective way of referring: recalling the names of the victims. This was also of primary importance in the TRC hearings: by naming the victims, their suffering is evoked as an experience that is not yet over, that belongs to the present and that gives us, the third person, at least an intimation of what wrongdoing is about. By this act (or perhaps gesture) of naming, the continuity with the past is restored. It strongly suggests, at the same time, that the past will never be recuperable in historical reports establishing guilt. But there is more to the question of truth.

THE EMBARRASSMENT OF THE FIRST PERSON PLURAL

The continuity mentioned above allows those who survived the oppression to speak "on behalf of the victims". It enables them to fill out the place left open in Babalwa Mhlawuli's question: the place of the pronoun "we": "*We* want to forgive." I now want to draw attention to this first person plural, so characteristic of politics. It is the focus of a bunch of questions that are no less than embarrassing. They aim at the problem of "right" hiding in this pronoun. Where does this "we" come from? What are its boundaries?

Whose title does it express? If it is true that the initiative of reconciliation lies with the oppressed in the precise sense of the *previously* oppressed, then in fact it lies with those who *are no longer* oppressed. There is a gap between the past in which they were oppressed and the present in which they enjoy, by presupposition, a significant degree of freedom. To bridge the gap, they have to pose as "the survivors of oppression". Many quotes from Claude Lanzmann's documentary *Shoah* or from the books by Primo Levi could bear testimony to the horrible experience of being a survivor of oppression. It virtually resembles the position of a suspect: somehow the appearances are against him, but he is believed innocent for the sole reason that there is not enough evidence against him. To bridge the gap by claiming to speak in the name of the victims is an enterprise that is liable to suspicion. It can be explained as the first effort by the (previously) oppressed to turn the tables and to appropriate the past as victors themselves.

Carl Schmitt reminds us of the fact that "Name" and "Nahme" are of the same root, that "to name" is "to nail", or that naming is both giving and grasping in one and the same act.[9] Naming, as well as recalling names, is not just neutral enumeration, but also narrative construction of a meaningful world. The narrative under construction is not only *about* something non-discursive that has happened, but it also tries to make sense *out of* these non-discursive events.[10] It functions within the life project of the narrators, in this case the survivors of an era that tried to deny their right to exist. The narrative will only make sense, if it relates the past in such a way that it justifies surviving this period of history. It can, in turn, only do so by articulating how the survivors preserved their dignity in suffering. The suffering is to be told in such a way that it can be heard as a victory for human dignity, that is: that "there was something to liberate". The oppressed must be enabled to believe that they preserved their identity as humans and that they did not yield completely to oppression. Their surviving should not be the contingent effect of a causal process, but the original, and therefore final, perspective of their acting. This is one of the reasons why survivors very often want to know exactly what has happened to their loved ones, as well as what the perpetrators had in mind with their acts. The reason is not that, for a lot of people, it is easier to live with

[9] See C Schmitt, "Nehmen/Teilen/Weiden. Ein Versuch die Grundfragen jeder Sozial- und Wirtschaftsordnung vom NOMOS her richtig zu stellen", (1953) 1 *Gemeinschaft und Politik. Zeitschrift für soziale und politische Gestalt*, 18–27; C Schmitt, "Nomos, Nahme, Name", in *Staat, Grossraum, Nomos. Arbeiten aus der Jahren 1916–1969* (Berlin, Duncker & Humblot, 1995 [1959], pp. 573–91 and R Cover, "Nomos and Narrative", in M Minow, M Ryan, A Sarat (eds), *Narrative, Violence and the Law* (Ann Arbor, University of Michigan Press, 1992 [1983], pp. 95–172.

[10] This thesis is amply argued in the first chapter of B Van Roermund, *Law, Narrative and Reality. An Essay in Intercepting Politics* (Dordrecht, Boston, London, Kluwer Academic Publishers, 1997).

certainties than with uncertainties, let alone that it is sheer curiosity. What they want to regain, in retrospect, is their dignity. The American theologian Robert Schreiter—following Samuel Solivan—speaks of "orthopathema".[11] The story should tell, not only how severely they suffered, but also that they suffered "in the right way". The legends of martyrs are often predominant in these policies of memory. Indeed, the very word "legend" suggests that here is a story that highlights how life should be "read", i.e. lived, under extreme circumstances.

There is, therefore, an inclination inherent in the initial stages of the freedom enjoyed by the previously oppressed to picture themselves as "the good people": the ones who, from now on, will have the absolute right to command because they were absolutely right in the way they suffered. This is a dangerous logic, the workings of which have been incisively explained by Yeshayahu Leibovitz: nationalism is the half-way house between humanness and bestiality.[12] Reconciliation can be regarded also as an effort to defer this transformation from the historical guilt of former perpetrators into the universal truth of the right to sovereign power of the survivors. This is what we can express by saying that in reconciliation discovering guilt is not tantamount to establishing truth. It takes us back to the same point that was already made (indeed, we looked at the two sides of the same coin): reconciliation is incompatible with the idea of "the good people". The new Constitution of South Africa opens with "We, the people of South Africa", leaving out all reference to a divine point of view from where eternal moral truth could be established. But it is not just a matter of tone or phrase. The crucial point here is that there is state continuity between the Republic of South Africa and its predecessor in spite of the constitutional discontinuity. Thus, the process of reconciliation here is also a process in which the nation commemorates the oppression of the past as *its own* inhuman cruelty, including the cruelty it took to liberate it from oppression. This has probably been the most daunting aspect of the truth and reconciliation process in the new South Africa: that it addressed political violence committed both by the defenders and the combatants of apartheid. Although, again, there is a principled distinction, pertaining to historical matters of fact, between these two positions, and although this distinction should be reflected in assessments from political morality, there is a profound sense in acknowledging that, though not equally justified,

---

[11] See R J Schreiter, *Reconciliation. Mission and Ministry in a Changing Social Order* (Maryknoll, Orbis Books, 1992), p. 37.

[12] He compares, in this respect, the ideology of the fascist state and the ideology of the state of Israel. He says as much (twice) in the impressive documentary by Eyal Sivan "Izkor: Slaves of Memory" (1991), with reference to Franz Grillparzer: "ein Rekurs von der Humanität, durch die Nationalität, zur Bestialität". In a different way, he asks the same question towards the end of the first part of Leibowitz, *Het geweten van Israel* (Amsterdam, Vert. R. Verhasselt, 1993): "Are we not heading towards a Jewish nationality in Mussolini's sense?" (my translation)

both forms of violence were equally *political*. That is to say, they share the basic conceptual structure of the political that starts out by including a first person plural with the exclusion of others. The problematic of inclusion and exclusion is at the bottom of all politics, and apartheid pushed it to its limits by repeating this very scheme once more within the unjustified inclusion already established. By hearing both oppressive and liberating acts of political violence, the TRC contributed to the awareness that political power is contaminated notwithstanding the justified intentions with which it is exercised.

RECONCILIATION AND LAW

If a student of legal philosophy wants to come to grips with the concept of reconciliation, s/he will find out soon enough that it is not regarded as a legal concept at all. Apart from the fact that reconciliation, though attempted and lived in various forms of socio-political life, is hardly ever brought into an institutionalised form, it is, apparently, not a topic in legal philosophy. This is surprising. For a considerable number of legal relationships are pervaded by the awareness that, at an earlier stage in time, the political agents involved were opposed to one another as oppressor and oppressed, violator and victim, possessor and possessed. One may think of relationships between members of a legal community torn apart by civil war, or ruled by a dictatorial regime, or based on discrimination. The same goes, though in a different way, for relationships that are the remnants of colonialisation, imperialism and slavery. It is, therefore, pertinent in the socio-economic sphere, where, on a global scale, the gap between rich and poor is still deepening.[13] Yet, the received accounts of the concept of law are very much at odds with reconciliation between political perpetrators and their former victims.

In situations like these, law can only be established on the ruins of an oppressive past. What is more, it can only be enacted and enforced between parties whose identity is mutually related to their respective roles in this past. For all of them, to live under the rule of law is to engage in the daily effort to find good reasons to do so. Any model deriving from reciprocity of interests will necessarily fall short of explaining what the basis of a legal order is in such a context. It is characteristic of most of these models that they conceive of law from an *abstract* point of view. The abstraction occurs in three steps. First, one imagines a "world without law" as the negative counterpart of the world we are familiar with. In classical philosophy, such world is often referred to as "the state of nature". Secondly, one relates the agents in this world without law to a point of view beyond it, a point of

---

[13] While at the same time the environmental problems of today in the rich countries evolve into the poverty problems of tomorrow.

view that would be of interest to all interests involved. This point of view truly embodies a meta-interest and, thus, a *theory* pertaining to the practical first-order interests. Thirdly, one attributes to the agents the ability to transform this theory into an overriding practical interest.

The Hobbesian model is a case in point, and it is paradigmatic of many modern alternatives. Hobbes argues that human individuals can unite in spite of their concurring interests or "motions"—their "warre"—if and when they acknowledge having one "motion" in common: the desire to be left in peace as far as the undisturbed pursuit of their needs is concerned. So much being established, Hobbes submits that the transition to a state of law can indeed be made, because the crucial horizontal acknowledgement of interests between the agents involved can rest on a vertical insight into their overarching interest in peace. Theirs is a "scientific" insight that derives from the overall point of view of philosophy and which he supposes to be available for these agents. Only by accepting this viewpoint of the "divine Legislator" (Rousseau), the "impartial spectator" (Adam Smith) or from "behind the veil of ignorance" (Rawls), the agents are able to see what their common interest is. This is how they come to think of their *common* interest as a *shared* interest. But note that this in fact boils down to giving up the point of departure from which the whole idea of the state of nature was sketched: that there is no higher order insight into a commonwealth for the agents. The bottom line of all these models is that legal subjects are philosophers and that a philosophical account of law is directly available and valid for them *qua* legal subjects. Inversely, all these models presuppose, in the final analysis, the legal status of their philosophising subjects. Strange as it may sound: whether one calls them "combatants" (Hobbes) or "prisoners" (modern game theory), they are implicitly conceived of as subjects before the law, that is: as legal subjects. The very presupposition of their interests being "theirs", the very picture of the walls of their cells separating them and warranting their existence as individuals, is neither more nor less than the concept of law tucked away in the model that is going to produce it. They are subjects before the law in the double sense of the word. First, they are considered to be accountable by virtue of a normative rule: their common, though not shared, interest. Secondly, they are supposed to be accountable well in advance of the legal order they are in the process of establishing. There is, I submit, a gross fallacy in any contract theory of law, in so far as it does not take into account oppression as the real opposite of the rule of law.

It may be thought that there is at least one notable exception in Western legal philosophy: a model that does acknowledge oppression as, in principle, the situation from which any conception of law has to start. It is, of course, Hegel's account of the master—slave relationship in his *Phänomenologie des Geistes*. But, quite apart from the fact that for Hegel this relationship develops as an account of "awareness", it seems doubtful to me if its political interpretation could substantiate the claim that an oppressive master is dependent on, in any sense of the word, recognition on the part of his slave.[14]

From a practical point of view, the opposite of a world governed by law is not a world without law, but this specific world without law that is a world of oppression. As I explained at the outset of this chapter, political oppression is not war. War presupposes (a number of) polities in mutual violent conflict. Political oppression, however, works within one polity. Its violence is accompanied by the claim that the interests of some members of this polity may lawfully be impeded by other members in the interest of the whole. Transition from such a state to the rule of law by those involved in both states does not require philosophy, but reconciliation between victims and perpetrators. To the victims' mind, the core concept of law cannot be described in terms of "order for the sake of order" (Hobbes); "universalisable rules of outward behaviour in accordance with everyone's liberty" (Kant); or "respect for another one's personhood" (Hegel). They have lived through the cynicism lurking in the background of these allegedly foundational principles. They know that the quality of order seldom prevails over its matter of fact; that outward accordance with rules can be abused without any defence from the part of the commonwealth; that respect for the personhood of the oppressor is precisely the attitude that no moral authority can demand from the oppressed. The perpetrators, on the other hand, will realise that the first thing they will have to expect from a legal order is retribution of their crimes, not recognition of their interests. For both victims and perpetrators, reconciliation, not contract, is at the bottom of justice under the rule of law. There may be an important lesson for legal philosophy to be learnt here.

Having said this, I want to make one final observation. The account of what I believe to detect in the process of truth and reconciliation in South Africa, is itself a philosophical statement. It cannot be transformed immediately to political advice for those wrestling with the evil of oppression in the wake of mass violence,[15] wherever in the world they may find themselves. On the contrary, I am inclined to think that the impressive achievement accomplished in South Africa by those engaged in the truth and reconciliation process could well be conditioned, to a significant extent, by a deeply rooted African culture. Such culture cannot be exported or imported as a last colonial commodity to other cultures. Nor can it be celebrated as an exotic rudiment of paradise. But if my African

---

[14] I believe that, if there is such dependence, it derives from the preceding economic division of labour hiding in feudal relationships, not in the oppressive character of slavery. Of course there is oppression in slavery; but being a victim of oppression is not all there is to being a slave. But of course far more would have to be said in order to settle these interpretative doubts.

[15] Cf. A Boraine, "Alternatives and Adjuncts to Criminal Prosecution", paper delivered in Brussels, 20 July, 1996.

colleagues tell me that I have grasped at least the beginnings of what *Ubuntu* means, then, perhaps, more people can understand.[16] And I can try harder.[17]

[16] Cf. J Sindane, "Democracy in African Societies and Ubuntu" (1995) *Focus HSRC*, 3, 1–16, M B Ramose, *African Philosophy Through Ubuntu* (Harare, Mond Books, 1999).

[17] My first materials were gathered during a lecture tour in South Africa in July–August 1996. I am indebted to my colleague at Tilburg University, Dr. Mogobe Ramose, at the time professor at the University of Venda, both for the invitation to his country and for incisive criticism and assistance. I remember with real gratitude the discussions on the campuses of Transkei, Sebokeng, Vista (Soweto), Venda and a few other universities, as well as with several colleagues of the Human Sciences Research Council in Pretoria and the Human Rights Commission in Johannesburg. I thank Dr. Ian Liebenberg, senior researcher of the Centre for Constitutional Analysis of the HRSC, for sharing his published and unpublished insights with me, as well as for extensive and supportive feedback on my manuscript notes. My former PhD student Afshin Ellian provided some useful documents. Over the years I was lucky to receive helpful and encouraging comments from Nico Schreurs, Thomas Mertens and Bobby Nel. Earlier versions of the paper were presented at the IVR World Congress in Buenos Aires (1997) and the IASL Conference in Sao Paolo (1997), where I received useful comments from the audience. I acknowledge support from the Netherlands Royal Academy of Arts and Sciences to participate in these conferences.

11

Reconciliation, Property and Rights

VALERIE KERRUISH

"We have to look at the word 'reconciliation'. What are we to reconcile ourselves to? To a holocaust, to massacre, to the removal of us from our land, from the taking of our land? The reconciliation process can achieve nothing because it does not at the end of the day promise justice. It does not promise a Treaty and it does not promise reparation for the taking away of our lives, our lands and our economic and political base. Unless it can return to us those very vital things, unless it can return to us an economic, a political and a viable land base, what have we? A handshake? A symbolic dance? An exchange of leaves or feathers or something like that?"[1]

"This is coming from the traditional Elders now, and all we want is our Religion and our Culture respected. And we want it left alone, because that is the sense of belonging that belongs to our grandsons and granddaughters of tomorrow, who will become such persons as men and women of tomorrow and have children of their own and pass on the Religion and Culture the same as in the white society, of one generation to another passing on their history."[2]

"Aboriginal people have never asked for reconciliation, we have never asked for the imposition of white culture or government over us. The term 'reconciliation' is premised on the notion of a pre-existing state of goodwill between the invaders and Aboriginal people. Such goodwill has never existed."[3]

No reconciliation when there was no pre-existing conciliation.

INTRODUCTION: CONTEXTS

We think infinite being and are finite beings. In this we experience a sense of rupture, a sense of being that is out of joint. This is our determinate being, our *Dasein*. We may try to avoid it, in the way we think, by pursuing one side of the duality to the exclusion of the other. Hegel, I think, saw

---

[1] K Gilbert, "What Are We To Reconcile Ourselves To?", in I Moores (ed.), *Voices of Aboriginal Australia* (Sydney, Butterfly Books, 1994), p. 287.

[2] R Bropho, "Interview with Roderick Pitty", in *Voices of Aboriginal Australia*, above n.1, p. 453.

[3] P Coe, in *Voices of Aboriginal Australia,* above n.1, p. 283.

that and sought to avoid it in a philosophy which attempts to recognise and reiterate this rupture; to bring modern Western self-consciousness into agreement with itself as ruptured; to reconcile modern Western man to himself and his society; to be, in Hegel's idea of truth, the truth of this self-consciousness.

> "The word of reconciliation is the *objectively* existent Spirit, which beholds the pure knowledge of itself *qua universal* essence, in its opposite, in the pure knowledge of itself *qua* absolutely self-contained and exclusive *individuality*—a reciprocal recognition which is *absolute* Spirit[4]. . .

> The reconciling *Yea* in which the two 'I's let go their antithetical *existence* (Dasein), is the *existence* (Dasein) of the 'I' which has expanded into a duality, and therein remains identical with itself, and, in its complete externalisation and opposite, possesses the certainty of itself: it is God manifested in the midst of those who know themselves in the form of pure knowledge."[5]

These passages occur in *The Phenomenology of Spirit* as part of a transition from a moral to a religious world view. The sequence is not temporal. The moral world view is that of Western modernity. It is a view, premised on the antinomical character of pure reason, which finds in the abstract "ought" the highest point of the resolution of the contradictions of Reason.[6] Represented by the moral and legal philosophy of Kant and Fichte, it is the view of which much of Hegel's philosophy is a critique. The transition that is made is to a sphere of representation that encompasses religion, art and ultimately philosophy: a distinct sphere for a third, roughly temporal traversing. The idea of religion as a foundation of ethics is in no way denied by this structure. If anything it is justified. The further sequences of *The Phenomenology* take us to the limits of religious and artistic representation as expressions of substance, of that literally on which we stand, to the realisation of substance as subject, that is, to the idea that knowledge is and is of a process of conceptualisation within which knower and known are integrated and embedded. As a secularisation of thought, Hegel's philosophy leaves religion in its place as an apprehension of truth based on "figurate conception" or picture-thinking. In what Hegel calls science, this substrate of thought is replaced by logical operations of predication and subsumption that inhere in pure reason and appear as the structure of Indo-European languages. The antinomies that attend the self-referential character of thought that is its own foundation, reveal that its innermost character is that which takes shape as this ruptured self-consciousness.

---

[4] G W F Hegel, *Phenomenology of Spirit* (A V Miller (trans.), Oxford, Oxford University Press, 1977), p. 408.

[5] *Ibid.*, p. 409.

[6] G W F Hegel, *The Science of Logic* (A V Miller (trans.), Atlantic Highlands, NJ, Humanities Press International, 1812), p. 136.

I take Hegel as providing the most thought out *secular* conception of reconciliation (*Versöhnung*).[7] As a fully secular concept however it is found only in the *Logic*. In the *Phenomenology*—Hegel's epistemology so to speak—the human experience of reconciliation, as a spiritual experience, is formative of religious community. But religious knowing remains veiled in its mythological and figurative way of being thought; and Spirit—some *x* that takes the place of grammatical subject in statements about consciousness and self-consciousness—travels on. I do not want here to recount Hegel's phenomenology of its journey. I follow Rose's[8] reading of the *Phenomenology* in her emphasis on its narrative of *unresolved* diremption[9] of ethics (religion) and law (politics) and Lukacs'[10] exposition of the structure of the text. Suffice it to say that the standpoint of absolute knowing to which, at the end, those of us who have followed the journey as also our own come, is not a happy one for Cartesian egos or Kantian individuals. Nor will I go further here with exposition of the idea of a fully secular concept of reconciliation that I take from my reading of Hegel's *Logic*. Taking philosophy to be a concrete thinking of reality that is itself a medium of reconciliation in, of and to an unredeemedly dualistic world, I rather appropriate Hegel to thinking through proposals for reconciliation in Australia.

Legislation to initiate "a process of reconciliation between Aboriginal and Torres Strait Islander people and the non-indigenous people of Australia" was passed unanimously by the Australian Parliament in August 1991. It proposed a ten-year process to address Aboriginal disadvantage and aspiration in relation to "land, housing, law and justice, cultural heritage, education, employment, health, infrastructure, economic development and other relevant matters" and to educate non-Aboriginal Australians about Aboriginal history and culture.[11] In the course of those ten years, native title rights to land have been judicially established as part of the common law of Australia[12] and then cut back by

---

[7] Differences of meaning in ordinary language between the English "reconciliation" and the German "*Versöhnung*" are discussed by M Hardimon in *Hegel's Social Philosophy: The Project of Reconciliation* (New York, Cambridge University Press, 1994), pp. 85–7. His claim is that the connotation of submission and resignation which is found in one sense of "reconciliation" is not present in the German.

[8] G Rose, *Hegel Contra Sociology* (London, The Athlone Press, 1981), ch. 5.

[9] Rose's use of the archaic term "diremption" to mean, as I understand it, the sundering of things which, in some sense, belong together, might presuppose too much. I use it nonetheless in acknowledgment of her reading of *The Phenomenology* and, more broadly, her interpretation of Hegel's ethical thought.

[10] G Lukacs, *The Young Hegel: Studies in the Relations between Dialectics and Economics* (R Livingstone (trans.), London, Merlin Press, 1975).

[11] T Duke, "Reconciliation . . . Who reckons What!", in *Voices of Aboriginal Australia*, above n.1, p. 282.

[12] In *Mabo v. The State of Queensland and others* (No.2) (1992) 175 CLR 1.

legislation[13] and judicial regression.[14] The High Court has avoided opportunities to find constitutional protection against genocide[15] and to construe the race-power so that it can only be exercised for the benefit of Aboriginal and Torres Strait Islander peoples.[16] Social indicators reveal increased rates of Aboriginal death in custody, of imprisonment and of institutionalisation of Aboriginal children, worsening morbidity and mortality, on-going discrimination in housing, employment and the provision of services.[17] But while the conservative Prime Minister, John Howard's promise of a second, reconciliatory term of office was evidently hollow, there is another side to all this. There is widespread support for reconciliation coming from a broadly liberal intelligentsia in Australia. Participatory reconciliation groups have been formed. Education initiatives in schools and tertiary institutions have multiplied and there has been a rethinking of Australian history by significant conservative intellectuals. An increasing and activist movement against racism in major cities has drawn groups into public demonstrations under a reconciliation banner. If it is the strength of this aspect of reconciliation that prompted Howard's change of tune, suspicions of bad faith should not be misdirected at those people whose practices and understandings of reconciliation occasioned the change.

In all of this, reconciliation, as a policy, has struck me as something which cannot be embraced and which cannot be spoken against. This works a vertiginous suspension of political will and it is this that I am trying to think through. The will, in the philosophical tradition in which I work, is a thinking will; a will that is constituted and determined by reason, as well as located in passion, moved by emotion and in need of intuition. It is a will that, at least after Hegel, suffers the rupture with

[13] Native Title Act (Commonwealth) 1993 amended by Native Title Act 1998. The 1993 legislation was characterised as beneficial in *State of Western Australia* v. *The Commonwealth* (1995) 183 CLR 373. Justification for that characterisation might be found in the Act's conferral of rights to negotiate given by it to registered native title claimants and in provisions formally equating native title rights with rights deriving from Crown grant in relation to "future acts". It is difficult to imagine such a characterisation of the 1998 Amendments.

[14] In particular in *Fejo and Another (on behalf of the Larrakia People)* v. *Northern Territory of Australia and Another* (1998) 156 ALR 721, with the decision that the grant of a fee simple estate in land, absolutely extinguishes native title, even where estate has come to an end.

[15] *Kruger* v. *The Commonwealth* (1997) 146 ALR 126; see V Kerruish, "Responding to *Kruger*: The Constitutionality of Genocide", (1998) 11 *Australian Feminist Law Journal*, 39.

[16] *Kartinyeri and Another* v. *The Commonwealth of Australia* (1998) 152 ALR 540; for comparative writing on Aboriginal and colonial law see I Watson, "Indigenous Peoples Law Ways: Survival against the Colonial State", (1997) 8 *Australian Feminist Law Journal* 39–59 and "Naked Peoples: Rules and Regulations", (1980) 4:1 *Law—Text—Culture: In the Wake of Terra Nullius* 1–17.

[17] H McGlade and J Purdy, "From Theory to Practice, or What is a Homeless Yamatji Grandmother Anyway?", (19980 11 *Australian Feminist Law Journal* 135.

which I began, that seeks reconciliation as integral to its freedom, and yet which knows, that to rest and float free of what it suffers in that vertiginous suspension of which I spoke, is the choice of the beautiful soul,[18] of she who cannot and will not engage in transformative political activity.

PROBLEMS

I begin with an old idea. Private property within a historical and cultural context that transforms such property, at the level of normative discourse, into rights of persons (moral subjects, citizens) is a mode of social organisation which has exhausted its emancipatory potential.[19] If what is needed now, in Australia, is a concept and practice of reconciliation that is supportive of rather than hostile to social transformation, then this idea would have it that private property in the means of production and liberal legal rights are barriers to, rather than means for the realisation of, that need. Not only, however, do we have no concrete idea of a property regime that would supplant private property, the classical regime of private property and the modern Western form of law that constituted and was constituted by it, has long been supplemented—some would say supplanted—by a corporatist regime.[20] Law has reflected this change. Formal rational law and its rights are both supplemented and undermined by use of substantive, equitable principles, alternative dispute resolution and negotiated outcomes. In this hybrid system it is too purist, too inattentive to its actual working, to disdain strategic thought and pragmatic action in favour of a theoretical high ground of merely negative rights critique. Negotiated outcomes may well have become an empty slogan, too easily thrown out as a cure-all to conflict and contradiction; more a slogan for an alternative dispute resolution industry than a reliable means of gaining land, employment, decent living conditions and political freedom for Aboriginal and Torres Strait Islander peoples. Even so, it is absurd to negate possibilities of and for negotiation by failing to acknowledge that it is only where people have something to negotiate with, that any such possibilities exist. And since, via the legal and political doctrine of *terra nullius*, everything was officially taken from Aboriginal peoples—their land, their law and their sovereignty—to the extent that the coloniser's legal system does offer rights and in so doing strengthens their negotiating position, it is a resource that is not without value.[21]

[18] The reference here is to Hegel's *Phenomenology of Spirit*, in particular to the subsection "Conscience. The Beautiful Soul, Evil and its Forgiveness", above n. 4, pp. 383–409. See also G Rose, *The Broken Middle* (Oxford, Blackwell, 1992), p. 183.

[19] V Kerruish, *Jurisprudence as Ideology* (London, Routledge, 1991), p. 187.

[20] A Pottage, "Instituting Property", (1998) 18 *Oxford Journal of Legal Studies* 329–44.

[21] This assertion has been questioned by Irene Watson in a personal exchange. It must be read as a particular perception of value; that is as a perception of value from within the standpoint of the coloniser. For the coloniser cannot but conceptualise value from within her own culture and in terms of her own law.

From here another idea presented itself: to argue for a redirection and expansion of the limited gains of native title rights in *Mabo (No. 2)* along jurisdictional rather than proprietary lines. Such an argument would press the recognition of Aboriginal and Torres Strait Islander laws as sources of common law native title rights, toward a full recognition of laws as a requirement of reconciliation. Reconciliation, understood as conditioned by recognition of laws, would be supportive of rather than hostile to social transformation. On the one hand, recognition of laws would be a practical deconstruction of the jurisdictional colonisation of Aboriginal peoples. Legal pluralism need not be touted as any kind of end or good here. The point is decolonisation or, to put the same thing another way, a thorough-going abandonment of the doctrine of *terra nullius*. On the other hand, recognition of Aboriginal law would bring into Australia concepts of property founded on Aboriginal relationship to country, in addition to concepts located in capitalist and corporatist production and in non-indigenous home-making. Resolution of conflicting titles that neither subordinates Aboriginal to colonial property forms nor the reverse, would be the transcendence of private property in the means of production that is sought.[22]

What further commended this idea to me was that the focus on recognition of laws gives apparently secular content to a term, "reconciliation" which, within my own, Western culture is heavily loaded with Judaic and Christian religious connotations. Secular from my perspective, reconciliation thus understood, would not the less respond to Robert Bropho's articulation of what those Aboriginal people for whom he is spokesperson want: respect for their religion and culture as that which constitutes their being and belonging in the world. It was thus consistent with my commitment to religious toleration as one of the most profoundly important principles of a democratic society, and with my persuasion that a wholly secular form of reason is necessary to foster and defend religious toleration. No doubt this appearance of consistency needs more rigorous scrutiny. No doubt these thoughts may blunder into questions of faith, tolerance and secular reason all unaware of that they carry an assumption that sets up a tyrannous hierarchy of secular over religious thought. These seemed like avenues that needed to be explored.

But then a number of problems occurred to me. As I have indicated, I am persuaded by Hegel, with help from Rose,[23] that religion is the latent

---

[22] This is both vague and problematic from two quite different perspectives. One such perspective might argue that private property in the means of production has already been transcended. The other would ask how recognition of Aboriginal property could accomplish a transcendence for non-Aboriginal people. This needs to be worked out, but my idea is that the transcendence in question has not taken place and would take place at the level of reason at which value-formation takes place.

[23] Rose, above n. 8.

and inner foundation of the ethical thought of Western modernity.[24] Is a secular concept of reconciliation possible? Perhaps reconciliation is an *essentially* religious idea, that presupposes God or an original goodwill between coloniser and colonised as an ideal unity or one-ness. In that case "the community" or "the nation" or "the constitution" is slid, in the name of secularity, into that pre-conceptual space, as the source of authority. The problem is less the spectre of ending up arguing for the nationalist far-right, as that the quest for a wholly secular form of reason is abandoned at the stage-post of community, nation or constitution, because what we have not yet worked out are non-mystical foundations of authority.

Perhaps in fully secular form, the concept of reconciliation becomes the Marxian concept of social revolution. The problem of authority and its hidden religious foundation remains. Marx, on a generous reading, envisaged secular authority constituted in practical political activity for the purpose of transcending private property relations, while maintaining the technological advances of capitalist production: a practical *Aufhebung* (sublation) in an historical and material dialectic of a well-developed contradiction between relations and forces of production. Can such a democratic constitution of secular authority be thought to meet the totalitarianism that was actually existent socialism? Did Marx's passion for revolutionary socialism move him to an incautious characterisation of religion as the opiate of the people, which was used to justify its repression?

The question comes too quickly. There is a deeper problem. There is to my mind no historical and material dialectic independent of its conceptualisation by conscious and self-conscious human beings. But human beings are located in cultures and societies and their conceptualisation is marked and shaped by their location. Marx's address to the question of how the social alienation of private property in the means of production and the fetishism of private production and social exchange is to be transcended, fails to conceive its own locatedness and particularity, and so misconceives its sphere of validity. The democratic constitution of authority, as a practice, is the political idea that meets the difficulty of religious foundations of our normative thought and then stalls on its own metaphysical foundation. Marx, repositioned in relation to Hegel—taken back and re-read with an eye to a discrepancy between the idealist dialectic of his discussion of commodity fetishism and his explicit rejection of an idealist dialectic—might yet have more to say about democracy. But the metaphysical issues on which I have touched now launch their strongest challenge to my idea of reconciliation that has as its condition the recognition of laws.

The dominant logical paradigm of Western thought remains that of classical logic. It assumes the validity, in truth functional terms, of two-valued, exclusive and exhaustive classification. This turns up as a law—

---

[24] See further, G W F Hegel, *Elements of the Philosophy of Right* (H B Nisbet(trans.), Cambridge, Cambridge University Press, 1991), § 270R, 270Z.

not-law characterisation. Both non-legal norms and facts fall within the category of non-law. Recognition of Aboriginal law demands its location within the category of law. But then, if a claim based on a norm of aboriginal law is radically inconsistent with one based on common law, how is the inconsistency to be resolved? It is all very well here to talk about negotiated outcomes, or new institutions, but this logic, now in the form of an axiom of identity (A = A), demands unity of "law". It will not allow, because it cannot cope with, the contradiction and can deal with it only by distinguishing the laws and placing them in a hierarchy. Justice, decolonisation, conscience, God—any singular and ultimate determinant—might demand that Aboriginal law, like equity, prevail. But if this makes recognition of laws logically possible within this paradigm, its practical possibility is, to say the least, remote. Only one other option is available here and that is to subordinate Aboriginal law to common law. One could still talk here of recognition of laws, but it would be a recognition of Aboriginal as subordinated, inferior law.

It might be said that this is the actuality of colonisation and there is nothing for it but to accept it in pragmatic compromise. But this response underestimates the actuality of colonisation, which is on-going destruction, assimilation or appropriation. Consider the failure of a campaign to defend native title and its cautious extension in *Wik*,[25] against legislative amendment to the Native Title Act. This campaign, in my observation, had very widespread support within the educated middle class, or as some would say, the intellectual elites. It failed to prevent the legislation. It failed to encourage the High Court to maintain the tendency of *Wik*, *Kruger*, *Kartinyeri* and *Fejo*,[26] reveal a High Court in flight from the promises of the common law. The so little that *Mabo (No. 2)*, the 1993 Native Title legislation and *Wik* offered Aboriginal people in the way of native title rights was even so, too much.

Is *all* argument for reconciliation conditioned by recognition of laws then vain? Is the only point in dressing it up in academic finery, show and illusion? In political terms, is it just another instance of privilege, maintaining and authorising itself by constituting itself as agent and spokesperson for the oppressed? In terms of where I began this section, might it be said that this idea leaves the high moral ground of rights critique for the higher ethical ground of recognition of laws? Few, I suppose, would dissent from the declamation that a politics of illusory truth and hypocrisy is worse then powerless. But it goes a very long way to say that *all* argument for the idea is vain. I do not see how legally and politically, we can be said to be done with *terra nullius* until there is recognition of laws. I would have thought such recognition is essential to

---

[25] *Wik Peoples v. The State of Queensland and others* (1996) 141 ALR 129 holding that, as a matter of (colonial) law, a pastoral lease will not necessarily extinguish native title.
[26] See above text and accompanying nn. 13–16.

according respect to Aboriginal religion and culture. Perhaps then, what is "out of whack" in all of this is reconciliation. Perhaps, in both Hegel and Marx, the hidden religious foundation in combination with a linear idea of historical progression, continues an anti-Semitism that is never lost. Perhaps we should be thinking in terms of respect or justice.

Against that however I have the idea that at some level or another, reconciliation is conceivable as a form of sublation. That is, as the thinking through a contradiction—indeed of particular *hard* contradictions, such as those between finite and infinite, or necessity and freedom. And my intuition is that theory must not give up on this attempt to find a fully secular notion of reconciliation that would be self-sublating, that is, would lift itself out of its religious foundation, while retaining a memory of its past, which warns, that to suppose it to be fully transcended is to court its repetition.

A set of questions thus emerge. Where does thought that is for the recognition of laws begin? To put that another way, if an argument for recognition of laws is to be made, where should that argument begin? Secondly, how can it be argued for in a way that avoids impossible or undesirable hierarchisation? Is there a concept, can a concept be developed—respect, justice, reconciliation etc.—that avoids such hierarchy? Finally, if a concept of reconciliation is proposed in answer to that question, what is it? Who precisely is to be reconciled to what?

IDEAS

These questions merely formulate lineaments of an inchoate idea. This idea is that a concept of reconciliation *is* what is needed; that its shape or function, that is, its most abstract form, is to be sought in metaphysics; and that since its scope or validity is confined to my own culture, the "who" of my last question is similarly confined. Aboriginal people are of course free to adopt this concept, for themselves, if they want to. It may have relevance for them insofar as they choose or are forced into this culture. But that is for their consideration. So far as I am concerned, any "We" of whom I speak, is formed by and located in my own law and culture. To what then is this we to be reconciled? Basically to our own ruptured being: the rupture with which I began of finite beings who think the infinite. This rupture assumes different forms of which, in the sphere of social and political philosophy, Rose's "diremption" of law and ethics is perhaps the most familiar in contemporary legal theory. In between, from Hegel's *Phenomenology*, the unresolved dialectic of master and slave, is transfigured as the shape of modern Western self-consciousness: an "I" torn between its having thought the good and confessed its evil, only to find itself confronted by an actuality which, having been characterised by it as indifferent or evil, insuperably opposes it. Prior to both, in terms of our conceptual apparatus, the rupture is of our reason in the form of a distinction between theoretical and practical reason.

The relevance of this idea to reconciliation in Australia is normative and negative. Its teaching is to give up any idea of unity other than an idea of that which is not, in an unredeemedly dualistic world. From here, a certain kind of thinking might construct another transcendent world, with greater spiritual value than this one, where unity is, from where redemption will come and where atonement is possible. But I take the negativity more literally. Unity is not to be sought in a beyond. It is an idea of that which is not, *in this world*. It is not a transcendent idea. It does not inhabit a world of ideal forms or any other beyond. A first corollary is therefore not to build a purely spiritual or future earthly heaven up on to the foundation of this idea of unity. Secondly, since unity is negative, is not, as implicated in a concept of reconciliation, it negates the static, absolute meaning of reconciliation as a finally arrived at state or product. Reconciliation is dynamic and relative, within time. It is on-going doing or activity that is without end while there is life to sustain it; like thinking. From this we can already say that a ten-year process of reconciliation, a process that will have the result of Aboriginal and non-Aboriginal Australia being reconciled in the year 2001, does not fall within this concept of reconciliation.[27] The negation of its static meaning works to consign that meaning to incomplete and momentary accomplishments. It is also a negation of reconciliation as a transcendental, regulative ideal. Reconciliation is not its own end. Its conceptual link is to freedom, in this context, decolonisation.

This, I think, is a sufficient basis from which to say that a conception of reconciliation that claims to apply and have the same normativity for Aboriginal peoples as it has within the culture that has thought it, is assimilationist. It is the imposition of white culture and, as a legislated policy, of government over those Aboriginal people who, like Coe, have never asked for it. If *we* propose and want reconciliation, we must ask what it and its decolonising purpose requires of *us*. I am suggesting that it requires recognition of laws, but also and as part of accomplishing that, it requires a re-thinking of the diremption of law and ethics within our own normative set up. This re-thinking goes, among other things, to property and rights. Whether or not this aspect is fundamental, the middle-class character of support for "reconciliation" as national policy gives it a particular relevance.

The dilemmas of conflicting rights, legal and moral, are dilemmas of reason and authority. The choice between affirming and denying the ethical universality of the idea of right that is premised on a prescriptive

---

[27] Indeed, this ten-year process idea of reconciliation reminds me of nothing more than Soviet declarations of the transition from socialism to communism in which the state has withered away.

recognition of legal personality is between inconsistency and self-serving righteousness. The affirmative is consistent with a concept of right that inaugurates personhood as the form of legal subjectivity and prescribes a basic obligation to be a person and respect others as persons.[28] Regarded also as ethical, it is an obligation to respect the rights of others and, if ethical norms are regarded as universal, it binds all who are eligible for personhood. But in context, when we consider *who* is speaking and *from where* in terms of property relations, "we"—a class whose material needs are met—are saying that "others" do wrong and do evil if they do not respect rights which, in one dimension, coercively protect our wealth. We thereby affirm the ethical propriety of punishment of poverty.

This dilemma can be avoided in all sorts of theoretical ways. But the actuality is that prisons are being filled by judgments enforcing this legal obligation and it seems reasonable to suppose that our judges and prosecutors do not regard themselves as acting immorally or unethically in so doing. Certainly, within a still strong culture of legal positivism, the judgments can be represented as legally and not necessarily ethically required. Those making them might find the ethical justification for their participation in the system elsewhere. But if legal positivism is not subscribed to its argumentation is not available. It might then be argued that ethical judgments must be particular: that this is the ethical stance necessitated by the effect of positivist hegemony, or of the modern distinction between right and good, or of a more ancient diremption of law and ethics. An appeal here to cultural reality, claims consistency with it as ground or justification for assigning universality to law and particularity to ethics. But this is too convenient. If our life-styles are secured in the actuality of others being punished for poverty, it is disingenuous to say we are at liberty to judge punishing poverty as ethically wrong. Law and ethics are indeed dirempted, but to take the benefit of that diremption by "staying pure" and writing theory which, assuming that liberty, constructs an ethics of and for such judgments is bogus. It is to place ourselves on the ethical as well as the material high ground; to take spiritual as well as material comfort from a property regime which is becoming increasingly punitive.

Reconciliation, as I understand it, must engage with this intra-cultural dilemma. Taken up, it leads quickly into questions of the authority of law. What is the justification of the prescriptive norm to be a person and respect persons as others? What I have been saying is that a merely negative critique of formalism supplemented by a turn to particularist ethics or, if these are, in the end, so very different, positivist or anarchist answers to the question of authority, use hierarchy (of ethics over law) or disjunction (of ethics/politics and law) rather than a concept of reconciliation to deal or not deal with this question. They do not undertake the theoretical task of

---

[28] Taken from Hegel's reconstruction of the categorical structure of legality ("Abstract Right") in *Elements of the Philosophy of Right*, above n. 24, § 36.

seeking a sublation of the dilemmas of rupture. Yet norms of formal justice and respect for rights come from *our* law, and the problem of authority is *our* problem. Contrary to the idea that we are ethically at liberty to disown or exploit the diremption, I am suggesting the necessity of implicating a concept of reconciliation in our thinking about right and rights. That path is taken by choosing consistency in our reasoning concerning the scope of our legal and ethical obligations to be and respect others as persons.

The conclusion which this draws us to on the question of what our law can provide in the way of benefits for Aboriginal peoples is salutary. A problem, that makes itself very apparent in Hegel's *Philosophy of Right,* is that "respecting others as persons" means not respecting others in their particular identity. Others as persons are not others as others. If "persons" is the form of legal subjectivity, if the law in question is the law in force, and if this is what we *must* do, then we are authorised to "pedagogically coerce"[29] others into being persons, that is, into being forcibly assimilated: taken from their families, brought up to despise their own people and culture and all the rest of it. Clearly the dilemmas of diremption are sharpened. Our law is a law which as interpreted, prescribed genocidal acts and which consistently thought through, still demands cultural genocide.

To say, in response to this dilemma, that we are "entitled and indeed obliged" to reinterpret its meaning when applied to Aboriginal peoples so as to include their concept of legal subjectivity within a more relaxed notion of "person" is sloppy. What could such a relaxed notion mean where there is head on conflict, such as, for example, sex-based or land-based "personality"?[30] This, it seems to me, is where a restriction of classical logic that is more fundamental than hermeneutics is necessary. It is to this necessity that I want to tie reconciliation as a form of sublation.

In formal terms this necessity is freedom—decolonisation in this context. But outside Hegel's reconceptualisation of the relation between necessity and freedom, this says next to nothing. Moreover, while there are abstract ideas in Hegel's *Logic* concerning that reconceptualisation, his accomplishment is limited. This limited accomplishment is such that his secular, logical notion of reconciliation, fails to assert itself against the notion that is grounded in religion and the hidden, mystical foundation of authority. What makes Hegel so intriguingly relevant to contemporary legal philosophy is that he is not unaware of this. He knows that his logical or metaphysical reconciliation of theoretical and practical reason (the form

[29] The phrase is Hegel's, *Elements of the Philosophy of Right,* above n. 24, §93R.
[30] In October 1997 the High Court refused leave to appeal from the Full Federal Court decision in *State of Western Australia* v. *Ward (on behalf of Mirruwung Gajjerong Peoples) and others* (1997) 145 ALR 512. This leaves in place a ruling that in native title cases, Aboriginal claimants may secure an order from a federal court to have evidence of secret men's and women's business withheld from members of the opposite sex other than the judges. No right of restriction is established. Any such ruling is in the discretion of the court.

taken by reason concerned with necessity and reason concerned with freedom in the Subjective Logic) is abstract. He knows that it is not realised in an unredeemedly dualistic world and that the very concepts of person and property that are realised or embodied in modern Western law, stand in the way of such realisation. He thus falls back in his philosophy of history, to theodicy and even in his *Logic*, is so constrained to illustrate his ideas by examples drawn from religion, that he is commonly and not unjustifiably read as writing ontotheology.

I think however that there is a secular, dialectical thought in Hegel's idea of the cunning of reason that withstands its theodicean content as the accomplishment of God's will in the world. But our world is not Hegel's and I do not want to lose it here in Hegelese. Suffice it say that what the abstractness of Hegel's reconciliation of theoretical and practical reason means within his own philosophical framework, is that modern Western law is not justifiable in terms of truth. It is not, in other words, true to or consistent with its own concept, namely freedom. It has in that sense a wrong to it and that wrong is to be unaware of its limitation; to think it can work itself pure, all unaware that in so thinking it stands in the way of realising its own concept, freedom.

My own appropriation of Hegel to the present and the present topic, begins from his idea of a logic that is also a metaphysics and that *takes the place* of ontology.[31] It has occasioned the thought, that we live within two invasions: of the realm of metaphysical sense by common sense and of Aboriginal Australia by British Europeans. In both cases, the coloniser declared the realm to be *terra nullius*. That neither declaration has been wholly successful in commanding belief is what makes my work possible. The first mentioned invasion is not an ideological or cultural correlate of the second, although the cultural imperialism of Britain and the USA affects it. It has more to do with relations between philosophy and science that condition the schools of Western philosophy.

On common sense, I only comment here, that it has at its core, a realism that gives epistemic significance to an external, physical world. What of metaphysical sense? From the axiom "there is nothing in thought which has not been in sense and experience"[32] which I accept, I infer that some sense or another occasioned several thousand years of metaphysical speculation within Western thought. I call that sense metaphysical sense, in contrast to common sense, and assign to it a sense of rupture, estrangement, or incompleteness. It is most certainly not the sense that leads us to think that arguments can be refuted by walking up and down (Diogenes refuting Zeno), kicking stones (Johnson refuting Berkeley) or holding up a

---

[31] G W F Hegel, *Science of Logic*, above n. 6, p. 63.

[32] Quoted from G W F Hegel, *Logic: Part One of the Encyclopaedia of the Philosophical Sciences* (1830) (W Wallace (trans.), Oxford, Clarendon Press, 1975), §8. I take it as an, if not the, axiom of empiricist thought.

hand for all to see (Moore refuting British idealism). It emerges in Hume's empiricist metaphysics as a sceptical sense and is tucked away by a Marx too busy with political economy to get back to philosophy and re-think its relation to science, as his favourite motto: *De omnibus dubitandum*.[33] In German idealism, it is a speculative sense, because as an idealism, it admits the further axiom: there is nothing in sense and experience which has not been in thought. In Kant, metaphysical sense is characterised as an urge to seek the totality, which Hegel in admitting its opposite, nothing, takes beyond transcendental logic and turns to the idea of a dialectical logic with negative (sceptical) and positive (speculative) moments. The substitution of antinomies for the "reality" of common sense at the core of our knowing, is the result.[34]

The hope of the concept of reconciliation that pits itself against both invasions, is not only to reveal the assimilationist character of conceptions informed by common law, common sense and mystified foundations of authority. It is that if, thinking in and through a duality that is never normalised or naturalised or justified as a doctrine of dualism because we *also* have sensed and conceived unity, albeit negatively; if actually, we give up justifying our selves and opinions, not by giving up truth as a guise of power, but by recognising that we have truth within our power only in ways we have not comprehended, then we will deal differently with contradictions and incompleteness. Extended to questions of law and politics, the inevitability of hard contradictions between claims founded in different laws, will not so threaten our own law as to make the necessity of professing its supremacy appear as truth, or an unavoidable diktat of actually existing power relations. Nor will they dictate abrogation of our reason if they are seen as part of it. If our notion of unity is not pre-conceptual; if it is thought, and thought through a metaphysical sense of its not being in our selves or our world, nor in any other, we can give up on projects of redemption and atonement that use Aboriginal peoples to absolve our sins and heal our suffering. "The community", "the nation", "the constitution" or "the people", figured over a unity that is not in this world, can be seen as patched on and over a gap, a rupture—without foundation or their own foundation, there is no difference. Nothing is less mystical unless we want to worship at this patch, fall on our knees to our own creation, rather than think that recognition of Aboriginal law would bring to law, in Australia, an obligation to respect others as others, constituted as subjects in and of their law.

---

[33] K Marx, "Confessions" (1865), in *Marx and Engels through the Eyes of Their Contemporaries* (Moscow, Progress, 1972), p. 226.

[34] A point here is that scepticism is constrained by acceptance of the empiricist axiom. Eleatic scepticism is not endorsed. That means simply that the existence of an external physical world is neither doubted nor given determinative epistemic significance.

I do not think that a notion of reconciliation that has as its condition, and reiterates as a requirement, the recognition of Aboriginal law, leaves the high ground of rights critique for the even higher ground of ethics. That is the point of beginning the argument for recognition of laws in metaphysics, and rethinking what has latterly become dogma: that truth is nothing more than a mystification of power. To rest in hope is delusive. But it is anciently thought[35] that hope brings insight and without insight we can only continue according to habits of the past. Then we do, what is currently being done. We repeat and continue a history of successive and increasingly destructive dispossessions of Aboriginal peoples from their land and culture. "We" who assume freedom to be a property of our wills and who want to think freely and for ourselves, like our law, stand in our own way. We do not want the identity of coloniser and in relation to Aboriginal and Torres Strait Islander peoples we are colonisers. We might refuse to think in terms of coloniser and colonised (too dualistic; too unaware of hybridity; too constructive of an us–them mentality). Does that not then align us to, if not indeed constitute us as, settlers of a *terra nullius*? Perhaps we can invoke discontinuities to cordon our selves off from the past and its settler culture. But how come these discontinuities, for us, leave the doctrine of *terra nullius* in place jurisdictionally and politically? To say that they have been discontinued is not correct. Admittedly legal doctrine is its own transported world and should never be thought to describe civil society. Equally the conditions, effects and practices of that transportation are part of civil society. Its role in the construction of historical narratives and what they authorise—dispossession—is a further facet of the doctrine of *terra nullius*, a further reason for stating it correctly, and for being rid of it.

---

[35] G W Oudemans and A P M H Lardinois, *Tragic Ambiguity: Anthropology, Philosophy and Sophocles' Antigone* (Leiden, E J Brill, 1987), pp. 103–6; and cf. Robert Bropho, Nyungah elder, describing living without human rights in terms of living without insight and in hopelessness; Robert Bropho, "Interview with Thomas Mutter and Susanne Neubert", unpublished, Perth, Western Australia, 1991.

12

Law's Immemorial

EMILIOS A CHRISTODOULIDIS

> "I felt the beating of the huge time-wound
> We lived inside."
>
> (Seamus Heaney, *The Spirit Level*)

Why should "we be astonished, . . . be scandalised by the contingent
constitution of our memory?" asks Paul Ricoeur in *The Symbolism of
Evil*.[1] Why indeed? Contingency, after all, breaks the sequences that establish unequivocal memories, it disturbs the continuities that work to iron
out incongruities. So, no scandal here; contingency *must* be invited in the
name of what is excluded. Let memory endorse contingency and let it run
another risk.

What did Nietzsche mean, in *The Uses and Disadvantages of History for
Life* by the disjunction between "a past from which we may spring rather
than that from which we seem to have derived"?[2] This is a disjunction
threatening to collapse even as it is stated: after all what future does not
seek its point of departure in some origin in the past? And yet the disjunction remains important from the point of view of releasing a future from
its overwhelming by the past, that condition that Joseph Conrad identifies
as the "heart of darkness": a vision of history as "the sea of inexorable
time . . . pervading the present, flooding it with a past that can neither be
[fully] known nor escaped in the future".[3]

There is undoubtedly a danger in reckonings with the past; in particular
when the urgency for new beginnings involves denials because the temptation to forget is strong. To mention but a few of those preoccupied with
this question: Nietzsche talks of memory as a "festering wound"[4] that calls

---

[1] P Ricoeur, *The Symbolism of Evil* (Boston, Beacon Press, 1967), p. 23.

[2] F Nietzsche, "The Uses and Disadvantages of History for Life", in *Untimely Mediations*
(Cambridge, Cambridge University Press, 1983).

[3] "We are cut off from the comprehension of our surroundings . . . We could not understand because we were too far gone and could not remember because we were travelling in
the night of first ages, leaving behind hardly a sign and no memories": J Conrad, *Heart of
Darkness* (London, Penguin, 1983), p. 51.

[4] F Nietzsche, *Ecce Homo* (Hammondsworth, Penguin, 1979), p. 15.

to be abandoned. Paul Ricoeur argues that where collective memory involves a collective imputation that visits the iniquity of one generation upon another, there is only one way to escape the "old Terror". "It is possible to free oneself from the chain of acts as it is possible to break the chain of generations: a revocable time is substituted for a supra-historical fate."[5] A new temporal economy breaks the law of hereditary debt. But at what price? The price is, in Herman Hempel's words, a certain "atrophy of the consciousness of historical continuity", as in Germany after the war, a loss of memory whose effect has been in this case the intrusion of a new racist, xenophobic nationalism in the politics of the united Germany. Saul Friedländer talks of the "intractable predicament" that "the Nazi past is too massive to be forgotten and too repellant to be integrated into the normal narrative of memory . . . For the last forty years Germans have been caught between the impossibility of remembering and the impossibility of forgetting".[6] In this context "What Does Coming to Terms With the Past Mean?"[7] Theodor Adorno writes this about history's vicious circularity, and it remains as pertinent as ever: "The fact that fascism lives on, that the work of reprocessing the Past has not yet succeeded and has instead degenerated into its distorted image, empty, cold, forgetting, is a result of the same objective conditions that brought about Fascism in the first place".[8] Whatever its conditions, this kind of abandonment of the past (or the "impossibility to remember it") creates what Alasdair MacIntyre described some decades ago as an "epistemological crisis":[9] a break-down of the communal narrative, no longer capable of upholding communal identity or hosting the understandings of the public sphere. The danger in the reckoning is in the denial "of the past from which we seem to have derived".

My interest in this chapter is to trace those mechanisms that hold the future captive to the past, and to explore whether memory can be released from their hold (by striking a balance such that might allow us to redress them without succumbing to an "epistemological crisis"); to explore whether this can be achieved institutionally; to identify, more specifically, what is forgotten in law, and to understand the law's mode of justifying what is forgotten. And to see whether there are ways of resisting what I will identify as "law's immemorial": the logic of a certain concealment both of *what* is forgotten and of *that* it is forgotten.

---

[5] Ricoeur, above n.1, p. 106.

[6] S Friedlander, "Some German Struggles With Memory", in Hartman (ed.), *Bitburg in Moral and Political Perspective* (Bloomington, Plymbridge, 1986), p. 27.

[7] T Adorno, "What Does Coming to Terms With the Past Mean?" in Hartman (ed.), *Bitburg in Moral and Political Perspective* (Bloomington, Plymbridge, 1986) p. 117.

[8] *Ibid.*

[9] A MacIntyre, "Epistemological Crises, Dramatic Narrative and the Philosophy of Science", in (1977) 60 *The Monist* 453.

POLITICISING MEMORY: MARXIST PERSPECTIVES

In *Eros and Civilisation*,[10] Herbert Marcuse returned to Freud to seek to supply Marxism with the social psychology that it lacked[11] and thus to explain the logic of the emergence of political consciousness in the working class. There are many reasons why one needs to go back to books like this.[12] For our purposes it is to look again at Marcuse's intriguing attempt *to forge a positive philosophical politics from the experience of political failure* and the role that he sees for memory in that undertaking.

Marcuse says this about the "liberation of memory":

"The therapeutic role of memory derives from the truth-value of memory . . . Its truth value lies in the specific function of memory to preserve promises and potentialities which are betrayed and even outlawed by the mature, civilised individual . . . The psychoanalytic liberation of memory explodes the rationality of the repressed individual. As cognition gives way to recognition the forbidden impulses and images of childhood begin to tell the truth that reason denies. Regression assumes a progressive function."

Here the analysis moves to social psychology:

"The rediscovered past yields critical standards that are tabooed in the present . . . The weight of these discoveries must eventually shatter the framework in which they were made and confined. The liberation of the past does not end in its reconciliation with the present. Against the self-imposed restraint of the discoverer, the orientation to the past tends towards an orientation to the future. The recherche du temps perdu becomes the vehicle of future liberation."[13]

"Enlightenment about what happened in the past", wrote Adorno, "must work, above all, against a forgetfulness that too easily goes along with and justifies what is forgotten".[14] Marcuse too is arguing against one of memory's most disarming features, its complicity with the past and thus also its inertia: "The flux of time is society's most natural ally in maintaining law and order . . . The flux of time helps men forget what was and what can be: it makes them oblivious to the better past and to the better future".[15] Like Nietzsche, Marcuse warns against the regressive pull of the past which passes as wisdom. This "wisdom" threatens because of

---

[10] H Marcuse, *Eros and Civilisation* (Boston, Beacon Press, 1966).

[11] Marx says nothing about how or why the workers will learn the truths which Marxism seeks to bring them. (On this see MacIntyre, *Marcuse* (London, Fontana, 1970), pp. 42–3).

[12] It is was a very novel attempt to cross disciplinary boundaries and in fact reconcile hostile perspectives—Marxism and psychoanalysis—and transfer insights from one field to another.

[13] Marcuse, above n. 10, p. 33.

[14] Adorno, above n. 7, p. 125.

[15] Marcuse, above n. 10, p. 33.

its complicity with a history which is overdetermined by loss, failure and mutability. Nietzsche says: "We ourselves bear visibly the traces of those sufferings which afflict contemporary mankind as a result of an excess of history".[16] Compare what the TRC Commissioner Malan said to justify his dissent from the TRC's *Final Report*: "Since we are the outcome of earlier generations we are also the outcome of their aberrations, passions and errors, and indeed of their crimes; it is not possible wholly to free oneself from this chain".[17] There is an evasion in this, a comfortable withdrawal behind a past that instills the present with inertia. This instilling of inertia characterises even the recall of past revolutionary moments, as Marx reminds us in his exhilarating *18th Brumaire of Louis Bonaparte*. Just at the moment when men seem most capable of "revolutionising themselves and things" they fall back on these past traditions and express themselves through them. In past revolutions "the awakening of the dead served the purpose of glorifying the new struggles". But the revolutions of the nineteenth century could not afford the risk of this relapsing into the past, of allowing the past to defeat revolution and praxis. "An entire people which had imagined that by means of a revolution it had imparted to itself an accelerated power of motion suddenly finds itself set back in a defunct epoch . . . the old dates arise again, the old names. . . *Let the dead bury the dead*".[18]

In short: Marcuse's endeavour to marshal memory in the service of praxis relies on countering its complicity and inertia and on tapping memory's disruptive potential, its ability to preserve promises and potentialities. Memory's "recovered past is not reconciled with the present but challenges it . . . Truth loses its power when remembrance redeems the past .. Without release of the repressed content of memory, without release of its liberating power, non-repressive sublimation is unimaginable".[19] And thus "[l]iberation is the most realistic, the most concrete of all historical possibilities and at the same time the most rationally and effectively repressed—the most abstract and remote possibility".[20]

Marcuse's conclusion is significant, it concerns the question of ideology, and as we proceed to look at the law in more detail, the limits of *its* representations. Can the repression of memory, its complicity with and redemption of the past, be redressed and can it be redressed in law? Can memory allow the past to be released from ideology's hold of it, and I use ideology in the broader, but still Marxist, sense of the term, that is, of the function that systems of meaning—here symbols—have of perpetuating oppression

---

[16] Nietszche, above n. 2, p. 233.

[17] *TRC Report*, vol. 5 "Findings and Conclusions".

[18] Marx, *Selected Writings* (D McLellan (ed.), Oxford, Oxford University Press, 1977), pp. 98–9.

[19] Marcuse, above n. 10, p. 163.

[20] *Ibid.*, p. xv ("Political Preface").

by a simultaneous move: that of keeping it latent ("glorifying the past") and undercutting the potential for resistance at the point of the recovery of meaning. Ideology here works through a linking up with a past and establishing *a continuity that is overdetermined by what is already in place*. The past is made commensurate with terms that allow social reproduction in a way that—to return to Nietzsche's words—establishes a continuity "with a past from which we seem to have derived rather than one from which we may spring": "To spring" as revolutionary subjects (in Marx and Marcuse) or more generally as subjects capable of a beginning that is neither a denial of history on the one hand, nor hostage to a past of iniquity and exploitation on the other.

My question in the next section—and this is a question directed to Marcuse too—is this: what resistance to this ideology and this appropriation of the past does the law offer us?

One way to read Marcuse's faith in the disruptive potential of memory is to see it as a move to deconstruct before its time; the pointers are there: suppressed alternatives, dangerous supplements, difference, traces. The function of the incongruent reference is to disrupt the way continuity works to justify what is forgotten. But in this respect let us confront Marcuse's Freud with Lyotard's. Lyotard says:

> "There is in Freud's own approach and tone a way of articulating a paradox of memory. Once the physical hypothesis of the mind is accepted, it suffices to imagine that an 'excitation'—that is a disturbance of the system of forces constituted by the psychic apparatus (with its internal tensions and counter-tensions, *its filtering of information onto the respective paths, the fixing in word and thing representations, and the evacuation of the non-fixed through the respective paths of the system*) affects the system when it cannot deal with it . . . It is an excitation that has not been 'introduced'; it affects but does not enter; it remains unpresented. It is thus a shock, since it affects a system, but a shock of which the shocked is unaware, and *which the apparatus (the mind) cannot register in accordance with and in its internal physics*".[21]

I will insist on what cannot register in accordance with the apparatus's own mechanisms of representation, to argue against Marcuse that a memory that defies memory's "respective paths" cannot surface except, possibly, as "an excess", i.e. as that which is in essence unrepresentable as such and thus defies memory's mode of registering it at all. But I will argue further, against those for whom such "excesses" are leads to what has been omitted,[22] that there is a certain un-recoverability of the past, of what is left behind when memorial events are picked out of the inventory of the

---

[21] Lyotard, *Heidegger and the Jews* (Minneapolis, University of Minnesota Press, 1990), p. 12, my emphasis.

[22] I have Lyotard in mind here: "But it is fair to say that the reality of the referent, always deferred, produced by difference (différend), never ceases to establish itself in the surcharge, in the erasure and in the better approximation of its truths". (*ibid.*, p10).

past, since any "shadow" of the excluded that might accompany the memorial event is too underdetermined to ever name.

But I will return to this. In the meantime, still in the realm of revolutionary politics, one can point with Marx but contra Marcuse to the serious limits that "the power of motion" towards emancipation encounters if it is to draw its leverage from the past because it will have to face this problem: since the system in place is one that secures the conditions of its own reproduction, the agent of emancipation can only be that by breaking with the past. But since the past determines the conditions of praxis, the discontinuity is one that becomes impossible to engender, structural determinants holding action pinned in place. With structural restraints impossible to address let alone redress, revolutionary praxis becomes either something that will be brought about by the objective conditions that will yield or activate the system's contradictions, as in Althusser, or, quite intriguingly in Lukacs, something that once initiated and in the process of its undergoing, shakes off structural constraints to establish praxis as revolutionary in spite of the conditions that led to it.

THE IMMEMORIAL

In his "Interpretation and the Politics of Memory",[23] Johannes Snyman argues that the role of the new Constitution of South Africa is to "articulate and guarantee a politics of memory". What is particularly significant, he says, is the Constitution's "inclusive recognition of the 'injustices of our past', preceding the undertaking of the healing of the divisions of [this very same] past". "One can speak", he says, "of a reciprocal reinforcement here: the constitution upholds an open politics of memory, and a politics of memory informs the functioning and legitimacy of the Constitution".[24] He concludes his paper with this: "The politics of memory is never completed because the norm for what we have to do today can never be stated in terms clear enough".[25]

I find this last phrase wonderfully evocative of an ethical demand to openness that calls us to responsibility and this is a responsibility we can never fully meet. And Snyman's article articulates this demand in the context of one of the most political of constitutions in a transition leaving behind the most traumatic of memories. But I want to argue against entrusting the demand for openness of memory to an institution that closes down memory ideologically. This is the link to our discussion of Marcuse's attempt to re-politicise memory, and retain its disruptive potential in the face of all that conspires to redeem the past in the service of perpetuating current structures.

---

[23] In (1998) *Acta Juridica* pp. 312–37.   [24] *Ibid.*, pp. 314–5.   [25] *Ibid.*, p. 337.

I want to contrast Snyman's trust in the Constitution as upholding the politics of memory to Lyotard's notion of the "immemorial" in *Heidegger and the Jews* which Lyotard describes as that "which cannot be represented without being missed, being forgotten anew",[26] that which can only be remembered *as* forgotten. The notion of the "immemorial" points to an undercutting of memory that remains latent. The immemorial is never part of any memory as such and remains that which any memory, as memory, forgets by representing it. What does memory mean in this context? What does it mean for the forgotten to remain immemorial, "unthought and unthinkable as such"?

Before we trace the notion back to the logic of memory's disclosures and concealments, let us note some resemblances: between the immemorial and the différend and what, in a different context, Foucault says of the occidental experience of madness: that "it remains silent in the composure of knowledge that forgets it".[27] Note that there *is* a différend here, in Lyotard's sense of a double silencing, of an objection that becomes impossible to raise: one cannot argue *against* a knowledge for what *it* cannot accommodate within *its* logic of disclosure and formation of options.

But we must take things a lot more gradually because the complexity is vast. Not only are we dealing here with an order by which things are gathered and named, but one where the gathering is a re-collection that depends on an imposition of a temporal economy on that complexity. To begin to untangle it I will put forward three statements about memory and tie them, in the next section, with three statements about the connection between memory and time.

(a) Any accounting of the past cannot but be *selective*. Not all can be remembered; a memory of everything cancels itself out even for the simple reason that there is not enough time to remember everything.

(b) Memory of the past, and with it any historical accounting of it, is a release from *sequence* and allows jumps within the sequence and thus omissions, each with its full complement of specific injuries (and differends).

(c) The *referent* of memory is not the reality of things past: it is instead the *stake of a question*, of several questions that we may ask about the past. Questions that, to borrow Lyotard's words, "lend [the past] form, diachrony, temporal succession, a quality in the spectrum of classifications, representation on the scene of various imaginaries and sentences." (p. 17).

Let me begin with the last of these. As famously expounded by Bultman in *Glauben und Verstehen*, "[a]ll understanding, like all interpretation, is continually oriented by the manner of posing the question and by what it

---

[26] Lyotard, above n. 21, p. 26.
[27] Foucault, *Madness and Civilization* (London, Vintage Books, 1970), xii.

aims at [by its *Woraufhin*]. Consequently it is never without presuppositions; it is always directed by a prior understanding of the thing about
which it interrogates the text".[28] Memory is the stake of a question, that
selects out and thus reduces the infinite complexity of potential renderings
of the past, and crucially here does it by means of "sequencing", releasing
established sequences and reconfiguring others, in each case establishing its
own temporal mode both in terms of links within the sequence and accel-
erations of time within it. I will need to say something more about time
before this aspect of memory can be fully developed (i.e. the connection
between time and the parcelling out of events as succession). But my aim is
to lead this gradually to the immemorial (and finally to law's immemorial)—to a forgetting that thwarts representation. I will argue that the
reality of the referent of memory is selected out and temporalised on the
basis of questions/expectations ((a)–(c) above) working backwards to pre-
structure the past. But unlike Lyotard I will not argue that in the process
the reality of the referent "never ceases to establish itself in the surcharge,
in the erasure" of what is represented and what eludes representation, since
the immemorial consists in the fact that the erasure cannot be accounted
for. The immemorial is memory's différend. What determines memory is a
"mark" we inflict upon the past that indicates what will count as a
memorial event by carving it out from what will not. The "erasure" we
associate with the immemorial has to do not with what was not indicated
and thus excluded, but with the fact that we inflicted the mark in the way
we did, and thus that other demarcations of possible indications *and* non-
indications are thereby forgotten. The immemorial thwarts representation
not because (event) "x was thus" and not "x was otherwise" but because
"x was thus and not otherwise" is a totalising description of the past that
purports to account for it fully. To borrow from Schürman (below, in a
different context), the immemorial is opposed to the indicated ("x was
thus") neither contrarily nor contradictorily but incongruently.

The exploration that follows is tentative and unsystematic because it
proceeds "aporetically", by pushing each time against the limits of the
conceptualisation of time, of memory and the linkage of the two in institutions. Through it I will follow the lead of the immemorial because its
essence too is an aporia: a memory that only ever "surfaces" as an excess,
that cannot be brought to representation as such, because unable to break
through memory's economy to find expression in its pathways, in a repre-
sentational space that may disclose and reveal it.

---

[28] Quoted in Ricoeur, above n.1 , p. 351.

MEMORY, TIME AND THE LAW

If to decipher the complexities of memory we need to unpick its elements and look at the way it manages time, we must break the circle (that would define the memory of past events in terms of memory's temporal economy) and try to address the question of time in terms that are properly its own. After all we must start from somewhere. And my frustration here comes from the fact that, at least in the analytical tradition, the question of time is *not* addressed in terms that are properly its own. This tradition tends sooner or later to define time in terms of something else, typically change or the succession of events. "Temporal relationism", for example, centres on the relationship between time and change, and as such reduces the temporal instance to some other category. "Causal theories of time"—at least an influential position within them—define temporal relations in terms of causal relations. The asymmetry of causation, temporal becoming, points to the directional element of time. Definitions in terms of "flow", "passage", and "irreversibility" either follow from or are connected with this. The Aristotelian question whether there can be "empty time", time not registered in experience, becomes particularly apposite. And then, of course, we have the question of the "unreality of time", as famously expounded by McTaggart. He argues that nothing "that exists" can be temporal; and that time is thus unreal because all statements that involve its reality ("tensed facts") are erroneous.[29] And while this is fascinating, is this philosophical in-breeding really pushing against the limits of the notion of time or merely the limits of analytical thinking about time?

These approaches are fundamentally unhelpful and do not get the theoretical exploration off the ground at all. Simply put: a theory that explains time in terms of change, i.e. as succession of events (or states) is unproductive for the reason that since events require time in order to be individuated as such it seems *at least paradoxical* to employ events to parcel out time—in order to understand it as succession. The mutual constitution is here completely self-undermining. Similarly, the event—that which counts as the indissoluble, elementary unity of happening—has a conferred, not an ontological character. Time is an aspect of what a system of meaning conditions as event. "Eventhood" is reconfigured and forever re-negotiated amongst systems on the basis of both different modalities and differential acceleration/condensation of time. It is nothing novel to say that during revolutions or other limit situations time accelerates compared to periods of stability; that suspense involves deceleration, even

---

[29] He concludes: "Nothing is really present, past or future. Nothing is really earlier or later than anything else or temporally simultaneous with it. Nothing really changes. And nothing is really in time": J M E McTaggart, "The Unreality of Time" (1908) 17 *Mind* 457–74 at 474.

the suspension of the flow of time. At the same time, acceleration and deceleration themselves are meaningless unless they register against a different time perception, a difference between enduring and changing (that which passes, passes in the mirror of what remains constant). Such a temporal economy is an indispensable condition for apprehension, one of Kant's elementary syntheses, a minimal condition for the manifold to be collected, in this instance as temporalised. But it is temporalisation that remains a condition of perception of the manifold, not the manifold a path to understanding time (as succession).

Let me explain this further by following what Lyotard says on Kant's theory of apprehension. "The most elementary syntheses . . . are those constitutive of time in the every day sense of diachrony. To apprehend sensible 'matter' . . . it is necessary to hold its flux within a self-same instance, be it infinitely small." But why say there is a flux? asks Lyotard. "How does one know this if time constitutes itself by its retention?" He answers brilliantly: "Because the retention, what is held back, is also constitutive of the flux. The flux only passes, only goes away and arrives because the imagination fixes and holds together the 'arrival' and the 'departure'".[30]

I would like to add this to the analysis: that the "fixing of an arrival and a departure" is a selection, and thus is specific to a system of meaning, to an order that collects and retains time and sets events in succession. Eventhood is an achievement of time, constituted in terms of the retention of time, and thus the creation of an "interstice" that the event can occupy (and only thus emerge as event). This time-border (or framework) that allows Kant's "matter"-in-flux to be represented in terms of events, does not cut across orders (or systems) of representation but sets the interstices on which events appear according to particular criteria. This is why, later on, I will argue that specific expectations are employed to pre-structure access to the past, make available the indices, and interstices, that will allow memorial events to emerge out of the horizon that is the past.

So, what do we keep from this, in order to proceed toward "the immemorial"?

(d) Time needs to be defined self-referentially, as a difference between past and future, or less crudely, as being constituted by its orientation to the double horizon of past and future.[31]

---

[30] Lyotard, above n.21, p. 31.

[31] N Luhmann, *Social Systems* (Stanford, Stanford University Press, 1995), pp. 74–82 and ch. 2 *passim*. Elsewhere Luhmann says: "The past and the future only 'are' as horizons for the present. The relevance of time depends upon a capacity to interrelate the past and the future in a present. All temporal structures relate to some sort of present". ("World Time and System History" in *The Differentiation of Society* (New York, Columbia University Press, 1977)). See also his "Temporalisierung von Komplexität" in *Gesellschaftstruktur und Semantik* (Frankfurt, Suhrkamp, 1980), vol. 1.

(e) This leaves time under-determined, lacking a substantive dimension that requires its parcelling out in terms of events and its registering as change. That is why memory holds the past in suspension: as under-determined the full scope of the past's potential never comes to presence; and yet what comes to presence is always subject to re-config-uration from a new observer. Every new observer will put the past to scrutiny: memory of the past is always in anticipation of its comple-ments and corrections.

(f) Finally, memory's determinations are not possible without a system reference that will provide the "lacking substantive dimension". This leads to a radical relativisation of what may count as event and thus as change—in the first case as *differentiation between* and in the second case as *succession of* events. Need one repeat here that the referent of memory is not the reality of things past? It is, instead, the stake of a question, of several questions that we may ask about the past. Questions that, to return to Lyotard's words, "lend [the past] form, diachrony, temporal succession, a quality in the spectrum of classifica-tions, representation on the scene of various imaginaries and sentences".[32]

Obviously (e) and (f) are what link time internally with memory. Past time can only be abstracted out of memory analytically; but past time cannot be otherwise differentiated from memory. And memory as truth to the past—as its "objective" recounting—does not exist. Memories are selections, selective re-configurations of the past. Of course one can talk at great length of the paradox of the past "already-being-there" yet possible otherwise;[33] but is this really fruitful? The past is not meaningful indepen-dently of its recall and memory's determinations consist of recognitions, evaluations and insights that of course could be otherwise re-configured. The past exists in terms of memorial events and in terms of how those memorial events are individuated. This links time directly to memory and through this analysis of memorial events (memory is its manifestation in terms of those events) in turn directly to orders of representation, that instill those events with significance. There are infinite templates of such selections. Time now to move this analysis to one of those templates, law.

LAW'S TIME

If time is an abstraction from meaningful experience, the meaning of the "past" can only be abstracted from the memory of the past, and that memory carries with it its institutional imprint. The referent of memory,

---

[32] Lyotard, above n. 21, p. 17.
[33] C Scott, *The Time of Memory* (Albany, SUNY Press, 1999), p. 12.

we said, is the stake of several questions; certain of these questions are the questions that the law asks of the past. The referent of memory thus becomes the stake of law. My argument is that that memory—law's memorial events—cannot stand independent of law, that memory is always-already institutional memory and that thus it cannot break free of the "trappings" of the institution because both time and eventhood are determined institutionally (above (d)–(f)) and this undercuts both Marcuse's ambition to sever memory's ideological ties—as if memory could be released from an institution that keeps it captive—as well as the less ambitious attempt to call upon the institution of law itself to articulate and guarantee the truth of a memory that is purportedly independent of it. To explain this I will need to say more about law's constitution of memory.

Law, wrote Jose Bengoextea, is a system *a posteriori*.[34] Its systematic character comes from its rationalising the past in a certain way, re-configuring it as appropriate to current and future legal decisions, to current and future attributions. This is a common premise, even if not stated as such, of theories as different as Edward Levi's and Ronald Dworkin's. In each case, in the name of coherence, legal memory calls up events as relevant to its current needs of classification and as relevant to expectations of how events will be classified in the future. In every case the recovered past can be nothing but reconciled with the present. The certainty of expectations and the exigencies of the rule of law dictate a minimisation of ambiguity here that looks both forward and backward: unambiguous future, unambiguous past, so far as possible. Law is after all about stabilising social expectations. The future is anticipated in terms of expectations which operate as forces of suppression to what might have otherwise functioned as disruptive memory.

There are two things that this does *not* mean. It does not mean that expectations work as rigid indicators, devices that cast a version of the past that is unaltering. No, as selective devices that are re-embedded as the system moves on, they allow a re-configuration of the past as appropriate to their re-casting. Levi comments that a classification changes as a classification is made. His brilliant analysis of reasoning in the common law[35] shows how this works through a forever shifting system of classification where selections are projected both forwards and backwards, reconfiguring the past to best pre-empt, anticipate or structure the future. There is no fixed structure as such but an evolving system whose unity and identity issue from the articulation of the order of a structured whole with the discordant events that call for regulation. In this dialectic of order and disorder, the law draws on its past to decipher and order what is contingent (and must be disciplined). In doing this and without committing the

---

[34] J Bengoextea, "Legal System as a Regulative Ideal", [1994] *ARSP Beiheft* 53, at 66–80.

[35] E Levi, "An Introduction to Legal Reasoning", in (1948) 16 *University of Chicago Law Review* 501–74.

law to an unambiguous stilling of its past, its reluctance to vary its struc-tures—because such readiness would undermine it as a system of regula-tion—does mean the loss of the future as a truly new beginning.

Secondly, it is true that memory cannot but be selective. What is forgotten, as Charles Scott puts it, "lets the remembered be vivid, by providing the gaps, as it were, in which other memories provide texture and instance".[36] So far so good. My concern is about the selectivity of legal memory and with *its* truth value. The redundancy that comes with all memory, the fact that things are selected out and then are left behind, and the function of memory that builds on this, compounding it, finds in law a privileged site. Legal memory is a special case in this respect. Files are closed and sealed and cannot be re-opened. In the common law, ratios distil memory and leave behind obiter dicta. Of course this "forgotten past" can be tapped but only *in spite* of law's organising principles and only after a special effort is invested. So yes, all memory is selective, but law's selectivity is policed and safeguarded through legal devices and anchored to nothing less than its very function that requires a restricting of ambiguities regarding what the past may require of us, in the name of the rule of law. No retro-activity, therefore no reading into the past of legal requirements that are not already enshrined in the official record, because that compromises legal certainty about the past.

With this we are already discussing the distinctiveness of legal memory, the legal delimitation of memory. Let me stress again that all access to the past, all selectivity that guides it allows its recall along specific pathways, determined by structures of expectations. This is just one rendering of the famous hermeneutic circle: hermeneutics proceeds from a prior under-standing of the very thing that it attempts to interpret. But I still want to claim a special case for law in this regard. Let us again pose our hypothesis that law remembers the past as forgotten: an impotent past, a past oriented to the present, where what is recovered can be nothing but reconciled with the present.

Legal memory is used to pre-structure access to the past. The legal system looks to the past as a repertoire from which to draw. In Luhmann's terms: "the system controls the environment by verifying the consistency of its own operations . . . recording agreement or disagreement. Without this form of consistency control no memory could arise and without memory there can be no reality".[37] There is a mutual constitution here of the meaning of past and present: without memory (without a past to fall back on) the meaning of any present operation is impossible: what are we to hold on to and give a name to in the present? At the same time the past is

[36] Scott, above n. 33, p. 4.
[37] Luhmann, "Closure and Openness: On the Reality in the World of Law". In G Teubner (ed.) *Autopoietic Law: A New Approach to Law and Society* (Berlin, de Gruyter 1988), pp. 335–48, at 337.

only a product of this "consistency control", a backward selection that reads as past what expectations can be carried into the present to be confirmed or disappointed. What happens in the present only registers if one knows what one is looking for—if memory can pre-select what is to be carved out as present experience, occurrence. But that pre-selection that makes the continuation of the system possible also imposes vast restrictions on possible renderings of events. Structures condense references to direct which possibilities of narrating the past will be selected as significant. It is through these expectations that identities are stamped onto experience so that the meaning of events, identities and concepts becomes possible.

Obviously the problem for those who entrust law to uphold the openness of the past or the disruptability of its memory is this: that such pre-selection of possibilities stands in the way of openness, of an attentiveness to the past and an inherent disruptability as an aspect of that attentiveness. There is, in other words, compulsion in the way law's memory works; how would we, as subjects of law, be in a position to speak to what has been suppressed if it is on the basis of selective suppression (and selective actualisation) that law—as a system of meaningful communication—emerges in the first place, carving out memorial events by endowing them with meaning? It is asking the system to remember what it forgot and to remember that it forgot it: a (double) recall that is impossible for it to perform.

THE EXAMPLE OF COLLECTIVE MEMORY

The Interim Constitution of South Africa of 1993 instituted the TRC on the basis that "there is a need for understanding but not for vengeance, a need for reparation but not retaliation". In this the need to provide a forum for story-telling ties in with a second "function": that of "facilitating the granting of amnesty to persons who make full disclosure of all the relevant facts". Truth-gathering, the determination of historical fact, links internally with reconciliation, understood as, or at least in the context of, the granting of indemnities to those who confess. The politics of amnesty link directly to the politics of memory: no amnesty without knowledge, thus without acknowledgement, thus without confession. So the TRC was seen crucially as a forum where the victims and perpetrators of apartheid would tell their stories. As "truth commission" it suspends its legal function, it aspires to recover the word; in this it shares the features of other truth commissions, more than fifteen of them in the last twenty years, all in the service of collecting memory; in this case a forum for its collection that might provide the new South Africa with a record of its past. Note its rationale as expressed by the Minister of Justice, Dullah Omar:[38]

---

[38] In a radio interview, October 1993.

"The idea of the TRC goes back to ANC decisions . . . [T]here was a strong feeling that some mechanism needed to be found to deal with all violations in a way that would ensure that we put our country on a sound moral basis. And so a view developed that what SA needs is a mechanism which would open up the truth for public scrutiny. But to humanise our society we had to put across the idea of moral responsibility—that is why I suggested a combination of the amnesty process with the process of victims' stories".

There is already here the trace of an elision that belies the collection of memory. Because why should one assume that the end result of our accounting of the past will move us any closer to a shared community rather than a break-down of community? What makes the danger impossible and the risk invisible? Memories collected from master and slave appear to be treated as constituting the inventory of communal experience, those proto-understandings that are shared in some *a priori* sense. They will be shared again, having undergone the "katharsis" of communication and in the process allowed a collective memory to crystallise around them. This move relies on a specific use of time that, as Scott Veitch puts it, "foster[s] a memory within which the idea of healing can be propounded as a progression and thus the problem of temporality dealt with on terms commensurate with its overcoming".[39] However convenient and desirable a demarcation the new community or nation might be, the question of shared memory cannot be pre-decided in this way without risking belying collected memories or over-determining them; in either case the purported transition from collected to collective memory is an *a priori*. And the history that the Constitution invokes, to paraphrase Veitch, is that of a collective memory that *may never have been* yet seemingly *must be.*[40]

This links to a second legal *a priori*: that collected memories will survive their transition to a (shared) collective memory in the first place. That there will be *consensus* over the explanation of the struggle is an unwarranted assumption, warranted merely by the fact that law is driven by a decisionist imperative and must "resolve" disagreement over the "truth of contested memories" and has devised a body of rules and criteria about what truly constitutes what, the terms of contestation, as well as *what* can be remembered, *what* forgotten.[41]

The argument about exclusion (that becomes immemorial) turns on the attempt to police the contours of institutional memory in a way that installs it as communal. In all this the institutional moment highjacks the

[39] S Veitch, "Pro Patria Mori" in D Manderson (ed.), *Courting Death* (London, Pluto Press, 1999), p. 157.
[40] *Ibid.*
[41] Czarnota, in Chapter 7 above: "Legal procedures and legal institutions have systematised remembering and forgetting. They have developed an impressive body of rules to prove the 'truth' of contested memories . . . Legal institutions . . . are [mechanisms] of systematic forgetting: files are closed conflicts are solved, offenders are rehabilitated, victims are compensated".

discursive by inserting at the social's most crucial junction the *a priori* of the existence of community. The TRC, the forum of collected memories, becomes the institution that marshals collective memory; the assumption that *collected* can become *collective* usurps and over-determines; it is an *a priori* assumption that when read into reconciliation cancels it out by doing violence to the understandings that might have established it.

Lyotard writes the following in *The Jews*, but it is pertinent to South Africa, to all politics of memory and forgetting and the "historico-political work of the memorial". He says:

> "As far as forgetting is concerned, this memory of the memorial is intensely selective; it requires the forgetting of that which may question the community and its legitimacy. This is not to say that memory does not address this problem; quite the contrary. It represents, may and must represent, tyranny, discord, civil war, the mutual sharing of shame, and conflicts born of rage and hate. It can and must represent [them] in a discourse that because of the single representation it makes of them, 'surmounts' them".[42]

The "single representation made of them" is in the use of the inclusive "collective" and with it the deployment of a temporality that "collects" past strife in the promise of its overcoming. Community is of course here as in every case "not-yet". But the promise of community allows the sidestepping of heterogeneity and non-communal conflict. The past returns here at the point of fusion of the present and future, stripped of all ambiguity. The future-anterior of the coming about of community allows the reading of the past in the service of the future, a past "collected" as collective. As I have argued elsewhere,[43] if this is what "coming to terms with the past" really means, then the promise of reconciliation is a lie.

LAW'S IMMEMORIAL

Let me summarise the argument about the immemorial. I argued that law pre-structured its past in such a way that the past was cast in terms commensurate with its overcoming, i.e. with its own projection of expectations into the future. There is no memory, I argued, independent of such disciplining, i.e. a selectivity that is specific to an observer, to a specific mode of reducing the complexity that applies equally to past and future selections. Yet that does not mean that memories cannot be re-configured, remembered through different selections. Of course reductions provide the platforms for what registers as remembered out of infinite possible renderings of events. But there are also infinite such templates, a radical contingency of points of observation of the past, each selecting out what is

---

[42] Lyotard, above n. 21, p. 7.
[43] "Truth and Reconciliation as Risks", (2000) 9:2 *Social and Legal Studies* 179–204.

remembered. In this context there is no truth of memory, no inventory of past facts per se, since past events are selections. Law's immemorial reminds us that law cannot inhabit all these points of observation, but inflicts upon the past a specific mode of remembering that has to do with its function and expectational structures.

In the context of this argument we discussed the example of the collapse of the distinction between collected and collective memory in the TRC's use of law, which was an imposition upon the plurality of memories of a unitary viewpoint that over-determines the incongruous and calls it into line. What is forgotten here is that which might have sustained itself as incongruous, as resistant to law's casting of conflict as pathology to be overcome, a pathology requiring healing in the name of our community. Law's technique here is its re-aligning the incongruous instance, its subsuming it under the logic that will allow it to overcome it. That which might have resisted such re-collection can only be exposed as an external, a supplement maybe, and in that sense remains immemorial; forgotten as such, and the act of forgetting it forgotten too.

There is another instance of law's immemorial that I would like to mention ever so tentatively. It is law's reducing memory to a sharing that trivialises: from stark singularity to banal familiarity.

What is meaningful as common memory depends crucially on the mode of sharing its meaning—as projected that is in the mirror of others co-experiencing that meaning. This "social" dimension of memories, Luhmann would say, "enables a constantly accompanying comparison with what others can or would experience and how others could position their actions".[44] Otherwise put, a meaning is experienced through shared interpretative perspectives that must be imposed to distil the experience of any "common" meaning. This accomplishment, in turn, depends on inserting the vocabularies, the grammars and the gathering orders to allow a common recollection, or at least the communicability of the memorial event. Law makes available here a template of interpretative possibilities that are peculiar to it and recalls the remembered event through its vocabularies and the distinctions and indications that allow it to attribute value. An abstract, co-experiencing third party—judge, juror, legal subject—is pivotal to collecting and registering meaningful experience. It is this "re-duplication" in the mirror of (co-experiencing) others, that is reductive and suppresses in what institutional memory actualises as past. What is

---

[44] Luhmann argues that the social dimension of meaning "emerges form the fact that alongside the ego-perspective one or many alter perspectives come into consideration . . . This means that one can ask of every meaning whether another experiences it in the same way I do . . . The concepts of ego and alter here do not stand for roles, persons or systems, but for special horizons that collect and bind together meaningful references": above, n. 31, pp. 80–1. He says: "If what is social in meaning themes is experienced as reference to (possibly distinct) interpretive perspectives then this experience can no longer be attributed to a subject" (*ibid.*).

disclosed as past is disclosed only by virtue of those structures of meaning, orders, "pathways" or systems that bestow disclosive power to it: and only thus is an interpretative perspective fashioned at all.

Hannah Arendt saw an aspect of banality in the evil perpetrated against the Jews, in its accounting by Nazism's functionaries and executioners. At the basis of it there was a "normality" that she found terrifying: in Eichmann she saw no standard signs of culpability, no duress or insanity, the states of mind of Nazi officials eluding characterisation, unfathomable, unclassifiable. On the one hand we have Adorno's urge not to stop at mere rejection but to risk understanding where "one endures the horror through a certain strength that comprehends even the incomprehensible".[45] Against this comes a *fear* of explanation, a fear to empathise, in the sense that Primo Levi warned that to attempt to understand these men risks contamination. My point is this: this fear to remember removes the interpretative perspective, and yet—in order to legally judge them— necessitates one, involving a terror that both *must yet cannot* be reduced to familiarity.

From this point of view, the point of view of law, evil becomes banal once a common focalisation *is* posited, a common interpretative perspective inserted and the singularity of memory denied. "Singularisation", writes Shürmann, "works on normative positions from within, depriving us of any appellate jurisdiction".[46] But of course law *is* an appellate jurisdiction for the settling of normative claims. And an appellate jurisdiction must claim a basis on a shared interpretative perspective, otherwise it is meaningless as such. This "social" dimension of understanding a memory as legal, that depends on the introduction of the abstract, co-experiencing third, cuts away at ethical terminology, because it comes to mediate the relation with the other at the expense of the openness that, aspirationally only, might have realised it. It is Levinas who argues that the other cannot find expression in such mediation of concepts that repeats the relation of self to self; the other is betrayed by a thematising language that belies the asymmetry between self and other. In addressing you as a legal subject I lose the uniqueness—or sacredness—in you to substitute it for the banality in us both.

In this context of a justice to the other that resists subsumption to rule, compare how Ricoeur contrasts the Platonic nature of justice as the "architectonic" virtue of man, to St Paul's notion of justice that comes to a man "from the future to the present, from the outward to the inward, from the transcendent to the immanent . . . To be 'just' is to be justified by an Other; more precisely it is to be declared just . . . Justice, in fact is the verdict of acquittal".[47] And this is precisely why justice to the particular falls within

---

[45] Adorno, above n. 7, p. 126.

[46] Schürman, "Conditions of Evil" in Rosenfeld *et al.* (eds), *Deconstruction and the Possibility of Justice* (N.York, Routledge, 1992), p. 387.

[47] Ricoeur, above n. 1, p. 147.

the economy of the gift whose logic exceeds that of reciprocity, and thus of course also that of contract and legal responsibility.

To develop this in a positive way, Ricoeur intriguingly re-aligns responsibility to *fragility*.[48] Fragility invites action by virtue of an intrinsic relation, incongruous to rule, that calls us to responsibility. We are here in the realm of first principles, the slate has been cleared to inscribe responsibility *ab initio*. "Responsibility" says Ricoeur, "has the fragile as its specific vis-à-vis". The importance of this placing cannot be exaggerated. Ricoeur calls it a principle because it is expressed from the very first instance as an imperative which nothing precedes. We "are rendered responsible by the fragile". The key here is Ricoeur's distancing himself from the traditional analysis in which responsibility consists in the ability to designate oneself as the author of one's own actions, obviously the *sine qua non* of legal attribution of responsibility. In fact, Ricoeur tries a double reversal here. First, this "traditional" responsibility occurs in the aftermath of action and is turned towards the past rather than the future (in the willingness to pay damages or suffer penal consequences of punishable actions). But retrospection misses fragility altogether; the question to ask is "what shall we do with this fragile being?" and this involves a reversal from past to future.

The second reversal is the one we spoke of above and involves what Levinas would call the substitution of ontology for ethical terminology; it concerns an invocation of the other that, again, cannot find a home in traditional notions of responsibility. Because, as we said, the latter relies on the ability to designate oneself as author of one's acts, it repeats the relation of self to self. But "the appeal, the injunction and also the trust which proceed from the fragile result in its being always *another* who declares us responsible or, as Levinas says, calls us to responsibility".[49] Responsibility, re-oriented to the fragile, introduces an *incompleteness* here, an asymmetry. Because it is directed to the future and thus is not-yet realised, it is *always* attentive to the fragile because one can never have exhausted the duty of caring, confirming beforehand that the fragile has been adequately provided for in the future.

So what about the immemorial? "How can one man take on the memories of even one other man, let alone five or ten or a thousand or ten thousand; how can they be sanctified each?" asks Primo Levi. This last argument about law's immemorial has been about its impotence to accommodate both the *singularity of memory*, its reduction to familiarity

---

[48] From a lecture given by Ricoeur at the Department of Philosophy of the University of Naples in May 1992. This edited version is included under the title "Responsibility and Fragility" in M Valdes (ed.), *Reflection and Imagination: A Ricoeur Reader* (Toronto, University of Toronto Press, 1991). For a more extensive elaboration see Ricoeur, "The Concept of Responsibility" in *The Just* (Chicago, University of Chicago Press, 2000), pp. 11–35.

[49] *Ibid.*, p. 19.

betraying it, and *responsibility*, the modes of (legal) attribution of which read the past in a way that misses the fragile altogether and thus render responsibility vacuous. "To rule and to regulate", says Shürmann, "is to speak in the name of the common. It is to simplify the manifold, produce evidence and thereby make oneself understood".[50] The interpretative structures on which the law relies to recall the memory of the singular reduce it to the mediation of a world of legal concepts and thus depict it as that which it is not. This is the argument about the reliance on interpretive perspectives that force memory into a betrayal. In this context Shürmann urges us to "see a dark light at the core of evidence, telling us 'you cannot understand; you must understand'".[51] This, I think, is Levi's cry too. But memory remains unrecoverable: the operation of criteria of criminal responsibility, which in Arendt's *Eichmann in Jerusalem* remain unable to pierce through and capture the heart of evil, the long lists of human rights violations, the categories of culpability and perpetrators, all trivialise, professionalise and rationalise, and thus fail to represent the memory of suffering, fail to make familiar what is senseless (what every representation misses), display a thinness of description, portray perpetrators as shallow in their evil and victims as sorrowful but not maddened with the sorrow of unbearable memory. Representation here lets suffering remain forgotten. With Lyotard "one will say, It was a great massacre, how horrible! Of course there have been others . . . Finally one will appeal to human rights, one cries out 'never again' and that's it! It is taken care of".[52] This is why Lyotard relegates humanism with its human rights talk to the order of "secondary repression",[53] and writes this about the problem of formulating political and ethical questions in terms of rights: "[n]ow, completely occupied with the legitimacy of exchanges with others in the community, we are inclined to neglect our duty to listen to this other; we are inclined to negate the second existence it requires of us. And thus we will become perfect ciphers, switching between public and private rights without remainder".[54]

CONCLUSION

Against Marcuse's faith in the recovery of memory as lever of liberation I have argued for a structural embedding of the immemorial in law, that not only imposes a reduction on memory (and undercuts its liberating potential), but leaves it unable to redress that reduction. What is reduced out is walled up in silence. Law's immemorial "remembers something as forgotten" because its memory of events, in each case, "is inseparable from

---

[50] Schurman, above n. 46, p. 399.   [51] *Ibid.*   [52] Lyotard, above n. 21, p. 26.
[53] *Ibid.*, p. 27.
[54] Lyotard, *Political Writings*, quoted in S Veitch, *Moral Conflict and Legal Reasoning* (Oxford, Hart Publishing, 1999), p. 183.

the performative process that recalls it as event".[55] It is this performative process that reduces the past in order to actualise it as memory, in all the ways described: it reduces to vocabularies and grammars that disclose its truth; it imposes a sharing that denies singularity in order to foster normative positions for an appellate jurisdiction. And, significantly, it deploys a temporality that allows the memory of the past to be recalled in ways that cannot but reconcile it with the present. The question of an assumed commonality becomes pertinent again here. Both as presupposition and as object of law's scrutiny of the past, commonality is an *a priori* inserted at memory's crucial junctions. As presupposition, since law's interpretative perspectives must rely on common expectations (law's social dimension, above). But as object, too, memory is the stake of a question that the law does not want to risk. Commonality *will* be recovered, in all the ambiguity of the term: remembered, re-established, covered-over-again. And the immemorial will redeem this: a question that cannot be asked cannot threaten. I have argued that the embedding of the immemorial in law is structural because it underlies in a constitutive way what can emerge as meaningful communication about the past. In this dialectic of memory what is actualised depends on what is suppressed. And it is this dependence that underlies the logic of the immemorial as the radical other of memory, at once represented and thwarted.

So where to premise our duty to listen to the other, to remain open to questions about the past and open to a non-reductive recognition of what is at stake in the past? In his book, *At The Mind's Limits*, the Belgian philosopher Jean Amery, victim of torture at the hands of the Gestapo, reminds us that when torture has been committed no "healing truth" can redeem the past, and the memory of horror, the only experience unchanged by recollection, cannot be shared. Amery talks to us of a debt that can be acknowledged yet remains impossible to settle. And it is not just any debt, but debt itself, the recognition of commonality cancelled, human solidarity cut at the root:

> "Whoever was tortured remains tortured. Whoever has succumb to torture can no longer feel at home in the world. The shame of destruction cannot be erased. Trust in the world will not be regained".[56]

---

[55] Veitch, Chapter 3 above.

[56] J Amery, *At The Mind's Limits: Contemplation by a Survivor on Auschwitz and Its Realities* (Bloomington, Indiana, 1980).

Index

230   *Index*